MODELLING WELFARE STATE REFORM

CONTRIBUTIONS TO ECONOMIC ANALYSIS

225

NORTH-HOLLAND
AMSTERDAM • LONDON • NEW YORK • TOKYO

MODELLING WELFARE STATE REFORM

G. M. M. GELAUFF
J. J. GRAAFLAND
Centraal Planbureau (CPB)
The Hague, The Netherlands

1994

NORTH-HOLLAND
AMSTERDAM • LONDON • NEW YORK • TOKYO

ELSEVIER SCIENCE B.V.
Sara Burgerhartstraat 25
P.O. Box 211, 1000 AE Amsterdam, The Netherlands

ISBN: 0 444 81886 3

This book is printed on acid-free paper.

PRINTED IN THE NETHERLANDS

INTRODUCTION TO THE SERIES

This series consists of a number of hitherto unpublished studies, which are introduced by the editors in the belief that they represent fresh contributions to economic science.

The term "economic analysis" as used in the title of the series has been adopted because it covers both the activities of the theoretical economist and the research worker.

Although the analytical methods used by the various contributors are not the same, they are nevertheless conditioned by the common origin of their studies, namely theoretical problems encountered in practical research. Since for this reason, business cycle research and national accounting, research work on behalf of economic policy, and problems of planning are the main sources of the subjects dealt with, they necessarily determine the manner of approach adopted by the authors. Their methods tend to be "practical" in the sense of not being too far remote from application to actual economic conditions. In additon they are quantitative.

It is the hope of the editors that the publication of these studies will help to stimulate the exchange of scientific information and to reinforce international cooperation in the field of economics.

The Editors

To Carolien and Petra

Preface

In the second quarter of 1987 a research project was initiated at the Dutch Central Planning Bureau to analyze the influence of taxation and social security on the economy by means of an applied general equilibrium model for The Netherlands. It took a five year period to devise and operationalize several versions of the model, to test its simulation properties and to implement it in such a way that it could handle many different policy questions. By the beginning of 1992 the model was judged to be mature enough to apply it to policy issues in the field of taxation and social security and to use it for providing policy advice to political parties, government advisory committees, and unions. By now the model is frequently used for that purpose not only in the Netherlands but occasionally also for outside executives. For instance, recently a number of simulations have been made at the request of European Commission officials.

For us it has been a challenging experience to be (former and current) head of the team that realized the project on the applied general equilibrium model. Perhaps being able to monitor at best the large amount of work that has been done, we are also most grateful to all those who contributed to its success. First of all we should mention André Nibbelink, who is part of the modelling team right from the beginning. André's structural design of large computer programs and data bases together with his systematic method of working have been of overriding importance in realizing the project. Moreover, he has developed a detailed knowledge of the Dutch system of taxation and social security. And most important, he is a person with whom it is a pleasure to cooperate.

Many other colleagues at the CPB contributed to the project in various ways. In the period before 1990 Frank van Erp operationalized a previous version of the household model. Nick Draper, who has been part of the team in the years 1990 – 1993, contributed to the simulation experiments and developed a savings model and a concept model for endogenizing the use of disability benefits, which are to be implemented in a next version of the model. Frits Nulle updated and refined the labour market data base, combining several statistical sources. Carel Eijgenraam assisted on the cumulated production structure approach and Rocus van Opstal on the submodel of firm behaviour. Helmer Vossers, Sjoerd Ottens, Anja van der Linden and Marein van Schaaijk patiently answered many questions about the system of taxation and social security in the Netherlands. To all of them our sincere thanks.

This book greatly benefitted from comments by CPB director prof. Gerrit Zalm and by professors Henk Don, Theo van der Klundert and Dale Jorgenson. We also highly appreciated the thorough and stimulating referee report by Erling Holmøy of the Norway Central Bureau of Statistics. Many CPB colleagues provided valuable suggestions on parts of the manuscript, which on many points led to improvements. Among them are Ton Manders, Ate Nieuwenhuis, Ruud Okker and Ed Westerhout. Last but certainly not least we owe special thanks to Nicole de Jager, who worked with us for her Masters thesis on negative income tax experiments in MIMIC and participated in writing Chapter 12 of this book.

The Hague, May 1994

George Gelauff and Johan Graafland
Former and current head of the
Applied General Equilibrium Models Division
of the Central Planning Bureau

Contents

List of figures

List of tables

1 Purpose and method

1.1 Introduction

An important characteristic of the economy of the Netherlands is the relatively large share of the government sector in combination with a high rate of labour market inactivity (see Figure 1.1 and Figure 1.2). The share of government income is one of the highest compared with other OECD countries, whereas the marginal tax rate on labour is even higher than in any other OECD country. The largest component of the total collective burden concerns social premiums paid by employers and employees. Here lies a direct relation with the labour market situation in the Netherlands. Because of a relatively high unemployment rate and disability rate, many social benefits are paid to inactive people, which must be financed by social premiums paid by employees and employers. Furthermore, labour participation of women is relatively low in the Netherlands, so the large collective burden must be produced by a relatively low number of actively working people, which makes the average collective burden even higher. The ratio between the total number of inactive people, receiving a benefit, and the active working

Figure 1.1 Government income in 1986 and total marginal rate of taxation and social security premiums in 1983 for a number of OECD countries

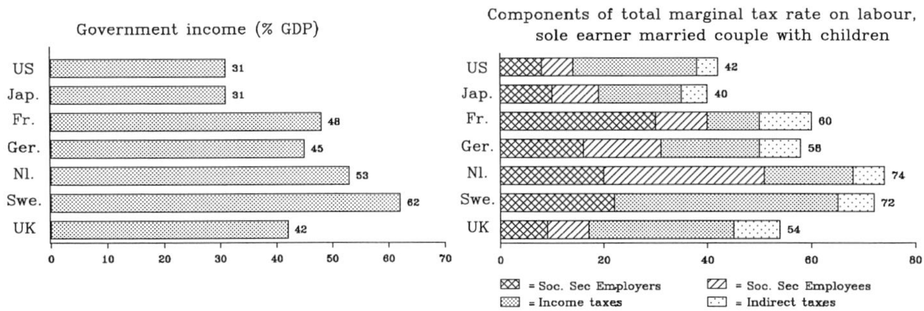

US = United States, Jap. = Japan, Fr. = France,
Ger. = Germany, Nl. = Netherlands, Swe. = Sweden and UK = United Kingdom.

Source: Government income, OECD (1989)
Marginal tax rates, Mc. Kee et al (1986)

Figure 1.2 Labour market characteristics of a number of OECD countries in 1985

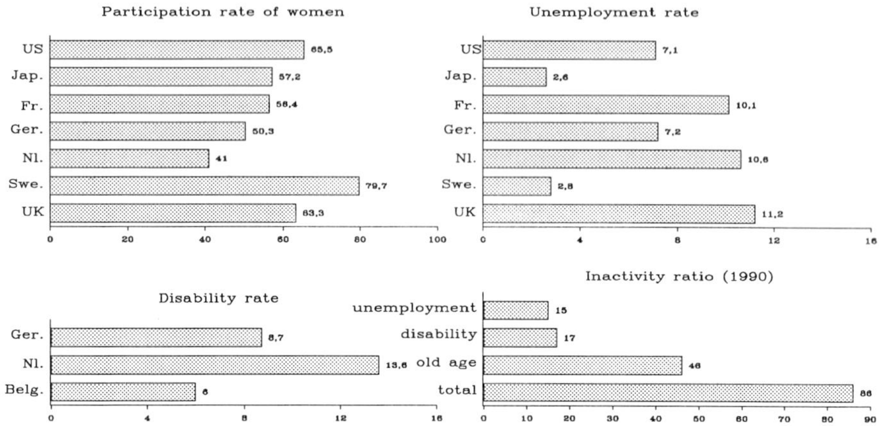

US = United States, Jap. = Japan, Fr. = France, Ger = Germany, Nl. = Netherlands, Swe. = Sweden, UK = United Kingdom and Belg. = Belgium.

Source: Participation rates, OECD labour force statistics 1969–1989
Unemployment rate, Central Planning Bureau (1990a)
Disability rate, Prins (1991)

population amounts to 90% in 1990. Although the Netherlands is a manifest example, this description characterizes the current problems in many Western European welfare states.

There is a growing awareness that the labour market situation and the large government share are interrelated through various mechanisms[1]. For example, if labour supply of women depends on net income earned by working, the progressivity of the income tax code may reduce the number of working hours they prefer or even hamper their labour market participation at all. Another important mechanism, which seems to be especially relevant for the Netherlands, is the forward shifting of higher income taxes and social premiums into higher wages. This may worsen the competitive position of Dutch industries, crowding out the private basis of the economy. The resulting rise in unemployment necessitates further increments in social security

[1] For reviews on the influence of taxation on behaviour of economic agents see for instance Saunders and Klau (1985), Hagemann *et al.* (1987) and Van Sinderen (1990).

premium rates, creating a spiral of growing inactivity and public incidence. As a by-effect also labour productivity increases, putting more pressure on the capabilities of the working population. This may induce the less productive working population to quit, voluntary or stimulated by the firm, by making use of the favourable disability schemes, further enforcing the spiral of inactivity and public incidence.

The current situation has become of great concern to policy makers, and various policy proposals have been put forward to reverse the spiral towards lower labour market inactivity and growing tax incidence on primary income. These proposals relate to various elements of the tax and social security system, like: reducing marginal tax rates of high income groups, as for example included in the tax reform-proposals by the Stevens Committee (Stevens, 1991; Social Economic Council, 1992); cancelling the transferability of the basic allowance between spouses to stimulate labour participation by women; increasing the supplementary income tax allowance for workers only, in order to make working more attractive compared to receiving a benefit income; decreasing value added tax rates to stimulate general wage reduction; reducing the attractiveness of inactivity by lowering the level of unemployment and disability benefits in relation to net wages; individualizing the social security system; and measures with respect to other government institutions that regulate the labour market, for example the minimum wage rate. The binding element in all these proposals is that they constitute various options for welfare state reform.

The purpose of the model for the Netherlands developed in this study is to analyze the effects of all these detailed proposals for welfare state reform. The model is called MIMIC[2] (MIcro Macro model to analyze the Institu-

[2] A previous version of MIMIC has been published in Gelauff *et al.* (1991). To experiment with different specifications of submodels a small scale version of MIMIC has been developed called MIDGET (MIni model Designed to experiment on Growth and Economic Theory). The purpose of MIDGET is comparable to that of the small scale ZOEM version (Gelauff and Okker, 1988) of the large scale macroeconomic model FREIA-KOMPAS (Van den Berg *et al.*, 1988). A description of MIDGET can be found in Gelauff and Graafland (1991) and Gelauff (1992).

tional Context) and belongs to the class of applied general equilibrium models. Applied general equilibrium models are often used to describe the influence of taxation on economic performance. The strength of these models lies in the explicit modelling of the microeconomic principles that underlie the behaviour of economic agents, and in the flexibility in the level of disaggregation in the model structure. In MIMIC especially the household sector is strongly disaggregated, in order to accurately describe the structure of income taxes and social premiums. Income distributions have been introduced in order to be able to use statutory tax functions which quite closely resemble the actual tax form of a household. The enterprises sector is more aggregated. The main distinction here concerns the exposed sector against the sheltered sector in order to stress the open character of the Dutch economy. Labour demand is subdivided into five categories, two types of low-skilled labour and three types of high-skilled labour. This is especially relevant for the analysis of the influence of those labour market institutions which mainly affect the labour market position of low income workers, like the minimum wage rate.

Construction of an economic model is a continuous process of selection. Choices relate to the theory embedded in the model, to the type of model chosen, to the level of aggregation, etc. To put in perspective the choices made while constructing MIMIC, we continue this chapter with a discussion of some general aspects relevant to modelling. Section 1.2 contains a short review on applied general equilibrium models. Section 1.3 discusses methodological aspects of MIMIC like modelling criteria and the concept of equilibrium. An overview of the structure of MIMIC is given in Section 1.4. Section 1.5 recapitulates the characteristics of MIMIC in light of those of other applied general equilibrium models. Finally, Section 1.6 presents an outline of the rest of this study.

1.2 Applied general equilibrium models

Economic modelling has developed in many directions since the disenchantment with large scale macroeconomic models in the 1970's. Especially in the United States, the interest in macroeconomic models has waned at academic research centres, but not that much in advisory bodies for government or business (Mankiw, 1988). Reasons for the disenchantment are twofold. Firstly, according to the critics actual economic events in the 1970's, like stagflation caused by supply shocks, could hardly be explained by the macroeconomic models of the 1960's[3]. Secondly, theoretical underpinnings of macroeconomic models were heavily questioned. Because the models are not derived from microeconomic principles, their parameters are not invariant to policy, as was stressed by the Lucas (1976) econometric policy evaluation critique[4]. Since then much research effort has been directed at providing macroeconomics with a solid microeconomic foundation. This has yielded a large increase in breadth and depth of economic modelling and theory. For extensive reviews we refer to Fischer (1988), Mankiw (1988, 1990) and Stiglitz (1991).

In this context the development of applied general equilibrium models became increasingly popular. The aim of applied general equilibrium modelling is to transform the abstract classical equilibrium models into realistic representations of actual economies and to use these models for policy analysis. Classical general equilibrium theory originated with Arrow and Debreu (1954) and Debreu (1959). In a static model, it distinguishes consumers who maximize utility, and producers who maximize profits. Markets are competitive and prices completely flexible. Equilibrium consists of a set of goods and prices in the economy, such that the market for each

[3] The validity of this argument has been challenged by Ando (1981) and Klein (1983a)

[4] Fischer (1988) finds, however, that the critique is not of any empirical significance in accounting for the failures of econometric models. Sims (1982) argues that the critique is not much more than a cautionary footnote, whereas Farmer (1991) shows that the critique can be bypassed in multiple equilibria rational expectations models.

good is cleared and agents have no incentives to change their behaviour. This Walrasian equilibrium is Pareto efficient. For expositions, see for instance Hahn (1981) or Ginsburgh and Mercenier (1988).

Applied general equilibrium models are applied to policy issues in the fields of development economics, international trade, resources, and taxation. An impression of the large number of applied general equilibrium models that have been developed over the last decades and of their structure can be obtained from surveys like Fullerton *et al.* (1984), Shoven and Whalley (1984 and 1992), Bovenberg (1985), Borges (1986), Bergman (1988), Decaluwe and Martens (1988), Ginsburgh and Mercenier (1988), De Melo (1988), Pereira and Shoven (1988), Bandara (1991) and Henderson (1991).

The major strength of an applied general equilibrium model is its solid theoretical foundation. Behaviour of agents is modelled explicitly and is based on microeconomic optimization principles. Parameters in utility functions and production functions are structural parameters, representing tastes and technology. Therefore, the model may be less vulnerable to the Lucas critique (Bovenberg, 1985). Given the number of markets distinguished, all agents acting on these markets are represented in the model. The inclusion of the complete set of budget constraints and equilibrium conditions implies internal consistency and a coherent structure.

First applications of applied general equilibrium models were disaggregated static market-clearing models with markets for goods and two factors of production. Since then, extensions have been developed in many directions such as asset markets, dynamics and expectations, price and wage rigidities, and imperfect competition. A common approach has been to extend an existing applied general equilibrium model in one or a few directions or to build a model which focuses on one of these aspects. Concentrating on one aspect often means a price must be paid with respect to some other aspect. For instance, Pereira and Shoven (1988) conclude that there is an inverse relation between the adoption of dynamic features in production and the level of disaggregation of the production side of the economy. Another approach is taken by Erlich *et al.* (1987), who use a finite horizon truncation of an infinite horizon model to be able to introduce several consumers and producers in an intertemporal model. In the words of Fullerton *et al.* (1984): 'Clearly, researchers always face a trade-off between simplicity and accuracy of detail and in several areas there is no "right" approach.' This calls for the introduction of different models for different purposes, using those aspects of theory in a model that are most relevant to the purpose for which the model will be constructed.

Applied general equilibrium models are well suited to implement the tax system at a detailed level, and to analyze its influence on the economy. Tax rates can be inserted in budget equations and decisions of optimizing agents may change when tax rates are altered. To study the interaction between various tax distortions, several tax instruments can be inserted in a model. Alternative approaches to applied general equilibrium modelling either model taxes on an highly aggregated level, or analyze distributional consequences of taxation in a very detailed way without incorporating economy wide consequences. An example of the first approach is the presence of average tax rates in linearized equations of empirical macroeconomic models. The second approach can be found in detailed accounting schemes that analyze the budgetary consequences of taxes and social security premiums[5] or in microsimulation models[6]. However, in applied general equilibrium models the measurement of tax rates and their relation to the actual tax code may present difficulties. In a number of models average tax rates are used, which are calculated by dividing tax receipts by the tax base in the year of calibration. This procedure may be too crude for taxes like the income tax, where average and marginal tax rates differ. That is why in some models income taxes are treated as a linear function (with intercept) of income for each household group (see for instance Ballard *et al.*, 1985). Although in this way average and marginal tax rates differ, marginal tax rates do not change with income

[5] For The Netherlands see Van Schaaijk and Verkade, 1988; for eight OECD countries see Central Planning Bureau, 1993a.

[6] See for instance Van Herwaarden *et al.* (1990) and Van Schaaijk *et al.* (1990). Nelissen (1991) discusses general features of microsimulation models.

and it is difficult to translate policy proposals into the parameters of these tax functions.

Another frequently quoted advantage of applied general equilibrium models is the possibility to analyze the welfare consequences of taxation. Computing compensating changes in income to restore utility of consumers after a change in tax rates yields an estimate of the welfare costs. In a static simulation this is a straightforward procedure, but in a dynamic setting without perfect foresight it becomes more difficult. Compensating variation measures also contain an element of arbitrariness. In policy proposals, distributional effects often play an important role and an aggregate compensating variation measure is not suited to describe these distributional effects (Bovenberg, 1985). In a non market-clearing model a related problem is how to measure the social disutility of unemployment.

Weaknesses of applied general equilibrium models can be divided into less appealing features of the specification of present day models and methodological aspects. The first category includes features like the perfect competition assumption, the specification of financial behaviour, etc. In principle these weaknesses can be overcome, and partly have already been overcome. To cite a few examples, Harris (1984) introduces economies of scale and imperfect competition in an applied general equilibrium model and shows that this leads to higher welfare gains from trade liberalization. Slemrod (1983) incorporates portfolio behaviour. Goulder and Bovenberg study open economy aspects, such as the influence of international capital flows[7]. At present many applied general equilibrium models contain dynamics. Pereira and Shoven (1988) present a survey of dynamic applied general equilibrium models. These examples show only a few aspects of a large research program, which is designed to overcome weaknesses in the current specification of models.

[7] See the series of papers starting with Goulder *et al.* (1983) and Bovenberg (1986). Bovenberg and Goulder (1991) incorporate intertemporal decision making.

The main methodological weakness concerns empirical validation. Generally applied general equilibrium models are calibrated[8], which means that relevant elasticities are taken from economic literature and other parameters, like scaling parameters, are computed in such a way as to match the base year solution of the model with a benchmark data set. This way of computing non-elasticity parameters is useful[9]. Using elasticities from other studies is more difficult to defend, because often these studies do not contain the same definitions of variables or level of disaggregation as the model that is being built. Also the functional forms used in applied general equilibrium models may impose restrictions on elasticities that are not in agreement with empirical studies. Modellers may react to the weakness of the calibration procedure in two ways (Bergman, 1986). The first is to stress the methodological aspects and broad themes of their results, which should be regarded as an illustration of a theory rather than precise numbers useful for policy decisions. The second reaction is, that calibration has been done seriously enough to warrant quantitative statements. Moreover, the use of micro data may strengthen the empirical basis of disaggregated applied general equilibrium models compared with more aggregated models, because disaggregated models incorporate detailed information on the structure of the economy.

1.3 Methodological aspects of MIMIC

The first methodological aspect of MIMIC relates to the theories incorporated in the model. Furthermore, this section pays attention to the equilibrium concept used and to the main criteria that have played a role in constructing MIMIC.

[8] Exceptions are the estimated applied general equilibrium models of Jorgenson and Yun (1986a, 1986b) and Jorgenson and Wilcoxen (1990), and the estimation of demand systems in Keller *et al.* (1988).

[9] At the same time it provides a way to check the model for coding errors.

An applied general equilibrium model with New Keynesian elements

MIMIC builds on the applied general equilibrium approach, and comprises some characteristics of New Keynesian Theory (see Gordon (1990) for a review). The basic reason to prefer an applied general equilibrium model is that behaviourial consequences of taxation and social security can be represented most adequately in this type of model. The representation of institutional detail has been done by inserting statutory rates of taxation and social security premiums in the budget constraints of households and by disaggregating households according to their sources of income. Advantages of using statutory tax and premium rates are that proper inputs can be computed for average and marginal tax and premium rates that influence labour supply and wage formation, and that policy proposals can easily be implemented. A consequence of using the statutory tax code is that sufficient disaggregation is required to avoid problems arising from kinks in the budget constraints of households. That is why the seventeen household types in MIMIC are further disaggregated with respect to classes of income of breadwinners. At this level of disaggregation the only data available is survey information for a single year. Using applied general equilibrium methodology, we rely for a large part on economic theory to provide a structure into which the statutory tax and premium rates can be incorporated.

Wage bargaining theory and monopolistic competition give MIMIC some major characteristics of New Keynesian models. New Keynesian theory attempts to give a theoretical underpinning of wage and price rigidity and analyses the consequences of introducing imperfect information and imperfect competition. Research in this field can be divided into research on nominal rigidities and on real rigidities.

Three groups of theories attempt to explain real wage rigidity. According to the implicit contract theory, workers are more risk averse than firms and firms insure workers against income fluctuations, by stabilizing the real wage. However, a number of difficulties shifted attention away from this approach (see for instance Blanchard and Fischer, 1989). The second group of theories explaining real wage rigidity, concern wage bargaining theories like the insider-outsider theory. These theories state that wage formation results from bargaining processes between employers and employees. Because of the bargaining power of employees the wage outcome of these bargains may lie above the market-clearing level and induce equilibrium unemployment. Under some conditions the level of equilibrium unemployment is not unique, but dependent on the course of the economy in the past, creating hysteresis in unemployment. Thirdly, efficiency wage theories are based on the hypothesis that worker productivity depends on the wage rate, which may induce firms to pay wages above the market-clearing level. One of the explanations for the relation between wages and productivity is the so-called fair wage theory, which stresses that the worker's feelings of loyalty to the firm depend on the perceived fairness of the wage. Workers may reduce their effort when the actual wage is less than this fair wage.

Bargaining plays a central role in Dutch wage formation. Therefore, we take the wage bargaining approach as the main building block in the wage model. Because in some sectors competitive wage determination is relevant and because in individual cases bargained wages can be supplemented by wage drift, total wage formation will be a mixture of an industry bargaining process and a atomistic wage drift process. Hence, we use a combined wage model, in which elements of the bargaining theory and of the efficiency wage theory play a role. Following Graafland (1990b) we will not use the extreme version of the insider-outsider model, in which unions take no account of outsiders at all. The efficiency wage element in the wage bargaining model involves the introduction of macro labour productivity. Macro labour productivity plays an important role in wage negotiations in The Netherlands and can be interpreted as an indicator for what is considered to be the fair wage in efficiency wage theory.

Another New Keynesian element in the model concerns price setting on goods markets. Firms are assumed to be price setters operating on monopolistically competitive markets. In this way prices are modelled as a mark-up over costs. Firms maximize profits, taking account of demand reactions to their price changes, and supply the resulting demand for goods. Because of the flexibility of firm behaviour with respect to prices and supply, the goods market always clears. Since issues related to the influences of taxes and social security on the labour market pertain to medium term adjustment effects, rather than short run stabilization effects, short run fluctuations and transitory real effects of nominal shocks are not our main interest. That is why we pay no attention to lags in price reactions and other lag structures. These aspects of New Keynesian theory are absent in MIMIC.

For a number of reasons the rational expectations hypothesis, which is a basic element of the New Classical paradigm and used in some dynamic applied general equilibrium models, will not be applied in MIMIC. Because of the high degree of disaggregation in MIMIC, using perfect foresight would substantially complicate the model. Notwithstanding the somewhat ad-hoc character, we model expectations in MIMIC therefore by means of small satellite models[10] or as being adaptive[11]. To this we may add that, although adaptive expectations are extreme in not implying any forward looking behaviour, the rational expectation hypothesis is at the other end of the spectrum in assuming perfect knowledge of the model. For example, Phelps (1988) dismisses rational expectations as being in contradiction with theory and evidence. Fischer (1988) cites evidence of systematic errors in expectations and repeated failures of joint tests of rational expectations and other hypotheses. According to Fischer, rational expectations has become the dominant expectations hypothesis, because there is as yet no clear way of choosing among alternative assumptions.

[10] See for instance the simplified model of the firm which is used in the wage bargaining model of Chapter 4 to take account of wage effects on employment and profits.

[11] This implies that the model cannot distinguish between the announcement of a policy change and the actual implementation, like for example in Jensen *et al.* (1993). Using an intertemporal general equilibrium model with overlapping generations they conclude that no benefits are obtained from pre-announcing a labour income tax cut. By contrast, a pre-announcement of a capital income tax cut some years in advance is found to generate a Pareto improvement.

The concept of equilibrium and model horizon

The first generation of static disaggregated applied general equilibrium models like Shoven and Whalley (1972, 1973), Keller (1980) for the Netherlands, Fullerton *et al.* (1981) and Piggott and Whalley (1985a) all started from the Walrasian equilibrium concept, in which all markets clear.

MIMIC diverts from this traditional equilibrium concept because of its New Keynesian characteristics. Although the goods market is assumed to clear, because of flexibility in firm behaviour with respect to prices and supply, the labour market does not clear. Since the outcome of the wage bargaining process between employers and employees lies above the market clearing level, persistent unemployment results. This unemployment can be denoted as equilibrium unemployment, because it exist in a situation in which individual decisions have had time to adjust to each other so as to be mutually consistent (Malinvaud, 1977).

When introducing dynamics, we have to take account of the time period for which an equilibrium is defined. In an annual model, a number of variables remain fixed when the model is solved for a particular year. This applies to stock variables, like the capital stock or stocks of financial assets at the beginning of the period, and to variables that are fixed in the short run, like rigid prices or short run exogenous government expenditure. Since expectations do not depend on future variables generated by the model, each period in the model simulation describes a *temporary equilibrium* in which individual decisions have been adjusted conditional on the variables that are fixed for the year (see Robinson and D'Andrea Tyson, 1984; Ginsburgh and Mercenier, 1988). By including adjustment equations for the stock variables, a sequence of temporary equilibria can be computed by the model, generating a simulation path of the economy through time. On this simulation path of the model, points in time can be chosen to compare the state of the economy under different policy settings.

A subsequent issue is which points of time on a counterfactual simulation path and on a base line simulation path will be compared to describe the economic effects of policy changes. In principle, both short-term (one year), medium-term (four years) and long-term (ten years and over) effects could be distinguished, but a serious concern should be whether the model has been designed to produce reliable outcomes in all these cases. For three reasons no attention whatsoever has been paid to the short-term and medium-term characteristics of MIMIC, while constructing the model. The first and most important reason is related to the fact that, being part of an applied general equilibrium model, behaviourial equations in MIMIC are strongly based on economic theory. Generally, economic theory only considers the state of affairs that will manifest itself if certain conditions are realized. A change in conditions generates a new state of affairs. Theories about adjustment processes and lags in behaviour are much more scarce. Often, especially in empirical macroeconomic models, lag structures are introduced in an *ad hoc* way or derived from goodness-of-fit considerations. Hence, theory is of little help in specifying the specific pattern of adjustment processes. Secondly, at the Central Planning Bureau already the empirical macroeconomic model FKSEC (Central Planning Bureau, 1992a) is operational to make short-term and medium-term forecasts for the Dutch economy and to analyze policy questions on their short-term and medium-term effects. The third reason is to avoid the additional complexities of having to construct an adequate base projection for the short and medium term and to produce and explain short-term effects of policy changes with a large and comprehensive model like MIMIC[12].

Because characteristics of adjustment processes have not been taken into account during model construction no reliable short-term and medium-term effects can be derived. Hence, only long-term policy effects can be computed from MIMIC. For the same reason the model cannot be tested[13] by assessing its ex-post tracking performance. In simulation exercises the long run is defined as the simulation path the economy will reach when all adjustments

[12] Currently, another modelling team at the CPB is working on the integration of MIMIC and the empirical macroeconomic model FKSEC.

[13] This feature of the model is common to most of the applied general equilibrium models currently operational.

have been completed in the sense that multipliers associated with exogenous shocks have stabilized. For a number of cases in which relatively small shocks are given, like the multiplier analysis in Chapter 8, results on a ten year horizon are presented. In other cases more complicated system adjustments will be simulated, which also are expected to be implemented more gradually. Therefore, in these cases a 25 year horizon was judged to be more adequate.

Modelling criteria

The reasons for the wide-spread use of models in economics are well-known (see for instance Britton, 1989; Siebrand, 1988; Zalm, 1988; Verbruggen, 1992). Models provide a consistent framework for organising thoughts about an economic issue. The assumptions underlying the conclusions are explicitly specified and open for discussion. Model exercises are reproducible and the sensitivity of conclusions to crucial parameters can be assessed. The user of a model is required to be precise about the question he is addressing, because it has to be incorporated in a formal structure. Moreover, because of this structure, no statements can be derived from a model that are in contradiction with definitional relationships in the model. Quantitative results from models can be used to guide policy. A specific model can function as a unifying framework to compare different policy proposals.

A useful distinction between two main types of models is made by Boland (1989). Models can be divided into pure models and applied models. Pure models are designed to improve the process of understanding. Assumptions that lead to one logically false statement are not acceptable, regardless of how many true statements can be derived. This leads to an axiomatic modelling approach, because mathematical theorems are convenient to establish whether a theory logically supports a particular conjecture. No statement is put forward with respect to the applicability of for instance utility maximization to a specific real world situation. Applied models are explicit, simplified representations of more general theories and are designed to apply to specific problems or situations. They can be subdivided into models for explanation, which are meant to give a description of a certain part of the economic process, and models for deriving policy advice like MIMIC. The logical status of the assumptions of these models is not the main issue, but is one of the criteria that can be used to evaluate the usefulness of a model.

Pesaran and Smith (1985) mention three criteria for model building: relevance, consistency and adequacy. Constructing MIMIC, a high weight has been given to the modelling criterium of relevance. Relevance means that a model is designed for a certain purpose and should be able to provide statements concerning that purpose. MIMIC is designed to play a role in current discussions about changes in the system of taxation and social security and about policy options to increase female labour force participation. Hence, the aspects that have been given most attention are wage formation, labour supply, labour demand and the representation of the system of taxation and social security in such a way that a direct link with the statutory tax and premium rates has been obtained. Explicit disaggregation is therefore largely confined to the influence of tax rates and social security premiums on household consumption and labour supply.

For an advising body like the Dutch Central Planning Bureau relevance is also related to the timeliness of results, since issues in the political debate come and go. Because of the time required to build a model, there is some danger that the policy question which it was intended to answer, has ceased to be relevant by the time the model is ready. To meet this type of deadline, some short-cuts have been applied in modelling less relevant parts of the model. For example, the allocation of household demand between different types of goods is modelled for all households together. Moreover, the saving rate has been kept exogenous, which is motivated by the fact that a large part of savings in The Netherlands consists of compulsory pension premiums and that free savings hardly influence the labour supply decision. The size and variability of free savings then become less important.[14]

[14] Modelling only those aspects that are of sufficient relevance to the simulation results of the model can also be illustrated by an example from the labour supply model. In the labour supply model we take account of kinked budget constraints, due to stepwise increas-

The second criterium of consistency relates to two aspects: to the internal structure of a model and to the theories applied in the model. Internally, MIMIC satisfies identities like budget constraints according to the definition structure implied by the National Accounts system. Consistency with theory is a less straightforward prerequisite. Theories can be modelled in many different ways. However, a dividing line can be drawn between representing a theory in structural form, for instance by explicitly optimizing a utility function under a budget restriction, and representation in reduced form. In MIMIC for the most part theories are described in structural form.

With the concept of adequacy, data and econometrics enter the scene. The main question is how adequately a model represents the phenomena it is assumed to describe. To provide MIMIC with an empirical basis, the wage formation model, which is crucial for the simulation results, has been based on estimation results with times series data. Parameters of the production functions of MIMIC have been calibrated in such a way, that the changes in employment of each of the five educational categories of labour distinguished, represent changes in the data available for 1979 and 1985. Base year income distributions have been calibrated on data from income distribution statistics. With regard to households, microeconometric estimates are taken from the literature on household labour supply to calibrate crucial parameters.

As a fourth modelling criterion we suggest comprehensibility. A model should not be a black box, the results of which are to be believed at face value. To improve comprehensibility, we preferred uniform reactions at a disaggregated level with MIMIC, when there were no strong theoretical or empirical reasons to impose heterogeneity. For example, as much as possible

ing marginal rates of taxation and social security premiums. Because of the interaction between the tax system and the social security system, small income intervals exist in which the combined marginal rate of taxation and social security premiums falls when income rises. This creates convexities in the budget constraint, which would require adjustments in the labour supply model that would lead to substantial complications. Inspection of the lengths of the relevant intervals showed that the non-convexities would only be relevant for a small number of partners. Hence, we decided not to take these intervals into account in the budget constraint of partners.

identical values of labour supply elasticities have been selected for different types of households.

1.4 An overview of the model structure of MIMIC

In this section the structure of MIMIC is illustrated by identifying the main markets in the model and the agents operating on these markets and by describing the characteristics of the behaviourial submodels. A subsection on closure of the model concentrates on the modelling of the public sector and on macro relationships, whereas the final subsection gives an overview of the most important relations between government institutions and the labour market in MIMIC.

Markets and agents

Three types of markets are distinguished in MIMIC, *viz.* goods markets, the labour market and financial markets. Agents operating on these markets are

Table 1.1 Markets and agents

	Goods markets				Labour markets		Financial markets	
	Domestic		Foreign					
	Quantity	Price	Quantity	Price	Quantity	Price	Quantity	Price
Firms								
– Domestic	Supply	Setting	Demand	Taking	Demand	Taking	Demand	Taking
– Foreign	Demand	Taking	Supply	Setting	–	–	–	–
Households								
– Domestic	Demand	Taking	Demand	Taking	Supply	Taking	Supply	Taking
– Foreign	Demand	Taking	–	–	–	–	Supply[a]	Setting
Public sector	Demand	Taking	Demand	Taking	Demand	Taking	Demand	Taking
Pension funds	–	–	–	–	–	–	Supply	Taking
Unions and employers' organisations	–	–	–	–	–	Setting	–	–

[a] In the calibration year 1985, net foreign supply of assets was positive. To have it fit in the table, 'supply' is inserted at the financial transactions of foreign households.

firms, households, the public sector, pension funds, employers' organisations and unions. Table 1.1 presents an overview of markets and agents in MIMIC.

Markets for goods are subdivided into domestic and foreign markets in order to stress the open character of the Dutch economy. Foreign firms, domestic and foreign households, and the public sector[15] demand domestic goods. In monopolistic competitive markets firms set prices so as to maximize profits given demand functions for their products and they supply the resulting demand for goods. Because of flexibility of firm behaviour with respect to prices and supply, the domestic goods market always clears. Domestic firms, households and the public sector demand foreign goods (imports). Import prices are fixed and exogenous, because domestic demand on the world market is too small to influence prices. By assumption, supply of foreign products is always sufficient to meet domestic demand.

As already described in the previous section, the labour market in MIMIC does not clear. Wages are set by bargaining processes between employed workers, who (partly) are organized in unions, and employers, who (partly) are organized in employers' organisations. It is assumed that the bargaining power of employed workers is negatively related to the unemployment rate. This introduces an inverse relation between unemployment and the wage rate, the so-called wage curve. The labour market situation is depicted in Figure 1.3. Labour demand follows from production decisions of individual firms and is negatively related to real wages, as expressed by the Ld-curve. Labour supply from individual households is positively related to real wages (Ls-curve). The wage curve is reflected by Ws[16]. Equilibrium unemployment is given by *u* in Figure 1.3.

[15] The model for pension funds describes the setting of pension premiums and financial transactions of pension funds. Goods transactions of pension funds, government and social security are aggregated and included in the public sector submodel.

[16] Unemployment is measured from right to left on the horizontal axis of Figure 1.3. Hence the wage curve is seen to represent an inverse relation between unemployment and wages in the figure.

Figure 1.3 Equilibrium unemployment on the labour market

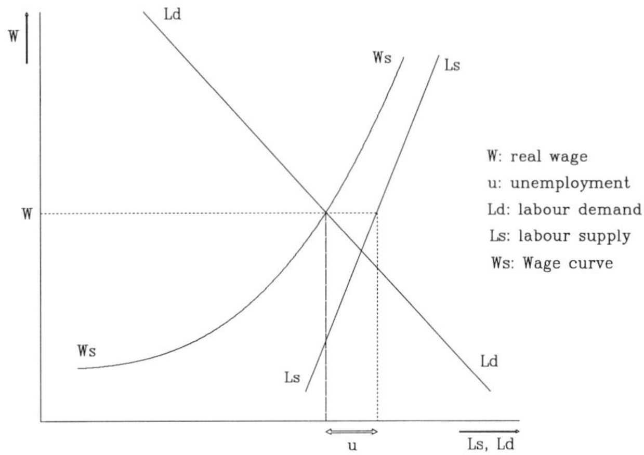

The financial market is treated in a simple way. Interest rates in the Netherlands and the value of the guilder are fully linked to German interest rates and the value of the Mark, because under standing monetary policy they follow these very closely. Hence, interest rates and exchange rates are exogenous. At given interest rates, firms and the public sector exert net demand on the financial market to finance investments and public deficits respectively. Households and pension funds offer net supply of financial assets. Foreign capital flows equilibrate demand and supply.

Characteristics of submodels

Broadly speaking, three submodels can be distinguished in MIMIC, describing respectively firm behaviour, household decisions and the confrontation between labour supply and labour demand in the matching process and wage formation.

Domestic firms are divided into six sectors of which the exposed and the sheltered sector are the most important ones. Firms maximize profits under monopolistic competition on the goods market. The production structure is described by means of nested CES production functions with intermediaries, capital and labour (disaggregated into five categories, *viz.* two types of low-skilled labour with a different level of income, technically high-skilled labour, economically high-skilled labour, and service-oriented high-skilled labour) as inputs. The output price is set as a mark-up over marginal cost and indirect taxes. The mark-up depends on the price elasticity of demand for the firms' product. At given world trade and foreign prices, domestic output prices determine production and employment. The latter is also negatively related to real wages because of substitution with capital. Because of flexibility of firm behaviour with respect to prices and supply, the domestic goods market always clears. Domestic firms, households and the public sector demand foreign goods (imports). Import prices are fixed and exogenous, because domestic demand on the world market is too small to influence foreign prices. By assumption, supply of foreign products is always sufficient to meet domestic demand. On the labour market the firm is assumed to have some monopsonic power, because it has a limited possibility to influence wages by offering an incidental wage component in addition to the contractual wage, which is given for individual employers. This incidental component of the wage rate is part of the search strategy of employers and can be used as an instrument to reduce search costs for attracting new employees.

The second submodel is the household model, describing labour supply and private consumption. To provide an adequate representation of households relevant for the labour supply decision, families are distinguished with respect to the presence of children, the educational level of the partner and, most important, the labour market situation of the breadwinner and the type of benefit (social insurance or social assistance) received by the breadwinner in case of unemployment or disability. In total, seventeen types of households are distinguished. For each type of household, the net income of the average breadwinner of the household is derived from the application of micro data based income distributions of gross breadwinner income, combined with the statutory rates of taxation and social security premiums.

In the household model only labour supply of partners is endogenized, because labour supply of breadwinners in families and of single persons is generally empirically found to be rather insensitive to income changes

(Theeuwes, 1988). Households are assumed to differ with respect to their relative preference for leisure versus consumption. Each household chooses the number of hours the partner wishes to work by maximizing a CES utility function in consumption and leisure given the kinked budget curve which follows from the income bracket tax system. The number of hours supplied depends positively on the net marginal wage of the partners (because of substitution from leisure to consumption) and negatively on other income components of the household (like the breadwinners income). Some of the partners will not participate because their relative preference for leisure is so high that the desired number of working hours becomes negative. Hence, the total labour supply effects for all partners in a specific type of households can be decomposed into a participation effect and an effect on the average number of hours supplied by participating partners in that type of household. The participation effect determines the change in labour supply measured in persons. The sum of the participation effect and the effect on the average number of hours supplied determines the labour supply effect measured in hours. Total labour supply follows from aggregating the optimal number of hours of individuals at different parts of the kinked budget curve. Based on empirical information, the average net wage elasticity of partner labour supply is set at one and the average other income elasticity of partner labour supply is set at –0.2 to –0.3.

The third submodel in MIMIC concerns contractual wage formation, the search intensity of unemployed and the matching process between vacancies and unemployed persons. Contractual wages are set by bargaining processes between employed workers who are organized in unions, and employers organized in employers' organisations. Wages are set above market-clearing levels, generating equilibrium unemployment. The level of equilibrium unemployment depends on the factors influencing the utility functions of the bargaining partners. Utility of employers is related to profits relative to fall back profits and utility of employed workers is partly related to net income relative to their fall back position and partly related to employment. The employers' fall back level of profits depends on profits obtained if no wage contract is concluded and all employees leave the industry so that all jobs have to be filled by new employees. The fall back position of employees depends partly on opportunities outside the industry and partly on a fair wage, which is linked to the consumer price and labour productivity.

The wage outcome of the bargaining model is related to the consumer price, the average rate of taxes and premiums, the net replacement ratio, which represents the average ratio between the net unemployment benefit rate and the net wage rate, the marginal rate of taxes and premiums, the unemployment rate and search costs of employers. A higher consumer price or a higher average rate of taxes and premiums lowers purchasing power of workers and raises the fair wage to offset the fall in purchasing power. The unemployment benefit level has a positive influence on wages, because it makes quitting the industry and searching for jobs outside the industry less expensive, thereby raising the attractiveness of opportunities outside the industry. In contrast to the positive influence of the average tax rate on wages, marginal tax rates of employees have a negative influence on the wage outcome. This can be explained by the fact that a rise in marginal tax rates (at constant average tax rates) reduces the rise in net income from a rise in wages, whereas the costs in terms of a reduction in employment remains the same.[17] Hence, the trade-off between net income and employment shifts in favour of the latter and this makes unions more willing to moderate wages in order to create additional employment. Hence, a higher marginal tax and premium rate stimulates wage moderation. Finally, a rise in search costs for new employees increases the wage outcome because it worsens the employers' fall back level of profits. The parameters of the model are set in such a way that the elasticities of explanatory variables are in accordance with empirical estimates of a linearized macro wage equation for The Netherlands.

Search costs for new employees are related to vacancy durations. In order to describe the relation between labour market institutions and vacancy duration, MIMIC includes a search model for unemployed persons and a

[17] See also Hersoug *et al.* (1986) and Malcomson and Sartor (1987). Hoel (1990) shows that a negative influence of the marginal tax rate on wages is also obtained if an efficiency wage model is considered.

matching model which relates the number of filled jobs to the number of vacancies, unemployed persons, and the search strategies of employers and unemployed. The effectiveness of the matching process depends on two types of government institutions, the official minimum wage and the level of the unemployment benefit. The minimum wage level determines the selectivity of employers in accepting new employees: if the official minimum wage is high, employers will only select relatively productive employees, reducing the number of potential candidates. Hence, the effectiveness of the matching process will be low and the search process for new employees more costly. The level of unemployment benefits determines the reservation wage of unemployed and hence their selectivity in accepting job offers. Moreover, the generosity of the unemployment benefit system also affects the search intensity of the unemployed by changing the relative attractiveness of working over unemployment. Hence, a rise in unemployment benefit levels will also reduce the effectiveness of the matching process, implying longer vacancy durations and higher search costs for employers.

Closure of the model

A model is closed when we have sufficient information to compute a meaningful solution. First of all this applies to the subdivision of variables into endogenous and exogenous variables. According to Cooper *et al.* (1985), for a linear model with m equations in k variables ($k > m$) closure consists of declaring a subset of $k - m$ variables to be exogenous and assigning values to these variables. According to the definition of closure above, the concept is much broader than merely declaring variables to be exogenous, because many more assumptions have to be made to make an applied general equilibrium model operational. The main areas for which closure assumptions have to be made are: the treatment of policy variables, the modelling of the external sector, the modelling of the public sector, the treatment of time, and of macro relationships (Piggott, 1985). The modelling of the external sector and the treatment of time have already been addressed above. Here we will pay attention to the modelling of the public sector and macro relationships.

In MIMIC government behaviour is largely exogenous. Tax rates and the volume of most public outlays are given, prices of government expenditure and the public sector wage rate are linked to private sector variables. The public deficit is endogenously determined and feeds back into government debt and interest charges on government debt. Pension premiums are adjusted to the level of the interest rate and the growth rates of wages and the population, in order to equilibrate the actuarial balance sheet of the pension funds in the long run.

MIMIC contains many relationships that link submodels with different degrees of disaggregation to each other. For example, with respect to the goods market, various types of goods are distinguished, like exports of goods, exports of services, investment in buildings, investment in equipment, various kinds of private consumption, all differentiated to the sector supplying these goods. However, with respect to the production structure and factor inputs, value added from all these types of goods is aggregated per sector, which implicitly assumes an identical production function for firms operating in different markets. Another example concerns the aggregation of sector-specific vacancies, determined in the model of the firm, to macro vacancies per type of labour, which is input in the matching function between vacancies and unemployment. Furthermore, many definitional relationships are necessary to link the types of labour distinguished in the model of the firm, consisting of five educational levels, to the types of labour distinguished in the household model. The latter model contains only two educational levels, but differentiates labour according to household situation and category of social benefits received. This implies that equations are needed to link employment, labour supply and wages for the types of labour distinguished in the firm model and the household model. In a similar way equations are used to link average tax rates and replacement ratios in both models in a consistent way.

Main links between government institutions and labour market

Figure 1.4 gives an overview of the most important relations between government institutions and the labour market in MIMIC. Four types of government institutions can be distinguished: indirect tax rates consisting of three value added tax rates; the official minimum wage rate; the statutory income tax and social security premium system; and social benefits for unemployment and disability.

Indirect tax rates have a direct influence on price setting by firms. Especially the value added tax rate on consumption goods is of great relevance in the model, because contractual wages are partly indexed to consumer prices. A rise in consumer prices induced by an increase in value added taxes will therefore cause additional wage claims and a decrease in employment, and this will in turn lead to higher equilibrium unemployment.

Minimum wages affect firm behaviour by creating a minimum productivity level per employee needed to earn the minimum wage. This restricts the employers' possibilities in attracting low-skilled employees, since workers with a productivity on the job which is lower than the minimum wages, will not be hired. A rise in minimum wages will reduce the number of candidates whose productivity exceeds the minimum wage and hence the acceptance rate of employers will fall. As a result the average vacancy duration rises, raising search costs for employers, with unfavourable consequences for labour demand and unemployment.

The income tax rates and social premiums are important determinants of labour supply of partners in households. Using micro data on gross income distributions a detailed description of marginal and average tax rates is given. The marginal tax rate has a negative influence on labour supply by partners, whereas average tax rates affect labour supply positively through income effects on both partner and breadwinner income. In addition, the average tax rate has an important direct influence on contractual wage formation, because of the forward shifting effect, implying that a rise in income tax rates will lead to higher wages with unfavourable consequences for equilibrium unemployment.

Figure 1.4 Links between institutions and labour market

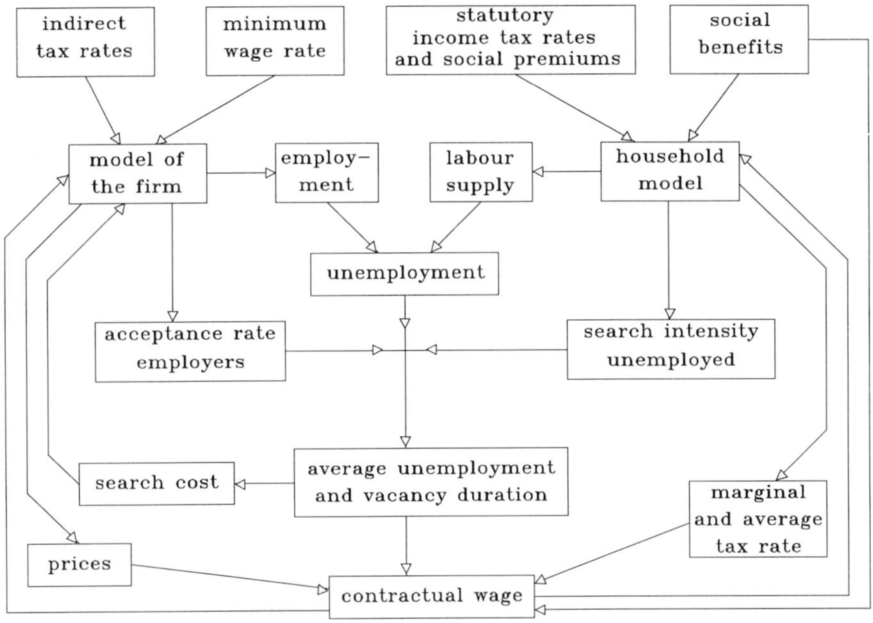

The fourth government institution that plays an important role in the labour market concerns the level and structure of unemployment and disability benefits. Two types of unemployment benefits are distinguished, unemployment benefits paid by the social security funds, and social assistance granted by the government. The ratio between the net unemployment benefit and the net wage rate, the so-called replacement ratio, has two effects. Firstly, a higher replacement ratio raises the reservation wage of unemployed persons and reduces their search intensity by lowering the utility of working compared to receiving a benefit. This has unfavourable consequences for average vacancy duration and incidental wages. Secondly, the level of unemployment benefits also has a direct influence on contractual wage formation by improving the threatpoint of employees.

1.5 Comparison of MIMIC with other applied general equilibrium models

After having presented the methodology and structure of MIMIC, in this section we compare MIMIC with other applied general equilibrium models. Because of the large number of applied general equilibrium models that have been developed until now, it is not possible to give a complete comparison. Instead we selected a small number of the models and present a table of characteristics that resembles tables in review papers like Shoven and Whalley (1984), Fullerton *et al.* (1984), Pereira and Shoven (1988), and Henderson (1991). Using these papers, comparison of MIMIC to other models can be performed by the reader.

The models selected for comparison are the model of Piggott and Whalley (1985a) for the United Kingdom, the models of Ballard, Fullerton, Shoven and Whalley (1985), and of Jorgenson and Yun (1986a and 1986b) for the United States and the model of Keller (1980) for The Netherlands. The model of Piggott and Whalley and the model of Ballard *et al.* are characteristic examples of fairly disaggregated applied general equilibrium models designed for the analysis of taxation. They are straight descendants of the first applied general equilibrium tax models of Shoven and Whalley (1972, 1973), and have been a starting point for further extensions in many directions. The model of Jorgenson and Yun is an example of a dynamic applied general equilibrium model. It is also characterized by the use of flexible functional forms and by being the only applied general equilibrium tax model that has not been calibrated but has been completely estimated[18]. Since MIMIC applies to The Netherlands, it is a natural choice to include the model of Keller (1980). For comparison we will use the specification in Keller *et al.* (1988), which is a much more disaggregated version of the original model. For further applications of this model see Zeelenberg *et al.* (1991).

[18] Jorgenson and Wilcoxen (1990) present an estimated general equilibrium model with 35 industrial sectors and 672 types of households, that is used for modelling environmental regulation.

The features of these models and of MIMIC are presented in Table 1.2, which largely speaks for itself. From the sections on producers and households in Table 1.2 it appears that increased complexity of the model specification combines with a lower degree of disaggregation. For instance, in the Jorgenson and Yun model intertemporal optimization with perfect foresight is modelled for one representative firm and one representative consumer, compared with 19 to 58 sectors and 12 to 100 household groups in the other models. In MIMIC only six enterprises sectors are distinguished, because much attention is paid to the modelling of employment through disaggregation into five types of schooling and a description of search strategies of employers. Also the complete input-output matrix is excluded from MIMIC, and replaced by the so-called cumulated production structure matrix, which is a reduced form representation of the input-output matrix.

The disaggregation of households in MIMIC is comparable to that in three of the other models, taking account of the fact that differences in income levels are incorporated by means of income distributions. For instance, in the Keller model the 40 groups of households consist of four family types times two social-economic categories times five income classes. In MIMIC there are on average ten income classes in the income distributions of breadwinners for each of the seventeen groups, which makes a comparable total of 170. Furthermore, in the labour supply model the heterogeneity with respect to relative preference for leisure also generates a distribution of incomes for partners in households (compare Section 3.2). Participation of partners and their average number of hours supplied are derived simultaneously in the labour supply model.

In the Netherlands a large part of household savings is obligatory through pension savings. Free savings are a relatively small component of the budget of households and hardly influence partner labour supply. In MIMIC an exogenous savings rate has been opted for to avoid the complexities of combining on the one hand a detailed analysis of the interaction of the statutory tax and premium system with the labour supply decision and on the other hand the intertemporal aspects of the savings decision. In all other models savings are endogenous. Because of the large share of pension

Table 1.2 Comparison of some applied general equilibrium models

	Piggott Whalley	Ballard Fullerton Shoven Whalley	Jorgenson Yun	Keller	MIMIC
Country	Un. Kingdom	United States	United States	Netherlands	Netherlands
Year of data	1973	1973	1955-80	1981	1985
Equilibrium					
Type	static	temporary	intertemporal	static	temporary
Expectations	myopic	myopic	perfect foresight	myopic	myopic
Time path	–	sequence static equilibria	dynamic	–	sequence static equilibria
Implementation					
Parameters	calibrated some estimated	calibrated	estimated	estimated and calibrated	calibrated some estimated
Solution algorithm	Newton	Merrill	multiple shooting	linear approximation	Newton
Producers					
Disaggregation	33 sectors	19 sectors	1 sector	58 sectors	6 sectors
Objective	costs	costs	costs	profits	profits
Competition	perfect	perfect	perfect	perfect	monopolistic
Technology	CES	CES	translog	CES	CES
Inputs	capital, labour	capital, labour	capital, labour	capital, 3 types of labour, imports	capital, 5 types of labour, imports
Capital stock	exogenous	endogenous	endogenous	exogenous	endogenous
Search costs	no	no	no	no	labour
I-O matrix	yes	yes	no	yes	cumulated production structure
Households					
Disaggregation	100 groups	12 groups	1 consumer	40 groups	17 types, 170 income classes
Objective	single period utility	intertemporal utility	intertemporal utility	single period utility	single period utility
Tastes	CES	CES	translog	CES	CES
Labour supply	endogenous	endogenous	endogenous	endogenous	endogenous participation, working hours
Savings	endogenous	endogenous	endogenous	endogenous	exogenous

Table 1.2 Comparison of some applied general equilibrium models (continued)

	Piggott Whalley	Ballard Fullerton Shoven Whalley	Jorgenson Yun	Keller	MIMIC
Pension funds					
Objective	–	–	–	–	Actuarial balance
Premiums	–	–	–	Exogenous	Endogenous
Public sector					
Objective	public utility	public utility	–	public utility	–
Budget	balanced	yearly balanced	yearly balanced	balanced	not balanced
Debt	no	no	no	no	yes
Taxes	all major	all major	all major	all major	all major
Implementation of tax rates	average marginal	average marginal	average marginal	average marginal	statutory tax code
Foreign sector					
Open economy	yes	yes	no	yes, small	yes, small
Current account	balanced	balanced	–	balanced	not balanced
Markets					
Goods	clears	clears	clears	clears	clears
Labour	clears	clears	clears	clears	equilibrium unemployment, matchings, search intensity
Financial assets	–	–	–	–	clears
Policy					
Evaluation indicators	compensating or equivalent variations, Gini, Atkinson measure welfare	compensating or equivalent variations	social welfare function	compensating variations	unemployment, employment, public budget
Issues	VAT, each tax, housing subsidies	integration, consumption tax, VAT, capital or labour tax	programs of tax reform	Capital tax and subsidies, VAT, labour tax	VAT, income tax reform, social security benefits, minimum wages, basic income

savings, MIMIC contains a model for pension funds in which pension premiums are derived from the actuarial balance of these funds.

The disaggregation of the household sector in MIMIC also opens the possibility to use the statutory tax code to model taxes and social security premiums. Table 1.2 shows that other models use average marginal tax rates, which are derived by specifying income taxes as linear functions of income. Using the actual tax code we take into account stepwise increasing marginal tax rates and we are able to compute the direct consequences of policy measures on important variables like the tax variables in the wage model and labour supply. Another aspect of the public sector in MIMIC is that the annual budget of the government does not balance, which coincides with the inclusion of government debt in the model. This also means that the current account does not have to be balanced in each year. Since the Keller model and MIMIC both apply to the small open economy of The Netherlands it is no surprise that both of them use the small country assumption to model the foreign sector.

Regarding the functioning of the markets, an important feature of MIMIC is the fact that the labour market does not clear. Equilibrium unemployment follows from the wage bargaining process between employers and employed workers and, through the influence of search costs on the wage outcome, is affected by the matching process between vacancies and unemployment and the search intensity of unemployed. Because of the arbitrariness of measuring the welfare consequences of unemployment, no single policy evaluation indicator is computed for MIMIC. Instead, in simulations the changes in the unemployment rate are presented together with effects on production and on the budget of the government, without any attempts to weigh these effects in a social welfare function.

The applications of MIMIC in policy simulations concentrate on the labour market. The implications are analyzed of various changes in indirect tax rates, income tax rates, social security benefits and government assistance, and minimum wages. Income tax issues relate to recently introduced or proposed changes in the structure of taxes and social security premiums. Applications on social security relate to the influence of unemployment benefits on unemployment, the inflow into disability schemes and proposals to individualize social assistance benefits.

1.6 Outline of the study

The subsequent presentation of MIMIC runs from a description of the behaviourial structure and the calibration of the model in Part I to the presentation of the simulation results of the model in Part II. The description of MIMIC in Part I focuses on the derivation of the various submodels of behaviour of agents. In Chapter 2 the model of firm behaviour is presented. The model simultaneously describes the demand for labour, disaggregated into five types of schooling, the demand for capital, output prices and the search strategy of employers on the labour market, including incidental wage formation. The decisions of the firm are derived from profit maximization given an oligopolistic market environment, a CES production function and a cost definition. The production structure differs among production sectors. Furthermore, the chapter contains a detailed description of the calibration of the model of the firm. In an appendix the cumulated production structure matrix and the treatment of indirect taxes are dealt with.

Chapter 3 presents the model of household behaviour. After an overview of the composition and structure of the household sector, labour supply of partners in households is modelled from maximization of a utility function depending on consumption and leisure. Because of the strong disaggregation of household consumption and labour supply behaviour, aspects of search behaviour of unemployed are not fully integrated in the labour supply model, but modelled at a more aggregated level. As indicated above, the saving rate of households is exogenous in MIMIC. The calibration of the household model is documented in the last section of this chapter. Attention is paid to calibrated elasticities that are important for the simulation results of the model and to the way policy variables are included in the model. Moreover, some interesting aspects of the database are presented, like a description of the number of households in the base year 1985, subdivided with respect to sex, skill level, labour market situation and household type.

Chapter 4 considers three aspects of contacts between employers and households. Firstly, the search strategy including reservation wage and job acceptance rate is described for those people, who officially participate on the labour market but cannot find a job. Secondly, the matchings function describes the number of jobs filled from contacts between unemployed people seeking a job and vacancies posted by employers to attract new employees. Thirdly, in the wage bargaining model the outcome of the wage bargain strategies of employers' organisations and unions is derived. The characteristics of the calibrated wage model are compared with empirical estimates of a macroeconomic wage equation for the Netherlands.

Chapter 5 contains a description of government outlays and the implementation in MIMIC of the system of taxes and social security premiums in The Netherlands. In addition, a simple pension model is included, which analyses the strategy of pension funds in setting pension premiums in line with the required actuarial reserve for pensioners and the working population.

Chapter 6 focuses on the interdependence between the different behaviourial subsystems described in Chapters 2 up to and including 5. It identifies exogenous variables for the total model, provides a review of variables that link the various submodels and elaborates on some systems of definitional equations in MIMIC that convert output variables from one submodel into more disaggregated input variables for other submodels.

Part II contains an elaborate presentation of the simulation results of MIMIC. Firstly, Chapter 7 presents a description of the reference path on which the simulation analysis is based. Chapter 8 deals with various tax policies which yield an identical effect on the government budget. Thus, the effectivity of various tax parameters on influencing government policy target variables like unemployment, employment growth and inflation are assessed. This chapter closes with a presentation of a kind of 'Laffer curve', which can be generated by MIMIC. After an international comparison of income tax reform policies, Chapter 9 proceeds with a detailed analyses of the consequences of the 1990 income tax reform and of the proposals by the Stevens Committee on further income tax reform.

Chapter 10 discusses the effects of introducing a 'mini welfare state' in the Netherlands. Under this heading all kinds of proposals can be grouped that aim at a reduction of the ratio between the number of benefit recipients and the working population. We concentrate on three aspects in the political discussion about a mini welfare state: a reduction of the large inflow into the disability schemes by lowering the level of disability benefits; an increase of search intensity and acceptance rate of unemployed persons by reducing the level of unemployment benefits; and increasing the acceptance rate of employers, especially in hiring the low-skilled unemployed, by lowering the official minimum wage.

Chapter 11 deals with issues related to discussions about individualizing the tax and social security system. Individualization is aimed at creating equal rights and opportunities for women on the labour market and increasing female labour market participation. The issue is subdivided into individualizing the tax and premium system and individualizing the social security benefit system. Using MIMIC we compute the effects of abolishing the transfer of the basic allowance for income taxes and of individualizing the social assistance benefit system.

Chapter 12 treats a specific form of individualization of the tax system and social security system, namely by the introduction of a basic income for all individuals in combination with a less generous welfare system through the abolishment of the basic allowance and of social insurance and government assistance for unemployed and disabled workers. In this chapter also the effects of reinsurance of the loss in welfare arrangements by collective employers' and employees' organisations is considered, which might obstruct the introduction of a reduced welfare system.

Chapter 13 summarizes the main results of the simulation study, and evaluates the strengths and weaknesses of MIMIC in the light of the modelling criteria of relevance, consistency and adequacy.

PART I

THE STRUCTURE OF MIMIC

2 The model of the firm

The main elements of the model of the firm are an monopolistic competitive output market environment, a monopsonistic (labour) input market, a CES production function and a cost function that includes factor adjustment costs. Given these four elements, the firm sets its output price and wage offer and determines production and demand for inputs in such a way that profits are maximized. In this chapter we will present the modelling of these aspects of firm behaviour. Section 2.1 describes the output market, Section 2.2 discusses the cost function and input market characteristics and Section 2.3 the production function. Firm behaviour is derived in Section 2.4, followed by a discussion of the calibration of the model of the firm in Section 2.5.

2.1 Output market environment

On the macro level various groups of agents in the model exert demand for a certain category of goods. Domestic firms and the public sector demand investment goods, households demand consumption goods and services, the public sector demands public consumption goods and services, and foreign agents demand export goods. Investment goods are differentiated into investment in equipment and investment in buildings.

The structure of the demand for the products of the firm is presented in Figure 2.1. For expositional purposes, only the structure of demand for private consumption goods is presented. Households allocate consumption among five types of consumption goods: medical consumption (including other non-market services), residential consumption, other necessary consumption with a 0% value added tax rate, normal consumption with a 5% value added tax rate, and luxury consumption with a 19% value added tax rate. In this way the influence of value added tax rates on consumption demand can be modelled adequately.

At a second stage, each type of goods is further allocated over six production sectors: the exposed sector, the sheltered sector, the construction sector, the medical sector (including other non-market services), the mining

Figure 2.1 Structure of market environment of the firm

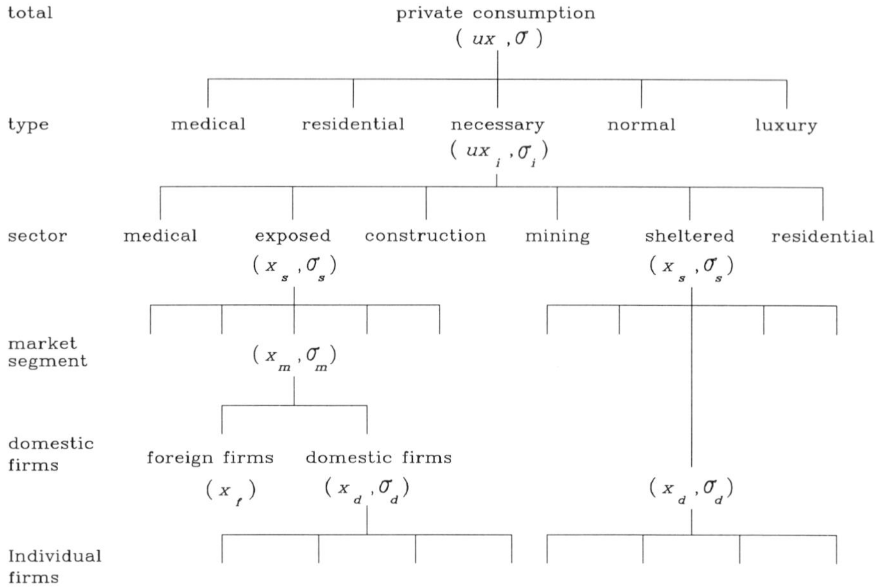

sector (natural gas) and the residential sector (exploitation of real estate). The exposed sector consists mainly of manufacturing, agriculture and transport. The sheltered sector consists of trade, banking and insurances and other private services. The construction sector is treated separately because its production structure differs markedly from that in the rest of the sheltered sector. Direct regulation was a reason to distinguish the medical sector. The mining sector and the residential sector are distinguished because they do not have much in common with other enterprises sectors. The labour income share in these sectors (about 5%) is clearly different from other sectors and demand and prices are strongly regulated.

The utility function, which underlies the allocation of total consumption to sector demand in the first two stages is assumed to have a nested MCES-structure. Allocation of total consumption demand among demand for a type of consumption goods in the first stage is given by:

$$ux = \left(\sum_{i=1}^{n} \alpha_i^{1+\rho} \, ux_i^{-\rho} \right)^{-1/\rho} , \qquad \sum_{i=1}^{n} \alpha_i = 1, \tag{2.1}$$

and allocation of demand for a type of consumption goods among demand for output of a production sector in the second stage by:

$$ux_i = \left(\sum_{s=1}^{n_i} \alpha_s^{1+\rho_i} \, (x_s - \bar{x}_s)^{-\rho_i} \right)^{-1/\rho_i} , \qquad \sum_{s\varepsilon i} \alpha_s = 1, \tag{2.2}$$

where ux denotes utility, n denotes the number of types of goods, n_i denotes the number of enterprises sectors delivering good i, ux_i denotes utility of consumption of type of goods i, x_s denotes consumption of type i delivered by sector s, $\bar{x}_s$ denotes minimal necessary consumption of x_s, and α_i and α_s denote (above minimal necessary consumption) market shares in the base year[19]. The MCES utility function has been used to be able to calibrate income elasticities not equal to one, while retaining the convenient nested CES structure.

Utility maximization under a budget constraint yields equations for utility of consumption of type i (ux_i) (Keller, 1976):

$$ux_i = \alpha_i \, ((X - \sum_{i=1}^{n} \sum_{s\in i} px_s \, \bar{x}_s) \, / \, px) \, (px_i \, / \, px)^{-\sigma} , \qquad \sigma = 1/(1+\rho), \tag{2.3}$$

with $X = \sum_{s=1}^{n_i} \sum_{s\in i} px_s \, x_s ,$

[19] All prices in the utility functions are normalised at unity in the base year.

where x denotes aggregate consumption, and an equation for consumption of type i delivered by sector s:

$$x_s = \bar{x}_s + \alpha_s\, ux_i \;(px_s \,/\, px_i)^{-\sigma_i}, \qquad \sigma_i = 1/(1+\rho_i), \tag{2.4}$$

where σ and σ_i denote partial elasticities of substitution between, respectively, different components of total demand and components of demand delivered by different sectors. The prices of total demand (px) and demand per type of good (px_i) can be expressed as weighted averages of component prices:

$$px = \left(\sum_{i=1}^{n} \alpha_i\, px_i^{1-\sigma} \right)^{1/(1-\sigma)}, \tag{2.5}$$

$$px_i = \left(\sum_{s=1}^{n_i} \alpha_s\, px_s^{1-\sigma_i} \right)^{1/(1-\sigma_i)}. \tag{2.6}$$

In the third stage, sector demand is allocated among market segments. In each sector various market segments exist. Products from these market segments do not differ very much, but are not identical from the point of view of the buyer. The number of market segments is so large, that monopolistic competition exists between market segments. This implies that firms within a given market segment ignore price competition from firms in other segments. For instance, a retailer pays attention to prices in other retail shops nearby, but neglects the price competition from banking services.

Within each market segment several domestic firms operate with a high degree of competition. Foreign firms are assumed to operate only on exposed markets. For a given domestic firm in a market segment in the exposed sector, products of other domestic firms are assumed to be closer substitutes than products of foreign firms, because of a higher degree of homogeneity between domestic products and because of locational aspects. This demand structure implies that domestic firms primarily take prices of domestic competitors into account and to a much lesser extent adjust their prices to prices of foreign competitors. The relevance of this assumption is confirmed by the empirical notion that substitution elasticities between domestic and foreign products are on average not much larger than two (see for instance Van den Berg *et al.*, 1988). Equal competition between domestic and foreign firms would imply a mark-up of prices over costs of over 50%. In reality profit margins are much lower, which can be explained by higher competition between domestic firms than between domestic and foreign firms[20].

The allocation of sector demand for goods (x_s) among market segments (x_m), domestic firms (x_d), foreign firms (x_f), and the individual domestic firm (x_k) is described by the following set of utility functions:

$$x_s = \left(\sum_{m=1}^{n_s} (1/n_s)^{1+\rho_s} \, x_m^{-\rho_s} \right)^{-1/\rho_s} , \tag{2.7}$$

$$x_m = \left(\alpha_d^{1+\rho_m} \, x_d^{-\rho_m} + (1-\alpha_d)^{1+\rho_m} \, x_f^{-\rho_m} \right)^{-1/\rho_m} , \tag{2.8}$$

$$x_d = \left(\sum_{k=1}^{n_d} (1/n_d)^{1+\rho_d} \, x_k^{-\rho_d} \right)^{-1/\rho_d} , \tag{2.9}$$

where n_s denotes the number of market segments in sector s, α_d denotes the market share of domestic firms in the base year, and n_d denotes the number

[20] According to this assumption domestic cost increases can to a large extent be shifted forward into prices of exports, improving terms of trade. Further inquiries into modelling market structures, pricing and profit margins are necessary in order to address this issue.

of domestic firms in a market segment. Utility maximization under a budget constraint yields the following standard demand equations:

$$x_m = (1/n_s)\, x_s\, (px_m \,/\, px_s)^{-\sigma_s}\,, \qquad \sigma_s = 1/(1+\rho_s)\,, \tag{2.10}$$

$$x_d = \alpha_d\, x_m\, (px_d \,/\, px_m)^{-\sigma_m}\,, \qquad \sigma_m = 1/(1+\rho_m)\,, \tag{2.11}$$

$$x_f = (1-\alpha_d)\, x_m\, (px_f \,/\, px_m)^{-\sigma_m}\,, \tag{2.12}$$

$$x_k = (1/n_d)\, x_d\, (px_k \,/\, px_d)^{-\sigma_d}\,, \qquad \sigma_d = 1/(1+\rho_d)\,, \tag{2.13}$$

where σ_s, σ_m and σ_d denote partial elasticities of substitution between, respectively, different components of sector demand, components of market segment demand, and components of demand delivered by domestic firms. The prices of total sector demand (px_s), of market segment demand (px_m), and of demand for domestic products (px_d) can again be expressed as weighted averages of component prices:

$$px_s = \left(\sum_{m=1}^{n_s} (1/n_s)\, px_m^{\,1-\sigma_s} \right)^{1/(1-\sigma_s)}\,, \tag{2.14}$$

$$px_m = \left(\alpha_d\, px_d^{\,1-\sigma_m} + (1-\alpha_d)\, px_f^{\,1-\sigma_m} \right)^{1/(1-\sigma_m)}\,, \tag{2.15}$$

$$px_d = \left(\sum_{k=1}^{n_d} (1/n_d)\, px_k^{\,1-\sigma_d} \right)^{1/(1-\sigma_d)} . \tag{2.16}$$

In order to arrive at demand equations for the full sector, it is assumed that all domestic firms and all market segments per sector are identical and that for the exposed sector the number of domestic firms and foreign firms is identical over market segments. In that case, px_k equals px_d for all k and px_m equals px_s for all m. Total demand for domestic and foreign products can be derived from substituting (2.10) into (2.11) and (2.12) and aggregating over all domestic firms and over all market segments. This yields the following demand and price equations:

$$x_D = \alpha_d\, x_s\, (px_d \,/\, px_s)^{-\sigma_m} , \tag{2.17}$$

$$x_F = (1-\alpha_d)\, x_s\, (px_f \,/\, px_s)^{-\sigma_m} , \tag{2.18}$$

$$px_s = \left(\alpha_k\, px_d^{\,1-\sigma_m} + (1-\alpha_d)\, px_f^{\,1-\sigma_m} \right)^{1/(1-\sigma_m)} . \tag{2.19}$$

Equations (2.17) and (2.18) are used to describe the demand for domestic goods and foreign goods in the exposed sector for the types of goods distinguished in the model, *i.e.* exports, private consumption, public non-wage consumption and investments in equipment and buildings. The sector price is a weighted average of the output price of the domestic firms and foreign firms that operate within the sector. The structure for other sectors is similar, apart from the absence of competition by foreign firms.

Finally, the demand structure described by equations (2.3) – (2.19) can also be used to derive an expression for the own price elasticity of demand for the individual firm, which is relevant for pricing behaviour of the firm (see Section 2.4). Since the number of market segments is so large that the market share of a single market segment can be neglected, the own price elasticity of demand is independent from competition between sectors. The own price elasticity corresponding to this demand structure equals:

$$\varepsilon^x = -\sigma_d - (\sigma_m - \sigma_d)\, s_k^{\,d} - (\sigma_s - \sigma_m)\, s_k^{\,m} , \tag{2.20}$$

where $s_k^{\,d}$ is the market share of the individual firm in total domestic output of a market segment, and $s_k^{\,m}$ is the market share of the individual firm in total output of a market segment.

2.2 Input market environment

The input market environment determines the way firms can hire input factors used in the production process. In the first subsection the costs of the input factors are considered and the way the firm can influence these costs in order to regulate the inflow of new input factors. The second subsection describes the selection strategy of the employer taking into account the heterogeneity of labour and the existence of minimum wage legislation.

The cost function of the individual firm

The individual firm uses seven types of input factors to produce its output: imports of intermediaries, capital, low-skilled labour, disaggregated into low-skilled with a minimum income and other low-skilled, and three types of high-skilled labour: technical, economical and service oriented. The costs for the individual firm are defined as:

$$C = ck\; k + pm_i\; m_i + \sum_j \left(w_j l_j + \bar{w}_j \gamma v_j + \frac{1}{2}\alpha_w\; l_j\; (w_j - \hat{w}_j)^2 / \hat{w}_j\right) . \tag{2.21}$$

C denotes total costs in period t, ck the costs per unit of capital, k the capital stock, pm_i the price of imports of intermediaries, m_i intermediaries, w_j the wage rate of a worker with average quality of labour type j, v_j the number of vacancies of labour type j, $\gamma\bar{w}_j$ search costs per vacancy of labour type j and $\hat{w}_j$ the contractual wage for labour type j.

The price of intermediaries and the costs per unit of capital are assumed to be given for the individual firm. Capital consists of buildings and equipment, which are assumed to be complementary and hence proportionally related to the total capital stock. The costs of capital (ck) are related to the interest rate and a weighted average of the costs of the stock of buildings (kb) and the stock of equipment capital (ko):

$$ck = \alpha_b \, pb \, (rf + \delta_b) + (1 - \alpha_b) \, po \, (rf + \delta_o) \, , \tag{2.22}$$

where δ_b and δ_o denote the rates of depreciation of buildings and equipment, α_b the share of capital costs of buildings, pb and po the prices of investments in buildings and equipment, and rf the interest rate charged to firms, which may include a risk premium.[21]

New employees have to be acquired by a costly search process of matching vacancies with unemployed workers. Search costs required for this matching process are related to the number of vacancies posted by the employer and to the average gross wage ($\bar{w}$) of labour type j. Search costs are assumed to be spent on services of other firms, for example labour offices and newspapers, hence $\bar{w}_j$ is exogenous for the firm. The number of vacancies depends on the employers' demand for new employees and the rate at which vacancies are filled. Assuming a voluntary quit rate of current employees δ, the required number of vacancies of type j equals:

[21] As yet no attention has been paid to the interaction between fiscal variables and investment. Profit taxes are considered to be lump sum transfers from firms to the government. That is why no fiscal variables appear in the cost of capital definition. Details on the role of taxes in capital costs can be found for instance in Nickell (1978) and Hasselman (1991) and references cited there. We also abstract from the growth rate of the price of investments in the cost of capital definition.

$$v_j = (dl_j/dt + \delta_j\, l_j) \,/\, z_j \,, \tag{2.23}$$

where l_j denotes employment of type j and z the rate at which vacancies are filled. The latter depends on the wage rate offered by the employer (w_j) compared to the wage rate paid by other employers ($\bar{w}_j$) and on the macro rate at which vacancies are filled for type j ($\bar{z}_j$):

$$z_j = (w_j/\bar{w}_j)^{\beta}\, \bar{z}_j \,. \tag{2.24}$$

It is assumed that the employer has some monopsonic power because of a limited possibility to influence the rate at which vacancies are filled by varying the offered wage through an incidental wage component. This incidental wage component is defined as the difference between the wage offered by the firm (w_j) and the contractual wage ($\hat{w}_j$). The contractual wage rate is given for the individual firm and follows from collective wage bargaining between unions and employers' organisations (see Chapter 4). The employer can use the incidental wage component to minimize search costs for labour. However, the firms' ability to use this instrument is restricted, because large incidental wage components in addition to contractual wages interfere with the solidarity between employees and are likely to create frictions with unions. As shown by the last term in equation (2.21) costs of frictions with unions are assumed to be progressively related to the incidental wage.

The minimum productivity standard

Because of the existence of search costs, the employer will hire all suitable candidates in order to save additional search costs. However, in the model not all candidates who are willing to accept the job are suitable, because the productivity of individual job-worker combinations is heterogeneous and because of the existence of minimum required wage levels. This minimum wage scale is exogenous for the individual employer and determined by the collective agreement between employers and labour unions at industry level.

Since the employer is bound to pay every employee at least the minimum wage, some candidates will not be accepted as their productivity profile on the job considered is too low.

In order to screen for suitable job-worker combinations, the employer uses a minimum productivity standard. For simplicity, the equation for this minimum productivity standard is not derived from the intertemporal model of firm behaviour in Section 2.4, in which all other variables of the firm are determined, but derived outside the model. It is assumed that only those candidates who meet this minimum productivity standard are accepted. Assuming perfect substitution between individual workers of type j, the minimum productivity standard can be derived from the condition that marginal labour costs per efficiency unit must be equal for workers with different labour productivity in the job. The minimum productivity index can then be related to the average productivity index of all new employees times the ratio between the minimum wage rate and the marginal labour costs for new employees:

$$he_j = \frac{hn_j \; wm}{w_j \left(1 + \frac{\gamma}{z_j} (\delta_j + r - \frac{\frac{d}{dt}(\bar{w}_j/z_j)}{\bar{w}_j/z_j}) + \frac{1}{2}\alpha_w \frac{(w_j - \hat{w}_j)^2}{w_j \hat{w}_j} \right)}, \tag{2.25}$$

where he_j denotes the minimum productivity standard per type of labour, hn_j the average productivity index of all new employees (see below), wm the sector-specific minimum wage scale. The marginal costs of labour include the wage rate of an employee with average productivity index (w_j) plus search costs, valued by a discount rate that equals the interest rate (r) plus quit rate (δ_j) minus the change in search costs over time, and the costs of frictions with unions (see also Section 2.4). Equation (2.25) implies that the number of candidates being accepted after an interview will fall if the ratio between the minimum wage rate and marginal labour costs rises.

It is assumed that the productivity index for type j of individual job-worker combinations (h_j) is fully match-specific and follows a lognormal distribution g with standard deviation sd_j and average productivity $\bar{h}_j$:

$$g(h_j) = N(\log \bar{h}_j - 0.5\, sd_j^2,\ sd_j^2), \qquad with\ E(h_j) = \bar{h}_j. \tag{2.26}$$

The average productivity of all potential job-worker combinations ($\bar{h}_j$) is normalized to one. The share of contacts that is acceptable for the employer can then be defined as:

$$fe_j = 1 - G((\log he_j)/sd_j + 0.5\, sd_j), \tag{2.27}$$

where G is the cumulative distribution function of the standard normal distribution[22].

Labour productivity being too low to match the minimum wage is not the only reason that a potential job-worker combination does not result in a job-match. Another reason for jobs not being filled is that the wage offered by the employer is not attractive for the candidate, because it falls below his or her reservation wage. This possibility will be dealt with in Chapter 4. The consequence of this second possibility that jobs are not filled is that the average minimum productivity standard not only depends on the minimum productivity standard of the employer (he_j), but also on the reservation wage of candidates. The formula for the minimum productivity standard combining the influence of the minimum wage productivity standard used by employers and the reservation wage set by the unemployed will be derived in Chapter 4. Here it suffices to note that, denoting hm_j as this combined minimum productivity standard and fm_j as the fraction of successful job-matches, the average productivity of accepted new employees (hn_j) is defined as the expected

[22] In the calibrated specification the cumulated normal distribution function is approximated by the following logistic distribution function (see Johnson and Kotz, 1970):

$$G(x) = [1 + \exp(-1.7x)]^{-1}\ .$$

productivity of all job matches with productivity larger than hm_j. Using the properties of truncated distributions as derived by Johnson and Kotz (1970), hn_j can be formulated as:

$$hn_j = E(h_j \mid h_j > hm_j) = [1 - G((\log hm_j)/sd_j - 0.5 sd_j)] \;/\; fm_j \;. \tag{2.28}$$

Changes in the minimum productivity standard used by employers to select new employees will also shift the average productivity index of all employees over time. Assuming that the average productivity index of all quitting employees is equal to that of all remaining employees, the average productivity index of all employees can be approximated as (in discrete times):

$$hg_j = \left\{(1-\delta_j) l_{j_{-1}} \, hg_{j_{-1}} + (l_j - (1-\delta_j) l_{j_{-1}}) hn_j\right\} \;/\; l_j \;. \tag{2.29}$$

According to equation (2.29) the average productivity index of all employees will slowly adjust after a change in the average productivity index of new employees, for example as a result of a fall in the minimum wage rate. In the long run hg_j will again be equal to hn_j.[23]

Finally, it is noted that the level of the minimum wage scale w_m is influenced by the official minimum wage. This influence is likely to be asymmetric. Empirical research on the development of minimum wage scales in collective agreements during 1983 to 1988 (Ministry of Social Affairs and Employment, 1990), in which period the official minimum wage fell by 7% relative to the collective wage rate, shows that a reduction in the official minimum wage affected the level of minimum wage scales in the collective agreements only for about 30%. Since the ratio between official minimum

[23] In order to prevent complex dynamic considerations, we abstract from the special case that relatively more workers with a low productivity exit the firm. This would be the case if the productivity of this group suddenly falls below the minimum standard, for instance after a jump in the minimum wage rate. In such a case, the firm may adjust to the new minimum productivity standard immediately by dismissing them. Then the mean productivity would jump instead of gradually adjusting to the new productivity level. See also Pissarides (1990), page 93.

wage and lowest wage scales is currently lower than in 1983, it is assumed that a further reduction in the official minimum wage will exert an even smaller influence on the lowest wage scales in collective agreements of about 25%. The research of Ministry of Social Affairs and Employment (1990) also shows that the average wage level in minimum wage scales is about 5% higher than the official minimum wage level. The influence of the official minimum wage on minimum wage scales is therefore likely to be higher in case the official minimum wage rises, becoming almost proportional once the official minimum wage level equals the level of the minimum wage scale.

2.3 Production structure of individual firm

Figure 2.2 reflects the production structure of the individual firm. In all sectors output is produced by a combination of intermediaries and value added. The latter factor is generated by the use of capital and labour. With respect to the use of capital and labour, the production function differs per sector.

Figure 2.2 Structure of the production function of the firm

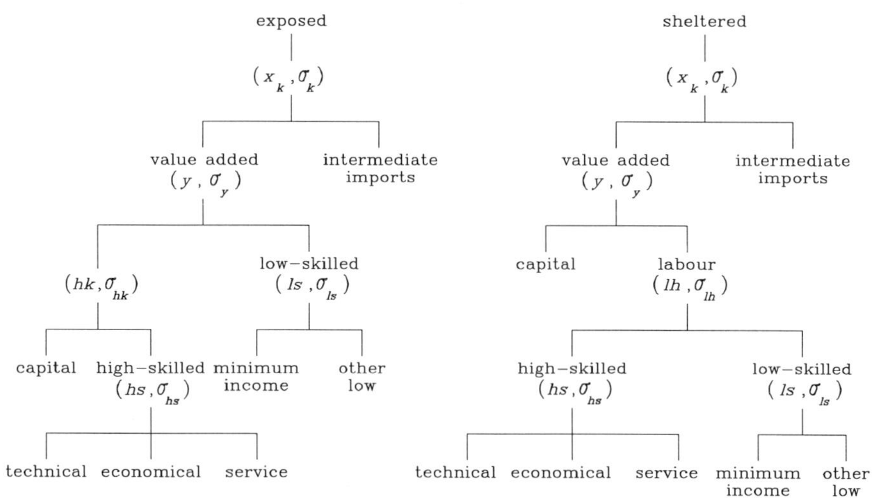

Table 2.1 Price and substitution elasticities for manufacturing in USA

Substitution between	high-skilled labour and capital	low and high-skilled labour	low-skilled labour and capital
Morrison and Berndt[a]	−0.20	1.20	0.10
Grant[b]	0.04 / 0.38	0.21 / 0.77	0.94
Clark and Freeman[b]	−1.98	0.91	2.10
Denny and Fuss[b]	−0.91	2.06	1.50
Kesselman *et al.*	−0.49	0.49	1.28
Berndt and White[b]	1.09	3.70	0.91
Berndt and Christensen[b]	−1.94	5.51	2.92

[a] Price-elasticity
[b] Allan partial elasticity of substitution

Source: Morrison and Berndt (1981), Freeman (1986), Hamermesh (1986)

For the exposed sector with a relatively high share of technically high-skilled labour and equipment capital the nesting structure is based on two characteristics. These are, firstly, a low propensity to substitute between capital and the combination of technically, economically and service-oriented high-skilled labour and, secondly, a relatively high propensity to substitute between low-skilled labour and the combined production factor of capital and high-skilled labour. Substitution of labour by capital in this sector entails the construction of technically and operationally complicated plants, requiring a relatively large input of these types of high-skilled labour. The empirical relevance of this nesting structure is confirmed by research for U.S. manufacturing (Morrison and Berndt, 1981; Freeman, 1986; Hamermesh, 1985) as is illustrated by Table 2.1. The (Alan) partial elasticity of substitution between high-skilled labour and capital is found to be negative in five out of seven studies, whereas the elasticity of substitution between low-skilled labour and either high-skilled labour and capital is positive in all cases. This confirms that high-skilled labour is complementary to capital, whereas low-skilled labour is highly substitutable with both high-skilled labour and capital.

Based on these postulates the production function reads:

$$x_k = \left(\alpha_y^{1+\rho_x} \, y^{-\rho_x} + (1-\alpha_y)^{1+\rho_x} \, m_i^{-\rho_x}\right)^{-1/\rho_x} , \tag{2.30}$$

$$y = \left(\alpha_{ls}^{1+\rho_y} \, ls^{-\rho_y} + (1-\alpha_{ls})^{1+\rho_y} \, hk^{-\rho_y}\right)^{-\upsilon/\rho_y} , \tag{2.31}$$

$$hk = \left(\alpha_{hs}^{1+\rho_{hk}} \, hs^{-\rho_{hk}} + (1-\alpha_{hs})^{1+\rho_{hk}} \, (e^{\varepsilon_k} h^{\phi_k} k)^{-\rho_{hk}}\right)^{-1/\rho_{hk}} , \tag{2.32}$$

$$ls = \left(\sum_{j=m,l} \alpha_j^{1+\rho_{ls}} \, (e^{\varepsilon_j t} h^{\phi_j} hg_j l_j)^{-\rho_{ls}}\right)^{-1/\rho_{ls}} , \tag{2.33}$$

$$hs = \left(\sum_{j=t,e,v} \alpha_j^{1+\rho_{hs}} \, (e^{\varepsilon_j t} h^{\phi_j} hg_j l_j)^{-\rho_{hs}}\right)^{-1/\rho_{hs}} , \tag{2.34}$$

with x_k representing output of the individual firm, y value added, m_i imports of intermediaries, h the index of working time, ls the combined production factor of low-skilled labour, hk the combined production factor of capital and high-skilled labour, hs the combined production factor of high-skilled labour, ε_j the rate of technical progress associated with input j, ϕ_j the coefficients of working time for input j, hg_j the average of micro productivities of workers of type j, and ν the returns to scale parameter. With respect to the educational level of labour index m denotes low-skilled labour with a minimum income, index l denotes other low-skilled labour, t technically high-skilled labour, e economically high-skilled labour and v service-oriented high-skilled labour. This nesting structure has also been used for the production function of the construction sector.

For other sectors, like the sheltered sector, capital consists relatively more of buildings with little substitution possibilities with labour. Hence, capital is assumed to show limited substitutability with respect to both low-skilled and high-skilled labour, while low-skilled and high-skilled labour are assumed to be highly substitutable. This leads to the following specification of the value added production function:

$$x_k = \left(\alpha_y^{1+\rho_x} \, y^{-\rho_x} + (1-\alpha_y)^{1+\rho_x} \, m_i^{-\rho_x}\right)^{-1/\rho_x}, \tag{2.35}$$

$$y = \left(\alpha_k^{1+\rho_y} \, (e^{\varepsilon_k t} h^{\phi_k} k)^{-\rho_y} + (1-\alpha_k)^{1+\rho_y} \, lh^{-\rho_y}\right)^{-1/\rho_y}, \tag{2.36}$$

$$lh = \left(\alpha_{ls}^{1+\rho_{lh}} \, ls^{-\rho_{lh}} + (1-\alpha_{ls})^{1+\rho_{lh}} \, hs^{-\rho_{lh}}\right)^{-1/\rho_{lh}}, \tag{2.37}$$

$$ls = \left(\sum_{j=m,l} \alpha_j^{1+\rho_{ls}} \, (e^{\varepsilon_j t} h^{\phi_j} hg_j l_j)^{-\rho_{ls}}\right)^{-1/\rho_{ls}}, \tag{2.38}$$

$$hs = \left(\sum_{j=t,e,v} \alpha_j^{1+\rho_{hs}} \, (e^{\varepsilon_j t} h^{\phi_j} hg_j l_j)^{-\rho_{hs}}\right)^{-1/\rho_{hs}}, \tag{2.39}$$

where lh is the combined production factor of low-skilled and high-skilled labour. This nesting structure has also been assumed for the production function of the medical sector.

2.4 Firm behaviour

The objective of the employer is to maximize profits over the planning period.[24] In general terms the Hamiltonian can be defined as:

$$H = e^{-rt}[px_k(1-\tau_{ind})\,x_k - C + \lambda_p(x_k - x_{output}(.)) + \Sigma\psi_j(-\delta_j l_j + (w_j/\bar{w}_j)^{\beta}\,\bar{z}_j v_j) + \lambda_x(x_k - x_{input}(.))\,]\,. \tag{2.40}$$

In (2.40) τ_{ind} denotes the rate of indirect taxes, C total production costs as defined in equation (2.21), and λ_p, ψ_j and λ_x are the Lagrange multipliers of the constraints. In choosing the optimal price, input demand and incidental wage, the firm has to consider its output demand relation (λ_p), the required inflow of new employees (ψ_j) (with equation (2.24) substituted into equation (2.23)) and the production function (λ_x), as presented in Sections 2.1 – 2.3 respectively.

From the first-order conditions for maximum profits the firm's individual output price can be expressed as a mark-up over marginal costs per unit of output:

$$px_k = \frac{\varepsilon^x}{(1+\varepsilon^x)(1-\tau_{ind})}\,cx, \tag{2.41}$$

$$cx = \left(\alpha_y\, py^{1-\sigma_x} + (1-\alpha_y)\, pm_i^{1-\sigma_x}\right)^{1/(1-\sigma_x)}, \tag{2.42}$$

where ε^x is the own price elasticity of demand for products of the firm as defined in Section 2.1 and py the marginal costs per unit of value added.

[24] As noted in Section 2.2, the minimum productivity standard (hn_j) and average productivity standard (hg_j) are determined outside the intertemporal model and therefore considered to be exogenous in this section.

With constant returns to scale, marginal costs per unit of value added equal the weighted average of marginal costs of the underlying production factors (cy). With increasing or decreasing returns to scale, an adjustment has to be made for the scale parameter υ:

$$py = \frac{1}{\upsilon} cy \; y^{1/\upsilon - 1} . \tag{2.43}$$

For the exposed sector and the construction sector the following factor demand equations can be derived:

$$m_i = (1-\alpha_y) \; x_k \; (pm_i \,/\, cx)^{-\sigma_x} , \tag{2.44}$$

$$y = \alpha_y \; x_k \; (py \,/\, cx)^{-\sigma_x} , \tag{2.45}$$

$$l_j = \alpha_j \; \alpha_{ls} \frac{y^{1/\upsilon}}{e^{\varepsilon_j t} h^{\phi_j} hg_j} (pl_j \,/\, p_{ls})^{-\sigma_{ls}} (pl_{ls} \,/\, cy)^{-\sigma_y} , \quad j = m,l , \tag{2.46}$$

$$hk = (1-\alpha_{ls}) \; y^{1/\upsilon} \; (p_{hk} \,/\, cy)^{-\sigma_y} , \tag{2.47}$$

$$l_j = \alpha_j \; \alpha_{hs} \frac{hk}{e^{\varepsilon_j t} h^{\phi_j} hg_j} (pl_j \,/\, p_{hs})^{-\sigma_{hs}} (p_{hs} \,/\, p_{hk})^{-\sigma_{hk}} , \quad j = t,e,v , \tag{2.48}$$

$$k = \alpha_k \; hk \; (pk \,/\, p_{hk})^{-\sigma_{hk}} \,/\, (e^{\varepsilon_k t} h^{\phi_k}) , \tag{2.49}$$

with $\sigma_k = 1/(1+\rho_k)$ for $k = x, y, ls, hs, hk$. Equations (2.44) - (2.49) are factor demand equations, which relate the demand for a specific factor to its relative marginal costs, to the total demand for the combined production factor, and to the autonomous productivity of the production factor comprising autonomous technological progress, working time and the average productivity of job matches. For the labour intensive sectors, like the sheltered sector, similar equations are obtained except for differences following from the different nesting structure.

In equations (2.46) and (2.47) cy is a weighted average of the marginal costs of the underlying production factors measured in efficiency units:

$$cy = \left(\alpha_{ls}\, p_{ls}^{\;1-\sigma_y} + (1-\alpha_{ls})\, p_{hk}^{\;1-\sigma_y}\right)^{1/(1-\sigma_y)} . \tag{2.50}$$

Marginal costs of the other underlying production factors in efficiency units are defined as:

$$p_{ls} = \left(\sum_{j\,=\,m,l} \alpha_j\, pl_j^{\;1-\sigma_{ls}}\right)^{1/(1-\sigma_{ls})} , \tag{2.51}$$

$$p_{hk} = \left(\alpha_{hs}\, p_{hs}^{\;1-\sigma_{hk}} + (1-\alpha_{hs})\, pk^{\;1-\sigma_{hk}}\right)^{1/(1-\sigma_{hk})} , \tag{2.52}$$

$$p_{hs} = \left(\sum_{j\,=\,t,e,v} \alpha_j\, pl_j^{\;1-\sigma_{hs}}\right)^{1/(1-\sigma_{hs})} , \tag{2.53}$$

$$pl_j = \frac{w_j}{e^{\varepsilon_j t} h^{\phi_j} hn_j} \left(1 + \frac{\gamma}{z_j} \frac{\bar{w}_j}{w_j} (\delta_j + r - \frac{\frac{d}{dt}(\bar{w}_j/z_j)}{\bar{w}_j/z_j}) + \frac{1}{2}\alpha_w \frac{(w_j - \hat{w}_j)^2}{w_j \hat{w}_j} \right), \quad (2.54)$$

$$j = m,l,t,e,v$$

$$pk = ck \;/\; (e^{\varepsilon_k t} h^{\phi_k}) \;. \quad (2.55)$$

The marginal costs of labour (pl_j) consist of wage costs plus search costs, valued by a discount rate that equals the interest rate (r) plus quit rate (δ_j) minus the change in search costs over time. The variable hn_j denotes the average of micro productivities of workers of type j selected in the current period (see Section 2.2). Equation (2.54) implies that if search costs increase, for instance as a result of a fall in the ratio between the number of matchings and vacancies (z), marginal labour costs will increase. The marginal costs for capital (pk) are simply related to the average costs per unit of capital (ck) corrected for capital augmenting technological progress and effective machine time.

From the first-order conditions for maximum profits also a relation for the wage rate can be derived:

$$w_j = \hat{w}_j \; (\beta \; \gamma(v_j \;/\; l_j) \; (\bar{w}_j/w_j) + \alpha_w - 1) \;/\; \alpha_w \;, \qquad j = m,l,t,e,v. \quad (2.56)$$

The wage rate is set as a mark-up over the contractual wage rate ($\hat{w}_j$). The mark-up depends on the ratio between the number of vacancies and employment. This implies that the employer will increase the incidental wage component if vacancy duration increases, for example if labour supply becomes scarce, in order to attract additional labour supply and reduce search costs.

Having derived equations for employment, the capital stock and the wage offered by the employer, equations (2.23) - (2.24) can be used to model the number of vacancies and the rate at which vacancies are filled. Investments in buildings (*ib*) and investments (*io*) in equipment can be determined from:

$$ib = kb - (1 - \delta_b)\, kb_{-1} ,$$
$$io = ko - (1 - \delta_o)\, ko_{-1} . \tag{2.57}$$

Finally, regarding aggregation, we assume that the production functions of firms, producing different types of goods, are identical within a sector. Then the factor demand equations derived above, can be interpreted as sector demand equations relating sector factor demand to aggregate sector output demand for all types of goods.

2.5 Calibration of the model of the firm

The calibration of the model of the firm is described in two parts. In the first subsection attention is paid to the calibration of the demand structure outlined in Section 2.1. The second subsection concerns the calibration of the input market and production model outlined in Sections 2.2 and 2.3.

Table 2.2 Parameters model of allocation of consumption among types of consumer goods[a]

	Types of consumer goods				
	medical	residential	0% VAT	5% VAT	19% VAT
s_i	0.165	0.117	0.045	0.212	0.462
ε^i	*0.9*	*0.9*	*0.9*	*1.0*	1.071
α_i	0.148	0.105	0.043	0.212	0.493
$\bar{s}_i$	0.061	0.043	0.017	0.063	*0.115*
ε_i^i	−0.4	−0.4	−0.3	−0.4	−0.7

[a] Values that are set by assumption are printed in italics. With market shares (s_i) given from base year data all other values can be calibrated.

Table 2.3 Substitution elasticities and distribution parameters of model of allocation among sectors[a,b]

	Exports				Consumption						Investment	
	goods	natural gas	other energy	services	0% VAT	5% VAT	19% VAT	medical	resi-dential	govern-ment	buil-dings	equip-ment
σ_i	*0.0*	*0.0*	*0.0*	*0.0*	*0.5*	*1.0*	*2.0*	*0.5*	*0.5*	*0.25*	*0.1*	*0.1*
α_{ex}	0.40	0.08	0.95	0.63	0.42	0.56	0.48	0.08	0.04	0.52	0.20	0.85
α_{mi}	0.03	0.92	0.04	0.03	0.01	0.02	0.08	0.02	0.0	0.05	0.01	0.02
α_{co}	0.01	0.0	0.0	0.02	0.01	0.01	0.01	0.02	0.03	0.14	0.63	0.02
α_{re}	.	.	.	.	.	.	.	.	0.91	.	.	.
α_{sh}	0.11	0.01	0.01	0.29	0.55	0.41	0.27	0.05	0.01	0.15	0.15	0.11
α_{me}	0.01	0.0	0.0	0.03	0.01	0.0	0.0	0.84	0.0	0.13	0.0	0.0
α_{ms}	0.45	.	.	.	.	.	0.16	.	.	.	.	.

[a] Values that are set by assumption are printed in italics.
[b] Subscripts of distribution parameters (α) denote sectors: *ex* = exposed, *mi* = mining, *co* = construction, *re* = residential, *sh* = sheltered, *me* = medical, *ms* = single sector imports.

The demand system and price formation

The calibration of the allocation model of the demand for goods depicted in Figure 2.1 is described in three steps. Firstly, Table 2.2 presents the parameters of the allocation of total demand over different types of goods. Table 2.3 and Table 2.5 present the calibration of the allocation of goods from total demand per type of good to sectoral demand. Table 2.4 presents the model-parameters for the allocation of goods within sectors.

In the model, the allocation of total demand over different types of goods is assumed to be relevant only for consumption, which is differentiated into five types of consumption goods. A moderate propensity to substitute between the different types of consumption goods has been assumed. Hence, a value of 0.5 has been selected for the elasticity of substitution σ. Furthermore, the income elasticities of necessary goods like medical consumption, residential consumption and consumption with a 0% VAT rate, have been set at 0.9 and the income elasticity of consumption with a 5% VAT rate at 1.0[25]. The market shares being given from base year data, the α_i parameters can be computed from the values of the income elasticities. Then the value of α_i and the income elasticity for luxury consumption with a 19% VAT rate follow from the restriction that the α_i sum to one. Minimal necessary quantities have been obtained by assuming that the minimal quantity for luxury consumption equals 25% of the total quantity. Applying (2.3) for luxury consumption, the sum of all $\bar{s}_i$ and the other values of $\bar{s}_i$ for each individual type of goods can be computed. Finally, the own price elasticities of demand ε_i^i for type of goods i follow from (Nieuwenhuis, 1986):

$$\varepsilon_i^i = - \varepsilon^i \left[s_i (1 - \sigma) + (\bar{s}_i + 1 - \sum_{i=1}^{n} \bar{s}_i) \sigma \right] . \tag{2.58}$$

From Table 2.2 the price elasticities are seen to be of comparable magnitudes, only luxury consumption is somewhat more price elastic.

The allocation of demand among sectors is based on the cumulated production structure matrix approach. Hence a shift in the allocation among sectors is a mixture of changes in the distribution of final demand among sectors and shifts in the composition of intermediary deliveries. A similar procedure has also been used in the empirical FKSEC model of the Central Planning Bureau (1992a).

For export products elasticities of substitution have been set at zero, because demand is characterized by a high degree of complementarity

[25] Because minimal necessary quantities are included income elasticities can differ from unity. The income elasticities can be derived from equation (2.3) if rewritten into the following equation for output per type of goods (x_i):

$$x_i = \sum_{s=1}^{n_i} px_s \, \bar{x}_s \, / \, px_i + \alpha_i \, ((X - \sum_{i=1}^{n} \sum_{s \subset i} px_s \, \bar{x}_s) \, / \, px) \, (px_i \, / \, px)^{-\sigma} .$$

The derivative of x_i with respect to X/px equals α_i. Multiplying this derivative by the ratio $(X/px)/x_i$ yields the elasticity $\varepsilon_i = \alpha_i / s_i$ since all prices have been normalized at unity in the base year 1985.

Table 2.4 Substitution elasticities and distribution parameters of model of allocation among market segments and firms for the exposed sector[a]

	Exports				Consumption						Investment	
	goods	natural gas	other energy	services	0% VAT	5% VAT	19% VAT	medical	resi-dential	govern-ment	build-ings	equip-ment
σ_s	*1.0*	*1.0*	*1.0*	*1.0*	*1.0*	*1.0*	*1.0*	*1.0*	*1.0*	*1.0*	*1.0*	*1.0*
σ_m	*1.5*			*1.5*	*1.25*	*1.25*	*1.25*			*1.25*		*1.25*
α_d	0.25			0.25	0.85	0.60	0.40			0.60		0.15
σ_d	*11.7*	*13.2*	*17.3*	*11.8*	9.2	9.8	9.0	8.8	9.6	8.9	8.7	*10.5*
n_d	5.	*10.*	*10.*	5.	5.	5.	5.	*10.*	*10.*	5.	*10.*	5.
ε^x	−9.8	−12.0	−15.7	−9.9	−7.6	−8.1	−7.5	−8.0	−8.7	−7.4	−7.9	−8.8

[a] Values that are set by assumption are printed in italics.

between products of different sectors. For the same reason low elasticities of substitution have been selected for most other domestic demand categories except for normal and luxury consumption. Partial income elasticities are equal to unity. Normalizing all prices at unity in the base year, the distribution parameters (α) and the share of minimal quantities per sector ($\bar{x}_s$) in minimal quantities of consumption per type of goods ($\bar{x}_i$) then equal the market shares. For normal and luxury consumption partial income elasticities (ε^s) are allowed to differ from unity and have been chosen more or less in line with two empirical models VINSEC (Draper *et al.*, 1987) and BETA (Eijgenraam and Verkade, 1988). The calibration procedure resembles the calibration of the model of allocation of total consumption among types of goods. The resulting own price elasticities concur reasonably well with the ones in the empirical models VINSEC and BETA.

Table 2.4 presents the modelparameters for the allocation of goods within sectors. Only the parameters for the exposed sector are presented. For the other sectors (sheltered sector, construction, medical sector) parameters are uniform for different types of goods and set in such a way that the profit rates in these sectors are about 5%. This is roughly in line with information from

Table 2.5 Parameters allocation models of 5% and 19% VAT rate consumption[a]

	5% VAT (normal)				19% VAT (luxury)			
	$s_s^{\ i}$	ε^s [b]	$\bar{s}_s^{\ i}$	$\varepsilon_s^{\ s}$	$s_s^{\ i}$	ε^s [b]	$\bar{s}_s^{\ i}$	$\varepsilon_s^{\ s}$
Exposed	0.560	1.0	0.168	–0.8	0.515	0.9	0.163	–1.2
Mining	0.020	*1.0*	0.006	–0.7	0.088	*0.9*	0.026	–1.3
Construction	0.004	*1.3*	0.000	–0.9	0.009	*1.2*	0.000	–1.8
Sheltered	0.412	*1.0*	0.123	–0.8	0.290	*0.9*	0.085	–1.3
Medical	0.004	*0.9*	0.001	–0.7	0.002	*0.9*	0.001	–1.3
Imports sector	.	.	.	.	0.096	*1.6*	–0.025	–2.2

[a] Values that are set by assumption are printed in italics. With market shares ($s_s^{\ i}$) given from base year data all other values can be calibrated.

[b] In this section all elasticities are defined for the specific allocation model under consideration, without taking interactions with upper nests into account. Hence, in this case the 'income elasticity' relates to the change of quantities per sector in response to a change of the quantity of a specific type of good.

Central Planning Bureau (1991) and Central Bureau of Statistics (1989b).[26] It is noted that the results are not very sensitive to a change in this calibrated profit rate by a few percentage points. Only if the calibrated rate is increased to a substantial number (about 10% or more), the calibrated share of capital costs (which is the complement of the sum of the labour income share plus the profit share) becomes too small. For the exposed sector the elasticity of substitution between market segments has been set at unity. The elasticity of substitution between domestic firms and foreign firms within a market segment is 1.5 for export goods and 1.25 for consumption and investment goods. At the given values of market shares of domestic firms (α_d) the resulting foreign price elasticities for the various types of goods are in line with foreign price elasticities in the empirical model ATHENA (Central Planning Bureau, 1990b). With respect to the income elasticity of imports MIMIC differs from empirical models like VINSEC (Draper *et al.*, 1987) and FKSEC (Central Planning Bureau, 1992a). In VINSEC and FKSEC the income elasticity of imports of consumer goods is larger than unity and the

[26] The profit rate can be written as $1-\upsilon(1+\varepsilon^x)/\varepsilon^x$, where υ denotes the returns to scale parameter. With a scaling parameter of 1.0, a profit rate of 5% implies that the substitution elasticities of the demand structure and the firm's output shares must be set in such a way that the own price elasticity equals –20.

rising share of imports over time is explained by the luxury character of imported goods. Except for imports of final services associated with luxury consumer goods (tourism), which according to Table 2.5 has an income elasticity of 1.6, in MIMIC we assume that the increase of the share of imports is the consequence of international specialization. Therefore, the rise of the share of imports has not been modelled through the income elasticity but through changes in the shares of domestic and foreign firms in a market segment[27]. The elasticity of substitution between domestic firms (σ_d) and the number of domestic firms operating within a market segment (n_d) are chosen in such a way that the own price elasticity varies between −7.5 for luxury goods and −15.7 for other energy. With a returns to scale parameter in the production function equal to 1.10 (see the next subsection), this implies an average profit rate of about 5% for the exposed sector.

The production model and selection strategy of the firm

Employment and wage data subdivided with respect to level of education are available for the years 1979 and 1985 only. The production functions have been calibrated so as to yield an adequate representation of the movements in employment of the different types of labour between those years.

Table 2.6 shows that imports of intermediaries are limitedly substitutable with output (σ_x=0.6), which is in line with FKSEC (Central Planning Bureau, 1992a). The value of σ_y of 2.5 for the exposed sector and construction sector indicates the high propensity to substitute between low-skilled labour and the combined production factor of capital and high-skilled labour. In the sheltered and medical sector a low value of 0.25 respectively 0 is used for σ_y because of the low degree of substitution between labour and capital in these sectors. In these sectors substitution occurs mainly between the two types of low-skilled labour and high-skilled labour (σ_{lh}). Furthermore, high substitution possibilities exist between the two types of low-skilled labour, whereas

[27] The distribution parameter α_d of the utility function per market segment has been specified as an 's' shaped function of time.

Table 2.6 Sector-specific parameters of production model and selection strategy firms

	Exposed	Construction		Sheltered	Medical		Exposed	Construction	Sheltered	Medical
σ_x	0.6	0.6	σ_x	0.6	0.6	α_w	1.4	1.4	1.4	1.4
α_y	0.60	0.71	α_y	0.85	0.96	β	1.5	1.5	1.5	1.5
σ_y	2.50	2.50	σ_y	0.25	0.0	γ	0.75	0.75	0.75	0.75
α_{ls}	0.35	0.44	α_k	0.12	0.21	ε_m	2.0	1.0	0.0	0.0
σ_{ls}	2.50	2.50	σ_{lh}	2.50	2.50	ε_l	2.0	1.0	0.0	0.0
α_m	0.20	0.25	α_{ls}	0.42	0.24	ε_t	4.0	2.5	2.0	2.0
σ_{hk}	0.75	0.75	σ_{ls}	2.50	2.50	ε_e	4.0	2.5	2.0	2.0
α_{hs}	0.52	0.77	α_m	0.24	0.25	ε_v	4.0	2.5	2.0	2.0
σ_{hs}	0.75	0.75	σ_{hs}	0.75	0.75	ε_k	2.0	1.5	0.0	0.0
α_t	0.68	0.84	α_t	0.29	0.10	υ	1.1	1.0	1.0	1.0
α_e	0.25	0.13	α_e	0.54	0.09	w_m	31.5	36.0	31.1	30.0
α_v	0.07	0.03	α_v	0.17	0.81					

limited substitution is possible between the types of high-skilled labour and capital in the exposed and construction sectors (σ_{hk}) and between components of high-skilled labour in all sectors (σ_{hs}).

The share parameters (α_i) are calculated from data on labour costs and capital costs shares for the base year 1985. In the exposed sector capital, other low-skilled labour and technically skilled labour are the dominant production factors, whereas in the construction sector the latter two production factors account for most of the production costs. This is also reflected by the values of the compensated price elasticities reported in Table 2.7, which show for example that employment of low-skilled labour with low income is most influenced by price changes for other low-skilled labour and technically skilled labour. In the sheltered sector economically skilled labour and other low-skilled labour are dominant production factors, whereas in the medical sector service-oriented skilled labour is an important production factor. From the compensated price elasticities it can further be seen that a rise in costs for one of the types of high-skilled labour hardly affects employment of other types of high-skilled labour. This applies to all sectors and follows from the low degree of substitution between the different types of high-skilled labour.

Table 2.7 Compensated price elasticities of production factors[a]

	Exposed						Construction					
volume	M	L	T	E	V	C	M	L	T	E	V	C
price												
Minimum (M)	−2.27	.19	.19	.19	.19	.19	−2.19	.27	.27	.27	.27	.27
Other low (L)	.69	−1.79	.69	.69	.69	.69	.81	−1.66	.81	.81	.81	.81
Technical (T)	.57	.57	−.79	−.05	−.05	−.05	.91	.91	−.96	−.22	−.22	−.22
Economic (E)	.21	.21	−.02	−.76	−.02	−.02	.14	.14	−.03	−.78	−.03	−.03
Medical (V)	.01	.01	−.01	−.01	−.75	−.01	.03	.03	−.01	−.01	−.75	−.01
Capital (C)	.77	.77	−.06	−.06	−.06	−.81	.32	.32	−.08	−.08	−.08	−.82

	Sheltered						Medical					
volume	M	L	T	E	V	C	M	L	T	E	V	C
price												
Minimum (M)	−2.22	.24	.24	.24	.24	.02	−2.31	.14	.14	.14	.14	.00
Other low (L)	.78	−1.69	.78	.78	.78	.07	.44	−2.02	.54	.54	.54	.00
Technical (T)	.41	.41	−.83	−.09	−.09	.04	.18	.18	−.73	.01	.01	.00
Economic (E)	.78	.78	−.17	−.91	−.17	.07	.17	.17	.01	−.73	.01	.00
Medical (V)	.24	.24	−.05	−.05	−.80	.02	1.50	1.50	.09	.09	−.65	.00
Capital (C)	.03	.03	.03	.03	.03	−.22	.00	.00	.00	.00	.00	.00

[a] defined as $(\partial q_i/q_i)/(\partial p_j/p_j)$, with q_i denoting quantity of input *i* and *pj* price of input *j*.

The parameters determining incidental wage formation (α_w, β) have been set in accordance with an estimated macro wage equation for incidental wage formation.[28] Because empirical information per type of labour is lacking, the parameters are set at uniform values. The search costs parameter (γ) is set

[28] The estimation result is : $\triangle \log (w \,/\, \hat{w}) = \underset{(4.41)}{0.31} \triangle \log h + \triangle \log (\underset{(2.50)}{2.79}\, vr + 1) + \underset{(2.62)}{0.01}$

$$R2 = 0.51,\ SE = 0.81,\ DW = 1.73$$

t-values are reported between parenthesis, *h* denotes labour productivity and *vr* a distributed lag of the vacancy rate. The sample period is 1966-1988. The estimation method is OLS. The estimation implies that with $\gamma = 0.75$ and assuming $\beta = 1.5$, α must be equal to 1.4. Labour productivity is a proxy for wage drift caused by structural shifts (like, for example, in age profile of the working population). This structural part is excluded in the definition of the incidental wage used in MIMIC.

in such a way that average search costs per new employee amount to 10% of the annual wage in 1985.

Estimated rates of labour augmenting technical progress (ε_i) in the exposed sector are larger than in other sectors (see for instance Draper *et al.*, 1987, Eijgenraam and Verkade, 1988 and Central Planning Bureau, 1990b). In the exposed and construction sectors, labour augmenting technical progress has been set at 2% and 1% respectively for all basic types of labour. For the combined production factor of high-skilled labour and capital an additional rate of technical progress has been assumed of 2% and 1.5% respectively. In the two other sectors the rate of high-skilled labour augmenting technical progress has been set at 2%. Employment movements per type of labour between 1979 and 1985 can reasonably be simulated with these figures.

Moderately increasing returns to scale (υ) have been introduced for the exposed sector to take some account of the scale effects that have been found with the estimation of production functions for The Netherlands (see for instance Gelauff *et al.*, 1985, and Gelauff, 1986). Production functions for the other sectors show constant returns to scale.

The minimum wage scales per sector (w_m) are based on Ministry of Social Affairs and Employment (1990) which provides a detailed analysis of minimum wage scales per industry. The average minimum wage scale appears to be highest in the construction sector (20% above the official minimum wage in 1988) and lowest in the sheltered sector (3% above the official minimum wage rate in 1988). The minimum wage scale in the medical sector is assumed to be equal to the official minimum wage rate. Since the average wage rate is lowest for low-skilled labour with minimum income, the ratio between the minimum wage rate and the average wage costs per worker is highest for this type of labour. This implies that the acceptance rate for this group is lower than that for other types of labour.

Table 2.8 presents the other parameters of the production and selection model of firms, which are uniform per sector but differ per type of labour. The quit rates (δ) for the various types of labour follow from the restriction that the number of vacancies per type of labour must equal data obtained from Central Bureau of Statistics (1986). The depreciation rates for capital are

Table 2.8 Other (sector-uniform) parameters of production and selection model firms

	Low skilled labour at minimum income (m)	Other low skilled labour (l)	Technically skilled labour (t)	Economically skilled labour (e)	Service-oriented skilled labour (v)	Capital buildings (kb)	Capital equipment (ko)
δ	0.18	0.17	0.06	0.05	0.09	0.04	0.09
sd	0.15	0.20	0.25	0.25	0.25		
ϕ	0.90	0.90	0.75	0.75	0.75	0.65	0.65

based on Central Bureau of Statistics (1987b) and Blades (1983) and amount to 4% for buildings and 9% for equipment. The values of the standard deviation of the productivity distribution (*sd*) are based on micro data of the wage distribution per type of labour (Central Bureau of Statistics, 1989). The coefficients transforming working time in efficiency units (ϕ) are similar to coefficients for labour and capital in FREIA (Central Planning Bureau, 1983). By assumption the coefficients for working time are set higher for low-skilled labour than for high-skilled labour.

Appendix 2.A Cumulated production structure matrix, imports and indirect taxes

To allocate demand among enterprises sectors, a cumulated production structure (CPS) matrix is used. The CPS matrix is a reduced form representation of the input-output matrix, which relates primary inputs directly to final outputs by substituting out the matrix of domestic intermediaries. The main reason for using a CPS matrix is to allow for flexibility in choosing the most adequate classification of final demand categories.[29] For instance, the CPS-matrix easily enables a disaggregation of consumption with respect to value added tax rates, without requiring an allocation of these categories among production sectors. Such an allocation would increase the size of the model,

[29] For derivations and applications of the CPS matrix see Klein (1983b), Central Planning Bureau (1992a) and Gelauff (1992).

Table 2.9 The cumulated production structure matrix of MIMIC in 1985 (billion guilders)

	Exports				Consumption						Investment		Total
	goods	natural gas	other energy	servi-ces	0% VAT	5% VAT	19% VAT	medi-cal	resi-dential	gov. ment	buil-dings	equip-ment	
Value added													
exposed	63.4	0.1	1.8	14.0	4.6	15.9	12.4	1.9	0.4	4.4	3.8	4.6	127.3
mining	5.9	15.3	1.4	0.6	0.1	1.0	8.2	0.7	0.1	1.0	0.5	0.6	35.3
construction	1.0	0.0	0.0	0.9	0.1	0.2	0.8	0.3	1.0	1.4	14.9	0.7	21.3
residential	.	.	.	.	.	.	.	.	27.4	.	.	.	27.4
sheltered	21.0	0.1	0.2	8.3	4.8	14.2	20.8	1.8	0.4	2.8	5.1	4.1	83.6
medical	0.9	0.0	0.0	1.1	0.1	0.2	0.2	31.3	0.0	2.5	0.1	0.0	36.4
Imports													
energy	9.7	0.4	26.2	2.0	0.4	0.9	3.9	0.5	0.1	1.2	1.1	0.4	46.8
other	81.7	0.7	0.6	9.6	2.0	16.3	33.0	2.8	0.7	5.4	8.0	27.1	187.9
fin. services	.	.	.	.	.	.	10.9	.	.	.	.	.	10.9
Ind. taxes[a]	−1.8	0.0	0.0	1.4	−1.0	3.6	23.5	1.5	−1.3	2.6	5.5	3.2	37.2
Value added government	0.5	0.0	0.0	0.8	0.7	0.2	0.2	0.2	0.0	2.9	0.6	0.0	6.1
Total	182.1	16.7	30.3	38.9	11.8	52.5	113.9	40.8	28.8	24.1	39.5	40.8	620.2

[a] Indirect taxes minus subsidies.

without contributing much to the purpose of the model. The CPS-matrix for 1985 is presented by Table 2.9.

The final demand categories distinguished in the model can be attributed to three types of inputs: value added of the six enterprise sectors, imports and indirect taxes. Three types of imports are distinguished, imports of energy, imports of final services, and other imports. Imports of energy are conceived as intermediaries and therefore modelled as part of the production structure. Imports of final services are associated with tourism and modelled as a sector in the allocation model for luxury goods with a 19% VAT-rate. Other imports consist partly of goods that compete with domestic products in exposed domestic markets. This is assumed to be relevant for exports of services, private consumption goods with either a 0%, 5% and 19% VAT-rate, non-wage government consumption, and for investment in equipment. Another part of other imports is considered as a separate sector in the allocation model for exports of goods. This applies to transit trade in the exports of goods category, since it can not be regarded as competitive imports nor as a factor of production. The remaining components of other imports are considered to be inputs in production, analogous to imports of energy.

Indirect taxes consist of value added taxes (VAT) and other indirect taxes like: indirect taxes on intermediaries referring to excise duties, for instance on oil products; taxes on factors of production like taxes on real estate and on motor vehicles paid by firms; indirect taxes paid on inputs by firms who are exempt from charging VAT on their products; excise duties on final products like liquor, tobacco, oil products and cars, and import duties.

Value added taxes on consumption by households amount to over 50% of the total of indirect taxes minus subsidies. In The Netherlands value added taxes consist of three tax rates: 0%, 5%, and 19% in the base year 1985. These rates can be introduced in the cumulated production structure matrix by distinguishing final demand categories according to value added tax rate. Because of the importance of VAT on consumption and to limit the number of final demand categories, this is only done for consumption. For other categories the value added tax rate is a weighted average of the three statutory rates.

Since value added taxes are also levied on excise duties, these duties have been allocated with respect to VAT rate too. Other indirect taxes are divided proportionally among value added of different sectors. Import duties are directly attributed to imports of final consumer goods.

3 The model of household behaviour

MIMIC contains a rather elaborate household sector and an intricate model of household behaviour which concentrates on the labour supply reactions of households in relation to the tax and social security system. Section 3.1 presents an overview of the composition of the household sector and of the structure of the household model. The labour supply model is presented in Section 3.2. Only labour supply of partners in families has been endogenized. Microeconometric research shows that labour supply of breadwinners in families and of single persons is not very sensitive to changes in their wage rates (see for instance Killingsworth, 1983; Theeuwes, 1988; and Theeuwes and Woittiez, 1992). Hence the participation rate and the number of labour hours supplied by breadwinners and by single persons are held exogenous.

In MIMIC the savings rate is also exogenous. The major part of household savings consist of pension savings with a compulsory character. Free savings are a relatively small component of the budget of households and hardly influence partner labour supply. To avoid the complexities of a detailed analysis of the interaction between the statutory tax and premium system and the labour supply decision in combination with the intertemporal aspects of the savings decision, an exogenous savings rate has been opted for.

The calibration of the household model is documented in Section 3.3. Attention is paid to calibrated elasticities that are important for the simulation results of the model and to the way policy variables are included in the model. Moreover, some interesting aspects of the database are presented, like a description of the number of households in the base year 1985, subdivided with respect to sex, skill level, labour market situation and household type.

3.1 The household sector

In MIMIC seventeen types of households are distinguished, which together represent the total population of sixteen years and older in The Netherlands. The types of households are depicted in Table 3.1. The largest number of households consists of families with children. Families with and without children are distinguished because the presence of children restricts the time available for working and influences the labour supply decision of the partner. Families are subdivided according to the labour market situation of the breadwinner of the household. For employed breadwinners a further division is made according to the educational level of the partner, since from Table 3.1 this also is seen to influence labour supply.

For households with unemployed breadwinners and with breadwinners who receive a disability benefit, the benefit regime of the breadwinner is thought to be the most relevant factor influencing labour supply of partners and no further distinction has been made as to the educational level of the partner. The importance of the type of benefit is evident for unemployed breadwinners, for whom two benefit regimes can apply. In the period directly after becoming unemployed a person is entitled to a benefit from the unemployment insurance fund. Depending on the number of years worked, eventually this benefit stops and unemployed persons receive social assistance, which is paid from the government budget. In the first situation the benefit level does not depend on the income earned by the partner, but in the second situation the social assistance benefit is reduced with the income of the partner. Since in the latter case partners face a 100% marginal 'tax' rate on their income, they hardly participate. In the model their participation rate has been set at zero.

Most of the breadwinners who receive a disability benefit are low-skilled. Because of the correlation between the educational level of the breadwinner and of the partner, most of the partners of breadwinners who receive a disability benefit are low-skilled too (see Table 3.2 in Section 3.3). That is why no further distinction as to the educational level of the partner has been made for these households either. Disability benefit levels of breadwinners are independent of income earned by the partner. The participation rates of partners of disabled breadwinners are comparable to those of partners of working breadwinners and of partners of breadwinners receiving an unemployment insurance benefit.

The other types of households distinguished in Table 3.1 are needed to model the influence of taxation and social security on the distribution of

Table 3.1 Types of households in MIMIC

	Number of households in 1985 (x 1000)	Participation rate of partners (%)
Families with children		
– breadwinner employed, partner high-skilled	626.	46.1
– breadwinner employed, partner low-skilled	1143.	25.3
– breadwinner, unemployment insurance benefit	60.	28.9
– breadwinner unemployed, social assistance benefit	46.	0.0
– breadwinner, disability benefit	205.	33.4
Families without children		
– breadwinner employed, partner high-skilled	319.	75.2
– breadwinner employed, partner low-skilled	451.	36.5
– breadwinner, unemployment insurance benefit	33.	46.8
– breadwinner unemployed, social assistance benefit	26.	0.0
– breadwinner, disability benefit	188.	45.3
Single parent families	304.	
Single persons		
– employed	1442.	
– unemployment insurance benefit	66.	
– unemployed, social assistance benefit	268.	
– receiving disability benefit	205.	
Students	1082.	
Aged households, over 65	1026.	
Total	7490.	

income, on consumption and on the marginal and average tax rates of employed and unemployed workers, which are explanatory variables in the wage model. Therefore, the large group of single person households is also differentiated according to labour market situation, including the distinction between the two types of unemployment benefits. Single parent households are treated separately because a large part of the social assistance benefits is received by divorced persons in this group, who have children to support. The two final groups complete the total population and are included to describe government expenditure on scholarships respectively social security payments and pension payments to the elderly.

Structure of the household model

As illustrated in Figure 3.1, at the most detailed level the household model consists of two blocks, the net income generator for breadwinners and the model of partner labour supply, if relevant. The complete household model applies to the first ten types of households in Table 3.1. For the other types of households only the net income generator is used to compute net incomes and weighted average and marginal tax rates[30].

In the net income generator, for a certain type of households, net income of breadwinners is derived from gross income and the statutory rates of taxation and social security premiums, through the use of class-frequency income distributions of gross breadwinner incomes. In the base year the class-intervals and frequencies are chosen in such a way that they represent data on the distribution of incomes and that they are consistent with macro data (see Section 3.3). When average gross breadwinner income rises the distribution is shifted to the right by multiplying the border values of the class intervals by the relative increase in average income. For each class[31] of the income distribution the social security premiums and taxes are computed by applying the statutory tax and premium rates. For 1992, the system of social security premiums and tax rates, which is used in the net income generator, is described in Section 5.2. The average net income of breadwinners in the type of households under consideration can be obtained from the resulting distribution of net income, together with the weighted average rate of taxation and social security premiums for the breadwinners. The marginal rates of taxation and social security premiums are also determined from the statutory tax rates and are weighted over income classes to yield the marginal rate for the

[30] In the net income generator aged households are treated as single persons. In the base year 1985 60% of the aged households consist of (mainly two person) families, the other 40% being single person households.

[31] Premiums and taxes are not computed for the average income of a class interval, but interpolated between lower and upper border values of that interval. In this way a continuous reaction of the amount of taxes to be paid to changes of income is obtained.

Figure 3.1 Structure of the household model

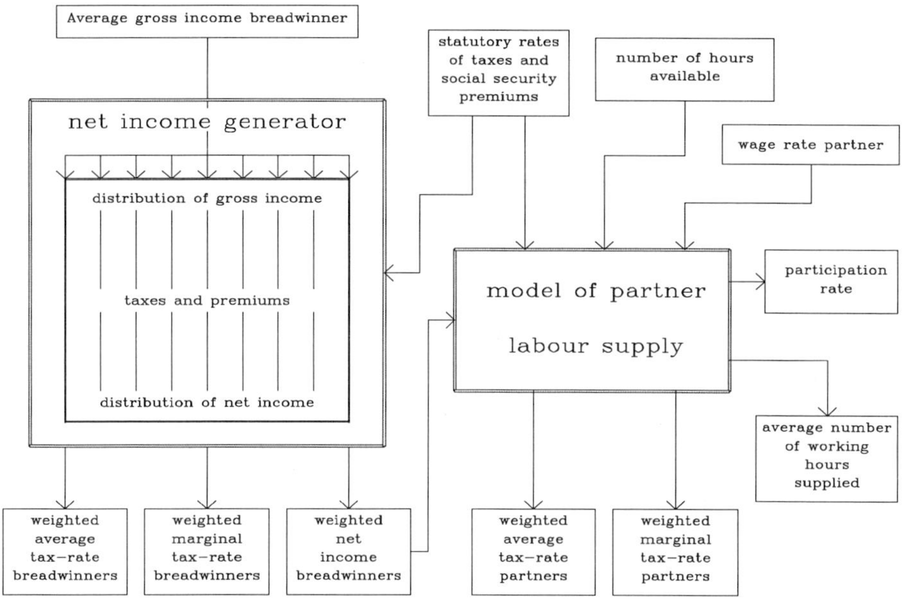

average breadwinner per type of household.

Figure 3.1 further shows that the average net income of breadwinners, the wage rate of partners, the total number of hours available for working, and the statutory tax and premium rates are inputs in the labour supply model of partners, which is described in Section 3.2 below. In the labour supply block the participation rate, the average number of working hours supplied, the weighted average tax rate, and the weighted marginal tax rate of partners are determined.

3.2 Labour supply

Three aspects of the labour supply model are important. Firstly, we must decide how to handle part-time work, either by restricting the choice of the partner to a specific number of jobs with a fixed number of working hours, or to assume flexibility in choosing a desired number of hours. The second aspect concerns how to model simultaneously the participation rate and the number of hours supplied by partners. Thirdly, we should pay attention to the functioning of the labour supply model in the long run, because MIMIC is used for long-term analysis.

In order to obtain insight in the variability of working hours, the cumulative distribution of the number of hours worked by partners in 1985 is depicted in Figure 3.2. From this figure we observe that 75% of the working partners with children work less than 20 hours a week, with significant variation in the number of hours. A large fraction of partners without children works over 36 hours a week. The distribution of hours worked for the remaining fraction rises markedly at 20 and 32 hours. These data show that not merely 20 or 40 hours jobs are available to partners, the diversity is larger. Although constraints on the number of hours that a partner might wish to work cannot be discarded as non-existent, it seems closer to reality to use a

Figure 3.2 Cumulative frequencies of working partners of employed breadwinners over the number of hours worked.

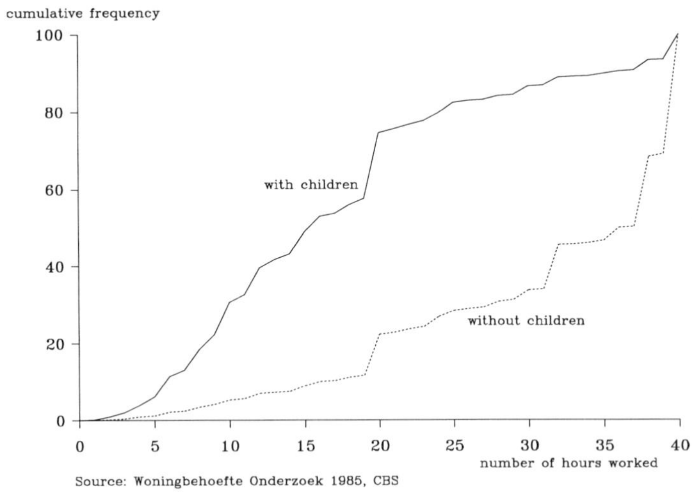

model with a flexible choice with respect to the number of hours worked, than a model in which partners can only apply for jobs with a fixed number of hours.

The second aspect of the labour supply model is the intention to model the participation decision together with the number of hours supplied by partners. To achieve this, households are assumed to differ with respect to their relative preference for leisure versus consumption, which is defined by means of a parameter in the utility function (De Ridder, 1987, Graafland, 1990a). The number of hours supplied will decrease with increasing relative preference for leisure. Partners do not participate if the relative preference for leisure is so high, that the desired number of working hours becomes non-positive. For partners who decide to participate, the average number of hours supplied is derived, taking into account the consequences of kinks in the budget constraint due to stepwise increasing marginal tax rates (see below).

The stability of labour supply reactions on the long run in a model with labour augmenting technical progress, is a third aspect that is important for the modelling of labour supply in MIMIC. In a standard labour supply model utility depends on consumption and leisure. On the long run real consumption per capita grows with technical progress and the total number of hours available for working remains constant through time. Depending on the elasticity of substitution between consumption and leisure, the result will be a permanent increase or decrease in labour supply. Stability will only occur if the value of the elasticity of substitution is such that the income effect and the substitution effect cancel. This assumption can sometimes be found in the literature on dynamic labour supply models (see Blanchard and Fischer, 1989), but is too restrictive for the calibration of the model. Another approach in the literature is to abandon technical progress or to impose a stationary process on technical progress (MacCurdy, 1981), which does not suit a realistic description of the model of the firm. Finally, Ballard and Goulder (1985) assume that individuals measure labour time in efficiency units, so that the number of hours available for work also increases by the rate of technical progress. This approach implies, that through time an individual derives an increasing amount of utility from leisure measured in hours per week[32]. Since it is doubtful whether an extra hour of leisure tomorrow is of greater value to an individual than an extra hour of leisure today, only because in the mean time production technologies have improved, we do not apply this assumption either.

The procedure we follow builds on the literature on the relativity of utility (see Van de Stadt *et al.* ,1985, Alessie and Kapteyn, 1991, and references cited there). To keep the model manageable we use a relatively simple procedure to implement interdependent preferences and replace consumption in the utility function by the relative consumption with respect to the reference group of the household. The reference group consists of households to which the representative household compares its consumption and status. The share of the representative household itself in the reference group is so small, that the average consumption of the reference group is independent of the actions of the representative household. In the complete model consumption of the reference group is related to average real consumption per capita over all households.

Finally, calibrating the model the assumption has been introduced that a fraction of the partners in each type of household does not consider participation al all. This exogenous fraction captures aspects that do not depend on wages, like the small disposition to apply for work of elderly partners, who have not had much work experience in the past.

Based on the above notions, a labour supply model is presented below with a flexible choice of the number of hours supplied. Except for the 'keeping up with the Jones' effect in the utility function, the model uses the standard approach to derive the number of hours supplied, that for instance can be found in Deaton and Muellbauer (1980). In the next subsection we

[32] Marginal utility of leisure measured in hours equals marginal utility of leisure measured in efficiency units times the increase of the number of efficiency units per hour. Because of the assumptions of Ballard and Goulder, marginal utility of leisure measured in efficiency units remains constant through time and the number of efficiency units per hour rises with technical progress. Consequently, marginal utility of leisure measured in hours rises with technical progress too.

start with the labour supply model for a single household. Heterogeneity is introduced in the subsequent two subsections.

Supply of working hours of a single household

Household utility depends on leisure (d) and on consumption (c) compared to the average consumption of their reference group $\tilde{c}$:

$$u = \left((c/\tilde{c})^{-\rho_d} + \alpha^{1+\rho_d} d^{-\rho_d}\right)^{-1/\rho_d}, \quad \alpha > 0 . \tag{3.1}$$

The coefficient of consumption has been set at unity in (3.1), which can be done without loss of generality, because units of measurement of utility can be chosen freely. The coefficient of leisure (α) can be interpreted as the relative preference for leisure of a household.

The budget constraint of the household can be written as:

$$p_c c = (1 - s_y) \left\{(1 - t_b)(w_b l_b + z_b) + (1 - t_p) w_p l_p + z_n\right\} , \tag{3.2}$$

with p_c the price of consumer goods, s_y the savings rate, t the average rate of taxation and social security premiums, w the wage rate per hour, l the number of hours worked, and z non-wage income. The subscripts b and p denote breadwinner and partner, respectively. Non-wage income is divided into a part subject to taxation (z_b) and a part exempt from taxation (z_n)[33]. The rate of taxation for non-wage income is the tax rate of the person who earns most, the breadwinner. The time constraint of the household can be written as:

[33] An example of non-wage income subject to taxation are interest receipts of households in excess of a threshold value. Exempt from taxation are various transfers like children's allowances or subsidies to compensate high rents for low income earners. These components of non-wage income are endogenous in the model.

$$h = l_b + l_p + d \,, \qquad l_b \geq 0 \,,\ l_p \geq 0 \,,\ d \geq 0 \,, \tag{3.3}$$

with h the total time available to the household.

Substitution of (3.2) and (3.3) in (3.1) and differentiation with respect to leisure (d) gives the first order condition:

$$\frac{\partial u}{\partial c}\frac{\partial c}{\partial d} + \frac{\partial u}{\partial d} = 0 \rightarrow \frac{\partial u}{\partial d} / \frac{\partial u}{\partial c} = - \frac{\partial c}{\partial d} \,. \tag{3.4}$$

Equation (3.2) implies:

$$\frac{\partial c}{\partial d} = -\,(1 - s_y)(1 - \tau_p) w_p / p_c \,, \tag{3.5}$$

with τ_p the marginal rate of taxation and premiums for the partner. Substitution of (3.5) in (3.4) together with the derivatives from (3.1) yields:

$$\frac{c}{\tilde{c}} = \frac{d}{\alpha} \left(\frac{(1 - \tau_p)\, w_p}{e} \right)^{\sigma_d} , \qquad \sigma_d = 1 \,/\, 1 + \rho_d \,, \tag{3.6}$$

where $e = p_c \tilde{c} / (1 - s_y)$ can be interpreted as available income of the average household from the reference group if the savings rate is equal for all households in the reference group. Together with (3.3) the budget constraint (3.2) can be written as:

$$\frac{c}{\tilde{c}} = \frac{yf}{e} - \frac{(1 - t_p) w_p d}{e} \,, \tag{3.7}$$

with $yf = (1 - t_b)(w_b l_b + z_b) + (1 - t_p)(h - l_b)\, w_p + z_n$ denoting full income. Elimination of c from (3.6) and (3.7) leads to the equation for the desired amount of leisure:

$$d = \frac{yf / e}{\frac{1}{\alpha}\left(\frac{(1-\tau_p)w_p}{e}\right)^{\sigma_d} + \frac{(1-t_p)w_p}{e}} . \tag{3.8}$$

Because working time of the breadwinner (l_b) is exogenous, (3.8) and (3.3) determine the desired working time of the partner. Conditional on α, the labour supply elasticities of partners can be obtained. The elasticity with respect to the wage rate of the breadwinner reads:

$$\varepsilon_b \equiv \frac{w_b}{l_p}\frac{\partial lp}{\partial w_b} = -(1-\tau_b)\frac{w_b l_b}{yf}\frac{d}{l_p} , \tag{3.9}$$

with τ_b the marginal tax rate of the breadwinner. The elasticity with respect to the own wage rate of the partner is:

$$\varepsilon_p \equiv \frac{w_p}{l_p}\frac{\partial l_p}{\partial w_p}$$

$$= \left[-(1-\tau_p)\frac{(h-l_b)w_p}{yf} + \frac{\frac{\sigma_d}{\alpha}\left(\frac{(1-\tau_p)w_p}{e}\right)^{\sigma_d} + \frac{(1-\tau_p)w_p}{e}}{\frac{1}{\alpha}\left(\frac{(1-\tau_p)w_p}{e}\right)^{\sigma_d} + \frac{(1-t_p)w_p}{e}} \right] \frac{d}{l_p} . \tag{3.10}$$

These elasticities apply to households with a participating partner. The income of the breadwinner has a negative influence on partner labour supply. The income of the partner has an income effect and a substitution effect. According to the income effect, a higher wage rate of the partner increases consumption possibilities and reduces labour supply. According to the substitution effect, rising partner wages make leisure more costly and raise labour supply. The net effect depends on the parameters of the utility function and on the average and marginal tax rates. The model implies that a rise in the marginal tax rate at given average tax rates will have a negative influence on the number of hours supplied, because it generates negative substitution effects without compensating income effects. Likewise, a rise in average tax rates at given marginal tax rates will only have income effects and exert a positive influence on the number of hours supplied.

Heterogeneity and the progressive tax system

It is well known that the existence of different tax brackets will lead to kinks in the budget constraint (3.2). This is depicted in Figure 3.3. The slopes of the budget constraint equal minus the wage rate times one minus the relevant marginal tax rate. The number of hours supplied is found at the point of tangency between the budget constraint and the indifference curve associated with the utility function (3.1).

Heterogeneity is introduced by assuming that households differ with respect to the relative preference for leisure as reflected by the parameter α in (3.1). Using a continuous density function for the distribution of the relative preference for leisure among households, an infinite number of indifference curves exists, which all may entail a different number of working hours supplied. Only on the kinks of the budget line there is a non-zero fraction of indifference curves that are tangent to the budget line at the same number of working hours. This concerns households whose indifference curves have a slope in between the slopes of the budget lines to the left and to the right of the kink.

Figure 3.4 shows the resulting relationship between the relative preference for leisure and the number of hours supplied. A relative preference for leisure larger than α_o means that non-participation will be the preferred choice. Denoting the distribution function of α by $G(\alpha)$, the fraction of partners participating then equals $G(\alpha_0)$. Households with a lower preference for leisure than α_o will supply a positive and rising number of hours until the value of $\alpha_l(\tau_1)$ has been reached, which is the lowest relative preference for leisure for which the indifference curve is tangent to the budget line with

Figure 3.3 Choosing the number of hours supplied with heterogeneity of relative preference for leisure

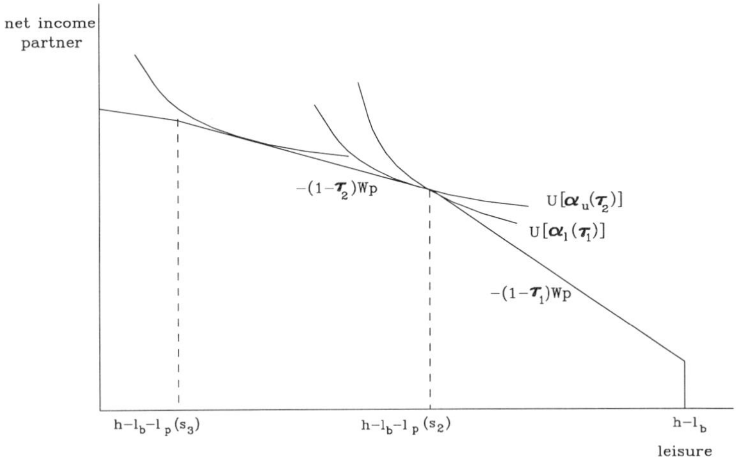

marginal tax rate τ_1 (see Figure 3.3). Let $\alpha_u(\tau_2)$ be the highest relative preference for leisure for which the indifference curve is tangent to the budget line with marginal tax rate τ_2. Then all households with relative preference for leisure between $\alpha_l(\tau_1)$ and $\alpha_u(\tau_2)$ will supply the same number of hours $l_p(s_2)$, *viz.* the number of hours associated with a taxable income of the partner equal to the lower border value, s_2, of the second tax bracket. Therefore, the curve in Figure 3.4 is horizontal over this interval. Households with relative preference for leisure less than $\alpha_u(\tau_2)$ will again prefer a higher number of hours and so on. The fraction of partners corresponding to each of the intervals in Figure 3.4 can be computed from the density function of α. A weighted average over the separate intervals yields the average number of hours supplied and the weighted marginal and average tax rates of partners.

Finally, the transfer of the basic allowance requires some further discussion. If the partner and breadwinner both earn a sufficiently high income, each of them is entitled to subtract a basic allowance from their taxable income before the tax rates have to be applied. If the partner does not work, her basic allowance is transferred to the breadwinner. Compared to a breadwinner with a single basic allowance, family income rises by the basic

Figure 3.4 Relative preference for leisure and number of hours supplied

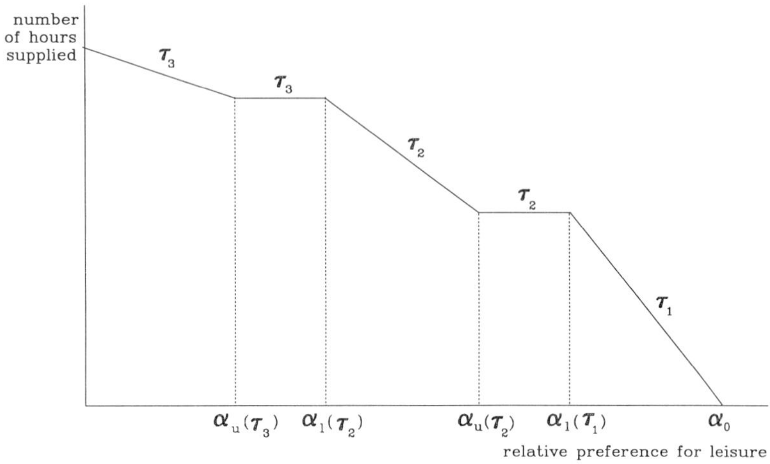

allowance (*tv*) times the marginal tax rate of the breadwinner, which equals θ_1 for a breadwinner with an income in the first tax bracket. This is depicted by the line segment AB in Figure 3.5, which is a magnification of the right side of Figure 3.3. In the current tax system, the complete basic allowance can be transferred to the breadwinner as long as taxable income of the partner is less than the basic allowance. This implies that a rise of partner income is taxed according to the tax rate in the lowest tax bracket, represented by the line segment BE. As is clear from Figure 3.5 for a household with breadwinner income in the first tax bracket there is no kink in the budget constraint associated with the basic allowance, since the marginal tax rates of breadwinner and partner are equal.

If the breadwinner is taxed according to the tax rate in a higher tax bracket (θ_2) and taxable income of the partner rises above the basic allowance, net family income falls, because the transfer of basic allowance is cancelled. The fall of net income (DE) equals the difference between the marginal tax rate of the breadwinner and the marginal tax rate of the partner,

Figure 3.5 Budget constraint with different ways of transferring the basic allowance

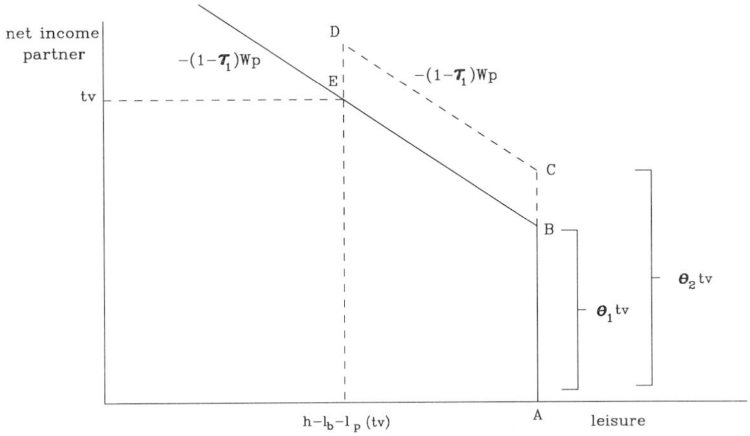

times the basic allowance[34]. Maximizing utility in the way described above, a number of indifference curves will be tangent to the budget line in point D. Yet, it is unlikely that many households will choose for the partner to earn exactly the basic allowance. In point D a small increase of taxable income or a small reduction of the basic allowance, will lead to a relatively large decline of net income[35]. To avoid this, not many households will select point D.

Because of the relatively small number of households with a partner who on the formal labour market earns less than the basic allowance, and with a breadwinner who is not taxed by the lowest marginal tax rate, we abstract from this case in the model. In the model the budget line BE is assumed to be relevant, and we do not consider a kink in the budget line at a partner income

[34] In the system of transfer of basic allowance before the 1990 income tax reform only the part of the basic allowance above taxable partner income could be transferred to the breadwinner. Hence, the marginal tax rate of the breadwinner applies to an increase of partner income. For a breadwinner with a marginal tax rate above the first bracket this would be depicted by a line segment CE in Figure 3.5.

[35] For the 1992 tax system the income reduction amounts to 600 guilders a year, if the breadwinner is taxed by the 50% marginal tax rate.

equal to the basic allowance. In this way a significant simplification has been achieved at a relatively moderate price.

The labour supply model with heterogeneity

The derivation of the labour supply model with heterogeneity starts at the kink in the budget line at a border value of a tax bracket. Define the lower border of tax bracket i by s_i and the marginal tax rate in this tax bracket by θ_i. If the basic allowance is denoted by tv, the total wage sum ys_i and the total number of hours worked by the partner $l_{p,i}$, corresponding to tax border s_i are:

$$ys_i = (s_i + tv)/(1 - p_w) , \tag{3.11}$$

$$l_{p,i} = ys_i/w_p , \tag{3.12}$$

where p_w denotes the sum of the average premium rate for employee insurances and the pension premium rate, supplemented by the general social security premium rate in the years before 1990. The value of $l_{p,i}$ denotes the height of a horizontal line segment in Figure 3.4. The net income of the partner corresponding to the border of the tax bracket can be computed directly from:

$$yn_{p,i} = s_i + tv - ts_i , \tag{3.13}$$

with ts_i the amount of taxes to be paid on income equal to the lower border of tax bracket i. The marginal rate of taxes and social security premiums τ_p can be determined as:

$$\tau_{p,i} = p_w + (1 - p_w)\theta_i . \tag{3.14}$$

To determine the corresponding border values for α of an interval on which the supplied number of hours is constant, we substitute the definitions of full income and household time in (3.8) and rewrite for α:

$$\alpha_l(\tau_{i-1}) = \frac{\left[(1 - \tau_{p,i-1}) w_p / e\right]^{\sigma_d} (h - l_b - l_{p,i})}{(yn_b + yn_{p,i})/e}, \tag{3.15}$$

$$\alpha_u(\tau_i) = \frac{\left[(1 - \tau_{p,i}) w_p / e\right]^{\sigma_d} (h - l_b - l_{p,i})}{(yn_b + yn_{p,i})/e}, \tag{3.16}$$

where $yn_b = (1 - t_b)(w_b l_b + z_b) + z_n$ is the net income of the breadwinner and $yn_{p,i}$ is the net income of the partner defined in (3.13). Both values of α are computed by means of the net income, $yn_{p,i}$, and the number of hours, $l_{p,i}$, corresponding to the border of the tax bracket. The upper border of the interval consists of the value of α corresponding to tax rate $i-1$ in (3.15); the lower border consists of the value of α corresponding to tax rate i in (3.16).

Denoting the distribution function of α by $G(\alpha)$, we can write the fraction of partners with number of hours supplied equal to $l_{p,i}$ as:

$$f_i = G[\alpha_l(\tau_{i-1})] - G[\alpha_u(\tau_i)] . \tag{3.17}$$

We can also determine the number of partners who decide to participate. The value of α for the household that is indifferent between participation and non-participation, can be derived from (3.16) with $l_{p,i} = 0$ and $\tau_{p,i} = \tau_{p,1}$:

$$\alpha_o = \frac{\left[(1 - \tau_{p,1}) w_p / e\right]^{\sigma_d} (h - l_b)}{yn_b \,/\, e} . \tag{3.18}$$

This value of α_o is on the right side in Figure 3.4. The fraction of partners participating then equals $G(\alpha_o)$.

Next the intervals with a varying number of hours in Figure 3.4 remain to be described. Where needed the subscript j will be used to distinguish variables in these intervals from those in intervals with a constant number of hours. The borders of an interval with a varying number of hours consist of $\alpha_l(\tau_i)$ and $\alpha_u(\tau_i)$, the lowest and highest value of α corresponding to the marginal rate of taxes and social security premiums τ_i. The fraction of partners in such an interval (f_j) can be computed analogously to (3.17). In the entire interval the marginal tax rate for the partner equals $\tau_{p,i}$. Determining the average number of hours supplied and the average tax rate is more complicated. We proceed as follows. Firstly, we can use the constancy of the marginal tax rate throughout the interval, to relate the net income of the partner to the number of working hours and to predetermined tax parameters. The definition of taxable income of the partner, yb_p, is:

$$yb_p = w_p l_p (1 - p_w) \ . \tag{3.19}$$

Taxable income is the difference between the total wage bill and all relevant premiums. The definition of net income of the partner, yn_p, equals:

$$yn_p = yb_p - ts_i - \theta_i \,(yb_p - tv - s_i) \ . \tag{3.20}$$

Net income is the difference between taxable income and the amount of taxes to be paid. Taxes consist of the amount to be paid on income equal to the lower border of the current tax bracket (ts_i), plus the marginal tax rate in the tax bracket (θ_i) times the difference between taxable income, adjusted for the basic allowance (tv), and the lower limit of the tax bracket (s_i). Substituting (3.19) in (3.20) yields:

$$yn_{p,j} \equiv (1 - t_{p,j}) w_p l_{p,j} = (1 - \tau_{p,i}) w_p l_{p,j} + d_i \ , \tag{3.21}$$

with $d_i = \theta_i(tv + s_i) - ts_i$.

In a second step, we can substitute the relationship between net income and the number of hours supplied from (3.21) into (3.16), and derive the number of hours supplied as a function of α:

$$l_{p,j}(\alpha) = \frac{\dfrac{h - l_b}{\alpha}\left(\dfrac{(1 - \tau_{p,i})w_p}{e}\right)^{\sigma_d} - \dfrac{yn_b + d_i}{e}}{\dfrac{1}{\alpha}\left(\dfrac{(1 - \tau_{p,i})w_p}{e}\right)^{\sigma_d} + \dfrac{(1 - \tau_{p,i})w_p}{e}} \,. \tag{3.22}$$

Thirdly, the average number of hours supplied in the interval follows from:

$$\int_{\alpha_l(\tau_i)}^{\alpha_u(\tau_i)} l_{p,j}(x) g(x) dx \; / \; f_j \,, \tag{3.23}$$

with $g(\alpha)$ the density function of α and f_j the fraction of partners in the interval (compare (3.17)). The integral in (3.23) can only be evaluated numerically, therefore a numerical integration routine is implemented in the model. Finally, the average value of the average tax rate follows straight from (3.21):

$$t_{p,j} = \tau_{p,i} - d_i / (w_p \; l_{p,j}) \,. \tag{3.24}$$

Now, for all intervals in Figure 3.4 we have identified: the average number of hours supplied from (3.12) and (3.23); the average value of the average tax rate from (3.11) combined with (3.13) and from (3.24); the marginal tax rate from (3.14) in both cases; and the fraction of participating partners from (3.17). A weighted average of hours supplied and tax rates over all intervals yields the average value of hours supplied and the average value of the marginal and average tax rates for all partners in a given type of household.

Because changes in income of breadwinner and partner affect the participation rate, the income elasticities for total labour supply are smaller than the income elasticities for the representative household derived in (3.9) and

(3.10). For example, if the breadwinners' wage rises some partners who previously supplied a small number of hours, would prefer to supply a negative number of hours and hence are now restricted to work zero hours. Therefore, the average number of hours falls by less than that of a representative partner at a given value of α. Note however, that the total influence of a higher income of the breadwinner on labour supply still is unambiguously negative since it causes some partners to stop working at all whereas all other previously working partners reduce the preferred number of hours supplied.

If the substitution effect dominates the income effect in (3.10) a higher wage rate of the partner raises the supplied number of hours for each individual household. This also applies to some households of which the partner initially did not participate, but who will supply a positive number of hours after the rise in wages. Therefore, the participation rate rises too. Moreover, according to (3.18) the influence of the wage rate of the partner on participation is unambiguously positive. Even if for individual households the income effect dominates the substitution effect, participation rises. This is because the income effect is not relevant for the indifferent household which is characterized by zero hours worked.

Equation (3.18) also shows that the marginal tax rate in the lowest tax bracket has a negative influence on participation. The effect is comparable to that of the wage rate of partners (with opposite sign). Tax rates in higher tax brackets do not influence participation, but do have a negative influence on hours supplied, as has been described on page 84.

On the long run in a model with labour augmenting technical progress, the nominal wage rates of the partner (w_p) and the breadwinner (w_b) and the full income (yf) grow by the sum of the rate of inflation and the rate of technical progress. With a constant savings rate, also the available income of the average household in the reference group (e) will have this growth rate. Because in the model the borders of the tax brackets and the basic allowance have been indexed to the wage rate, the participation rate and the preferred number of hours of participating partners will remain constant on the growth path, as is evident from (3.18), (3.12), (3.15), (3.16), (3.17) and (3.22). Also the elasticities conditional on the participation rate in (3.9) and (3.10) are constant.

If consumption would not have been defined relative to the reference group in the utility function, e would have to be replaced by p_c / (1−s) in the equations above. From (3.18) it follows, that for σ_d <1 (σ_d >1) a permanent increase (decrease) of the participation rate would result. Only σ_d =1 would imply stability of the participation rate. The preferred number of hours would be stable if σ_d =1 and if the marginal and average tax rates are equal.

3.3 Calibration of the household model

Calibrating the household model, various kinds of restrictions should be taken into account. Firstly, the distribution of the population over households has to comply with macro labour market information and data from population statistics. Secondly, the data from the National Accounts should be satisfied under the constraint that the average gross income derived from the class frequency income distributions must equal average gross incomes derived from wage costs and premiums paid by employers. Thirdly, the data of the labour supply models should be calibrated. In this section these aspects of the calibration procedure will be broadly outlined.

Population and labour market data

The major source of data about the structure of the labour market in 1985 is the Labour Force Survey conducted by Central Bureau of Statistics (1987a). At the Labour Market Division of the Central Planning Bureau this information has been compiled into a consistent set of data on participation, employment, unemployment, and persons in disability schemes, differentiated with respect to sex and eleven types of education and measured in persons and fulltime equivalents. After aggregation of types of education to the two skill levels distinguished in the household model, a household dimension has been added to these data, using the Households statistics of the Central Bureau of Statistics (1988) and the Labour Force Survey.

Table 3.2 People 15 – 65 years, subdivided with respect to sex, skill level, labour market situation and household type in 1985 (x1000).

	Single persons		One parent families		Families with children				Families without children				Total
Level education:	low	high	low	high									
– women					high	high	low	low	high	high	low	low	
– men					high	low	high	low	high	low	high	low	
Men													
Low skilled													
employed	492		14			75		631		43		246	1501
unemployed	139		4			8		69		6		33	259
disabled	115		9			17		145		21		117	424
not participating	10					2		14		5		29	60
High skilled													
employed		384		16	536		496		234		171		1837
unemployed		40		2	15		14		12		8		91
disabled		22		3	22		21		29		21		118
not participating		6		1	8		7		24		18		64
Total	756	452	27	22	581	102	538	859	299	75	218	425	4354
Women													
Low skilled													
employed	265		33				123	197			82	159	859
unemployed	74		31				17	27			6	13	168
disabled	63		24				15	23			10	19	154
not participating	95		98				383	612			120	234	1542
High skilled													
employed		301		37	234	42			229	59			902
unemployed		28		12	25	4			14	3			86
disabled		5		5	29	5			6	1			51
not participating		15		15	293	51			50	12			436
Total	497	349	186	69	581	102	538	859	299	75	218	425	4198
Total persons	1253	801	213	91	1162	204	1076	1718	598	150	436	850	8552

Table 3.3 Percentage distributions of people 15 – 65 years with respect to labour market situation and household type in 1985.

	Single persons		One parent families		Families with children				Families without children				Total
Level education:	low	high	low	high									
– women					high	high	low	low	high	high	low	low	
– men					high	low	high	low	high	low	high	low	
Men													
Low skilled													
employed	65		52			74		73		57		58	28
unemployed	18		15			8		8		8		8	5
disabled	15		33			17		17		28		28	7
not participating	1					2		2		7		7	19
High skilled													
employed		85		73	92		92		78		78		32
unemployed		9		9	3		3		4		4		2
disabled		5		14	4		4		10		10		2
not participating		1		5	1		1		8		8		6
Total	100	100	100	100	100	100	100	100	100	100	100	100	100
Women													
Low skilled													
employed	53		18				23	23			38	37	20
unemployed	15		17				3	3			3	3	4
disabled	13		13				3	3			5	4	4
not participating	19		53				71	71			55	55	37
High skilled													
employed		86		54	40	41			77	79			21
unemployed		8		17	4	4			5	4			2
disabled		1		7	5	5			2	1			1
not participating		4		22	50	50			17	16			10
Total	100	100	100	100	100	100	100	100	100	100	100	100	100
Men	17	10	1	1	13	2	12	20	7	2	5	10	100
Women	12	8	4	2	14	2	13	20	7	2	5	10	100

In this process some restrictions imposed by the model had to be satisfied. The most important of these is that the model expects the number of breadwinners and partners per family type of households to be the same, which restriction is less straightforward than appears at first sight. For instance, because on average in marriage men are older than women, drawing a dividing line at the age of 65 for men and women separately results in a group of persons in families younger than 65 with more women than men. Hence, a number of women have been registered with the aged households, although not yet being 65 years of age. Another aspect of the calibration process is that labour market characteristics have been given precedence over population characteristics. Since in the model we abstract from work by aged households, the (small) number of aged persons working have been registered with families younger than 65 years of age.

The resulting labour market data per type of household are presented in Table 3.2 and Table 3.3. Lines in Table 3.2 indicate numbers of men or women differentiated with respect to educational level and labour market situation. The columns show the distribution over household types. For instance, of the 1.5 million low-skilled employed men, 631 thousand form a family with a low-skilled woman and one or more children and 492 thousand live by themselves. The majority of high-skilled women live together with a high-skilled man (581 versus 102 thousand for families with children and 299 versus 75 thousand for families without children). Also for low-skilled women the educational levels of men and women in families are correlated, but less strongly so. These correlations can also be observed from the two bottom lines of Table 3.3, which represent the distribution of men and women over types of households.

The main part of Table 3.3 contains the percentage distribution of persons with respect to their labour market situation. It shows that in households with a high-skilled woman participation rates of women are higher than in households with a low-skilled woman: 17% of high-skilled women living together with a high-skilled man without children do not participate, of low-skilled women in the same family type 55% do not participate. Unemployment percentages are higher for single persons than for families. This can be explained by the high youth unemployment rate in 1985 and by the fact that many of the younger persons are single. Percentages of people who receive a disability benefit are highest for low-skilled men without children. This is because the disability risk is highest for low-skilled work and people often become disabled at an older age, when children have already left home to live on their own.

To construct a database for MIMIC two operations have been performed on the data in Table 3.2. Firstly, men who live in families and do not participate are registered as partners and women in these families are assumed to work and are registered as breadwinners. All other men in families are classified as breadwinners. Changing the row dimension of the table from men / women to breadwinners / partners a table with a comparable structure can be obtained, in which the cells of non-participating breadwinners are empty. In the second operation, family types are subdivided with respect to the labour market position of the breadwinner. This boils down to generating a division of labour market position of partners for each of the labour market positions of breadwinners per type of household in Table 3.2. Aggregating the relevant subgroups, data on the household types defined in the model can be obtained. The total number of these households and if relevant the participation rates of partners can be found in Table 3.1.

Once the distribution of persons over households is available, the link with the number of working hours per person can be made. Data on the number of working hours are available for the total column in Table 3.2, *viz.* for persons aggregated over households. In MIMIC for every person per type of household a so-called 'Persons / Labour-years ratio' exists which comprises the number of persons per standard labour year. The P/L ratios are exogenous for all persons except for partners, whose number of working hours supplied is determined endogenously in the labour supply submodel. Given the number of hours in a standard labour year the P/L ratios can be used to derive the number of working hours for a person in a specific type of households. Calibrating the model, three main types of P/L ratios are distinguished, *viz.* P/L ratios for single persons, for breadwinners and for partners. These ratios are determined in such a way that the known P/L ratios for the total column of Table 3.2 are satisfied. The resulting P/L ratio for breadwinners equals 1.03, indicating that breadwinners work almost the standard amount of time. The larger amount of part-time work done by partners is reflected in a calibrated P/L ratio of 1.75 for partners with children and 1.35 for partners without children. Single persons on average work somewhat less than the standard number of hours, their P/L ratio equals 1.07. Once the P/L ratios have been determined, the total data set on population and labour market data is available.

Income components and income distributions

Aggregated over household types, the total wage bill, sickness benefits, unemployment benefits, disability benefits, pension payments and children's allowances should equal the aggregates reported in the National Accounts. The same applies to non-wage income received by households, to total consumption and to the total amount of premiums and taxes generated by the model.

Data on the wage bill are available for men and women and per educational level. These figures are divided over persons in households, taking account of the Persons / Labour-years ratios derived in the previous step. Sickness benefits are assumed to be proportional to wages and children's allowances are divided over households with children. For unemployed persons gross replacement ratios of benefits from the Unemployment Insurance Act and from social assistance are calibrated, taking account of data on the distribution of unemployment benefits over these two sources of benefits. Also for other types of benefits, like disability and old age benefits, replacement ratios have been included in the model to index benefit levels to wages.

Data on the distribution of wage and benefit incomes over breadwinners are derived from the Housing Demand Survey by the Central Bureau of Statistics (1987c). In this survey, data on household types, housing, income levels and sources of income are recorded from 72 thousand persons, which are representative for the total population. In order to make the means of these distributions coincide with the wage or benefit rate per type of household derived from National Accounts information, the border values of the distributions are shifted proportionally until the average gross income rate from the distribution equals the gross wage or benefit rate from National Accounts data.

Taxes and premiums paid by households are computed using the statutory tax and premium rates. Not all persons included in the household sector of the model pay all social security premiums. For instance, employee insurances apply only to employees in the private sector. However, since employees in private firms, civil servants, and self-employed persons are not distinguished in the model, no differentiation can be made to apply the statutory premium rates only to a part of the households. In this case using the full statutory premium rates would result in too high an amount of premiums paid. Therefore the statutory premium rates are adjusted by means of proportionality factors, which are chosen in such a way as to equalize the premium payments generated by the model to the National Accounts data. The total amount of income taxes generated by the model has been set equal to the National Accounts figure by calibrating the amount of income tax deductions. Total calibrated deductions correspond reasonably well to information in Central Bureau of Statistics (1989a).

From the gross income distribution data and the statutory tax and premium system net income distributions per type of households can be derived. For the year of calibration, 1985, the net income distributions for several types of breadwinners and single persons distinguished in MIMIC are depicted in Figure 3.6 and Figure 3.7. Figure 3.6 shows that higher incomes arise most frequently with breadwinners with high-skilled partners. Since many of the breadwinners living together with high-skilled partners also have a high education their incomes are relatively high as well. Because a large number of young people can be found in the group of single persons the income distribution of this type of households lies to the left compared to breadwinners in families. A significant part of the mass of the distribution of aged people lies at low incomes because of the substantial number of aged people only receiving a basic benefit under the General Old Age Pension Act.

Figure 3.6 Net income distributions employed breadwinners and aged people

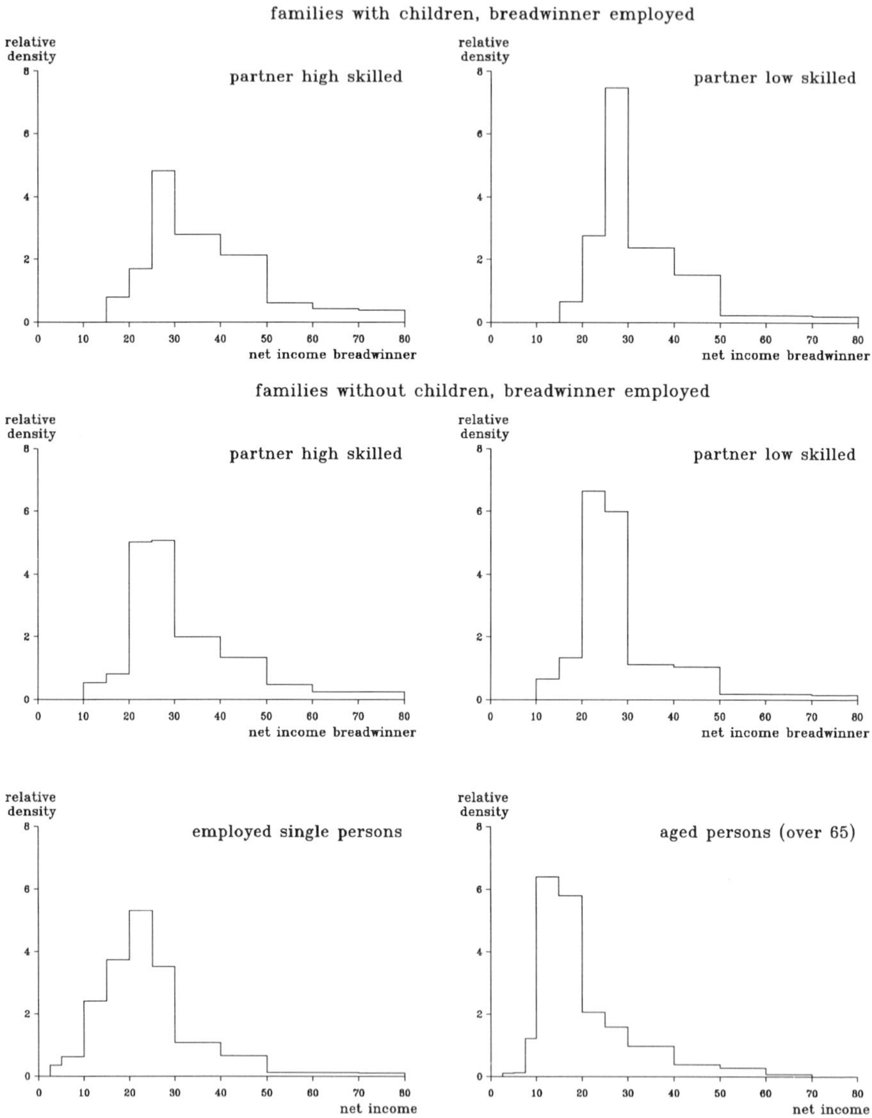

Figure 3.7 Net income distributions unemployed and disabled persons

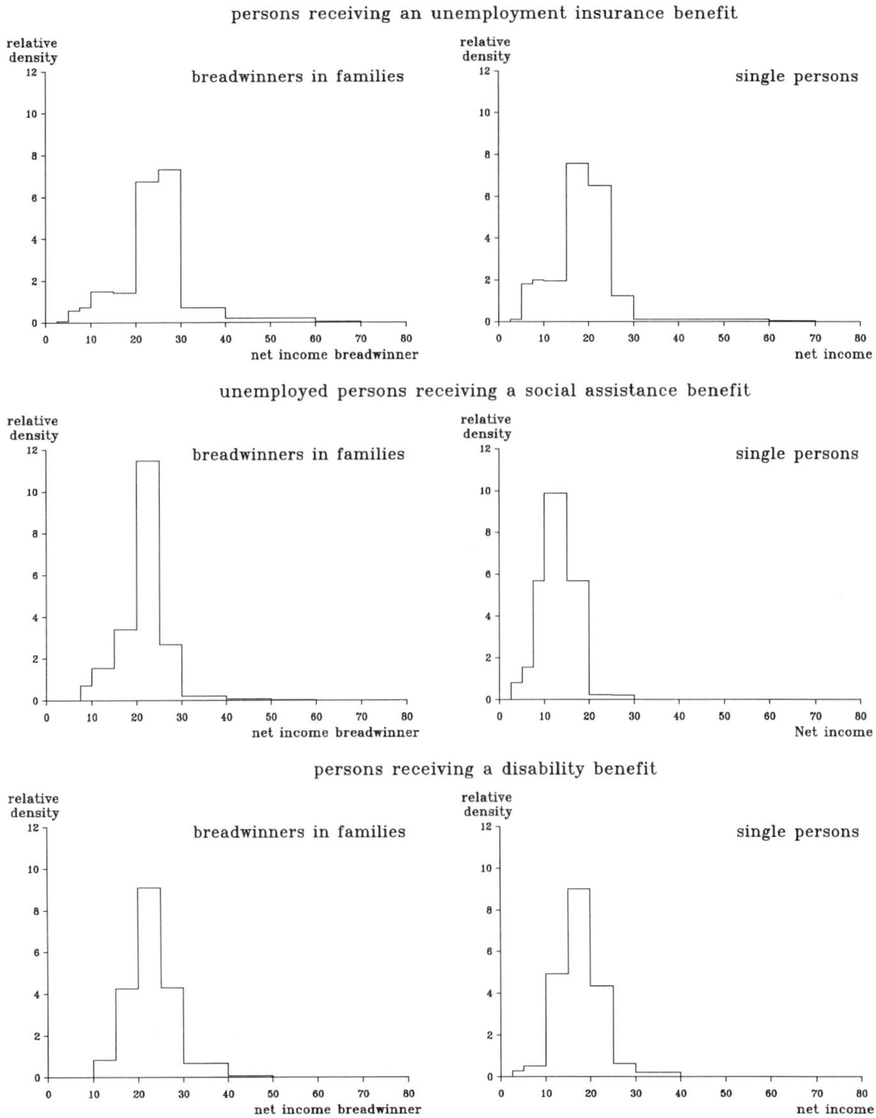

The income distributions of the unemployed are depicted in the first four graphs of Figure 3.7. Unemployment insurance benefits are related to the wage rate the person earned before becoming unemployed, while social assistance benefits are independent of previous earnings. This explains why the distributions of people receiving a social assistance benefit lie to the left of and are more peaked than the distributions of persons receiving an unemployment insurance benefit. For new entrants into the disability scheme the benefit level is comparable to the unemployment insurance benefit. Both equal 70% of previous wages. However, in Figure 3.7 the income distributions of disabled people lie somewhat to the left of the income distributions of persons receiving an unemployment insurance benefit. Two reasons can account for this phenomenon. Firstly, from Table 3.2 it can be seen that a larger percentage of disabled people is low-skilled compared to unemployed people. Hence, the average previous income of disabled people and consequently their current average benefit level will be lower. Secondly, in the four year period before the year of calibration 1985 the indexation of benefit levels to wage growth had been almost abolished. Since on average the group of people receiving a disability benefit is in the benefit scheme for a longer period of time compared to people in unemployment insurance schemes this also lowers their average benefit rate.

Once gross income components and total premiums and taxes equal data from the National Accounts, this is also the case for net incomes. Equalizing the savings rate per group of households to the macro savings rate implies that aggregate consumption over households equals the macro figure for 1985 as well.

Calibration

Firstly we discuss the calibration of the parameters of the labour supply submodel. Calibration concerns the selection of the maximum amount of hours available for work, and the parameters. The participation rate and the average number of hours supplied by participating partners are given from the base year data. In the calibration process we search for values of parameters that yield desired values of the own wage elasticity of the partner and of the wage elasticity of the breadwinner.

The average consumption of the reference group has been set at unity, because its size is not important. For units of time a scaling factor has been used in such a way that the number of hours supplied can be interpreted as hours per week. The total number of hours available for working has been differentiated with respect to the presence of children. For partners without children it equals 60 hours a week and for partners with children 40 hours a week. The logarithm of the relative preference for leisure α is assumed to have a normal distribution with expected value log μ and standard deviation ξ. As indicated above, an extra parameter (β_d) has been introduced, which denotes the fraction of partners that does not consider participation al all. This parameter captures factors influencing labour supply that do not depend on wages.

Table 3.4 contains the results of the calibration procedure. Based on information in Theeuwes (1988) and Theeuwes and Woittiez (1992) parameters corresponding to own wage partner labour supply elasticities of 1.0 have been selected. Because of insufficient empirical information on labour supply elasticities per type of households we opted for a uniform value of the own wage elasticity. The elasticity of breadwinner income appears hardly dependent on the parameter values. Its value of –0.2 is in line with empirical information. The parameters for the three types of households do not differ very much. Only the fraction of partners not participating (β_d) is lower for high-skilled partners, because of the high participation rates of these partners (compare Table 3.1). Since labour supply of breadwinners, single persons and single parent households is assumed to be exogenous in the model, all relevant elasticities of breadwinner labour supply are zero.

Comparison with micro econometric studies

Comparing estimated elasticities of labour supply over a number of micro econometric studies yields quite pronounced differences. For example, a survey of Dutch labour supply elasticities provided by Theeuwes and Woittiez

Table 3.4 Calibration of the labour supply model

	Elasticity for		Parameters			
	Partner income	Breadwinner income	β_d	μ	ξ	σ_d
Families with children[a]						
– breadwinner employed, partner high-skilled	1.0	–0.21	0.41	0.06	1.7	4.0
– breadwinner employed, partner low-skilled	1.0	–0.26	0.62	0.11	1.7	2.9
– breadwinner unemployment insurance benefit	1.0	–0.22	0.62	0.08	1.7	3.6
– breadwinner disability benefit	1.0	–0.20	0.57	0.07	1.7	3.8
Families without children[a]						
– breadwinner employed, partner high-skilled	1.0	–0.17	0.09	0.06	1.8	4.2
– breadwinner employed, partner low-skilled	1.0	–0.22	0.48	0.12	1.8	3.3
– breadwinner unemployment insurance benefit	1.0	–0.16	0.44	0.06	1.8	4.3
– breadwinner disability benefit	1.0	–0.14	0.48	0.04	1.8	4.8

[a] Families with unemployed breadwinners receiving a social assistance benefit are not included because partners of these breadwinners do not participate.

(1992) learns that the wage elasticity of married women ranges from 0.0 to 7.09, whereas for men and single women this elasticity ranges from –0.44 to 0.27 and from –0.83 to 3.84, respectively. According to the same writers, the discrepancies can be attributed to several factors. In the first place, the functional specification of the labour supply equation can vary greatly, ranging from a straightforward linear function to a full-fledged highly non-linear dynamic life cycle system. Secondly, data sources used in the estimations differ in kind, *e.g.* time series or cross sections, and with respect to the period or population they cover. Moreover, the development of econometric science has provided a variety of estimation techniques, which explains part of the pronounced variation in estimations.

To narrow the considerably wide ranges of estimations, Theeuwes and Woittiez (1992) present a list consisting of five criteria to be used as a checking device to select the best elasticity estimates from Dutch labour supply studies. The estimates are assessed with respect to definition of the elasticity, stochastic specification, reference to utility theory, calculation of the marginal wage and flexibility in the functional specification. It follows that none of the models underlying the estimated elasticities exactly satisfy the chosen criteria. Selecting the elasticity estimates from those studies that approach the first best practice in four criteria yields 22 second best estimates for married and single women which provide an average female wage labour supply elasticity of 1.2.

Assuming that the selected estimates of female labour supply elasticities are partial indicators of the true but unknown labour supply elasticity, a factor analysis model is used to estimate the relation of the indicators to the true elasticity. In the analysis it is explicitly accounted for the fact that the indicators stem from two types of data sources. For females, it follows that almost all indicators were significantly different from zero, implying that the indicators indeed contain information about the true elasticities. Conditional on the values of the indicators, prediction of the true elasticity provides a female wage elasticity of 1.1 with a small standard error of 0.11.

As a third road to follow, Theeuwes and Woittiez (1992) present the mixed estimation method, which takes extraneous information, *i.e.* previous estimates of labour supply elasticities, into account. The idea is that "old" elasticities estimated in previous studies can help to estimate the elasticity in a new study more accurately. This method provides a wage elasticity for married women of 0.8 with a standard error of 0.37.

Considered the values produced by the methodologies described above, Theeuwes and Woittiez (1992) conclude that the labour supply elasticity of Dutch women is approximately one, which is exactly in line with the wage elasticity of partner labour supply in MIMIC.

Starting from a modified version of a model introduced by earlier literature, van Soest (1990) presents a model which explicitly captures demand side restrictions by modelling a limited availability of jobs with different, distinct, numbers of hours. With respect to male labour supply in The Netherlands, the modified earlier model provides a wage elasticity of 0.12 whereas the extended van Soest model yields a wage elasticity of 0.10. Considered together with the average elasticity of 0.07 presented in a survey paper by Theeuwes in 1988, these values suggest that male labour supply is rather insensitive to wage changes. The assumption of exogenous breadwinner labour supply in MIMIC is therefore justifiable. As labour supply of Dutch women is concerned, the modified earlier model and the extended van Soest model produce a wage elasticity of 0.65 and 0.79, respectively. Compared to the average wage elasticity of 1.39 found by Theeuwes (1988), these values are low but not out of line. It should be noted that the wage elasticity of partners set in MIMIC is midway between these three values which is a second indication that it is well-founded.

In addition, the question should be asked whether the other-income elasticity set in MIMIC is justifiable on the basis of econometric estimates. Averaging over a number of Dutch labour supply studies, Theeuwes (1988) finds the male and female other-income elasticity to be –0.07 and –0.16, respectively. This suggests the value of the female other-income elasticity to be set a little to high. However, the study performed by van Mourik and Siegers (1991) which concentrates on analyzing the effects of unemployment on Dutch labour force participation provides more justification in this field. To their aim, the authors construct a model using a logistic specification of the labour supply equation. Regarding sensitivity to changes in income different from own wage earnings, an elasticity of –0.011 for Dutch men and an elasticity of –0.43 for married Dutch women is found. On the basis of these values, it can be concluded that the breadwinner and partner other-income elasticity of 0 and –0.2, respectively, are justifiable.

4 Matchings, search strategy of unemployed and contractual wage formation

Having presented the models for labour demand and labour supply in Chapter 2 and 3, this chapter deals with the confrontation of labour demand and labour supply in three respects.

Firstly, confrontation of labour supply and labour demand yields unemployment for all types of labour. It is assumed that persons becoming unemployed are randomly drawn from the pool of labour supply. Individuals entering the pool of unemployed face a new situation which differs from the situation of non-participating partners because of a legal right to an unemployment benefit. Because of this right, the behaviour of an unemployed person will differ from that of partners considering participation on the labour market. The model of the strategy followed by unemployed persons will be described in Section 4.1 and is akin the search model developed by Pissarides (1990). The model applies to a representative unemployed worker per type of education as distinguished in the model of the firm. In contrast to the household model the search model therefore abstracts from heterogeneity in the relative preferences for leisure and consumption. In the model two aspects of the strategy of the unemployed are analyzed, the intensity of searching for a job which is related to the number of hours spent actively searching, and the reservation wage defined as the wage offer at which the unemployed person is indifferent between accepting a job and searching for another job.

The second aspect of the confrontation between labour demand and labour supply relates to the matching process between unemployed persons looking for a job and vacancies posted by employers. At the micro economic level, a contact between an unemployed person and an employer will only succeed in a job match if the productivity of the matched job both exceeds the lowest wage scale and the reservation wage of the unemployed person. This implies some additional restrictions on the matching process. The model of the matching process is dealt with in Section 4.2.

The third aspect of confrontation of labour demand and labour supply concerns the bargaining processes between the representatives of firms and workers about contractual wage formation. Including legal extension to non-organized firms, in The Netherlands 80% of the private sector is covered by collective wage agreements. The bargaining processes take place at the industry level or at the firm level for individual large firms, and normally concern the wage rate of the subsequent year. Generally employment is not part of the bargain, but is set by individual firms. This means that an industry bargaining model akin to the right to manage model of Nickell and Andrews (1983) is relevant. Atomistic bargaining between employers and workers accounts for wages in some other sectors. As outlined in Chapter 2, employers may in individual cases supplement officially bargained wages by a wage drift component, for instance by raising the position of workers in official wage scales. Since this wage drift component is rather small compared to the contractual wage growth, it is assumed that the bargaining parties do not explicitly take into account the influence of wage drift on total wages when determining contractual wage growth. The model for contractual wage formation is described in Section 4.3.

Section 4.4 deals with the calibration of the search model of the unemployed, the matching process and contractual wage formation. The parameters of the search model of the unemployed and the matching process between vacancies and unemployed are based on Dutch microeconometric and macroeconomic research. Special attention has been paid to the empirical foundation of the model for contractual wage formation, because of its crucial importance for the simulation results[36]. The parameters of the model have been obtained from a detailed comparison with an estimated wage equation for the Netherlands. In this way the model captures the observed influence of tax rates and the replacement ratio on wages.

[36] For a theoretical and empirical analysis of wage models for The Netherlands, see Graafland (1990b and 1991a).

4.1 Search behaviour of unemployed persons

The search intensity of the unemployed

The strategy of the unemployed per type of labour contains two components, search intensity and reservation wage.[37] Search intensity is defined as an index of the number of interviews with potential employers per period. It is assumed that the search intensity (s) is positively related to the amount of time spent searching for a job (ts), but less than proportionally:

$$s = ts^{1/\zeta} , \qquad \zeta > 1 . \tag{4.1}$$

The positive utility from raising search time stems from a higher probability to find a job with an income that exceeds the unemployment benefit. The negative utility stems from a reduction in leisure. The optimal search intensity follows from the maximisation of the utility of the unemployed person which equals:

$$U_t = Uv_t + \eta \; Uc_t , \qquad \eta > 0 , \tag{4.2}$$

where Uv_t and Uc_t denote the utility from leisure and consumption respectively during the planning period of the unemployed person from period t onwards, where η measures the relative weight of consumption in total utility. For a representative unemployed person with search intensity s, Uv_t and Uc_t are defined as:[38]

[37] Because the theoretical specification of the models for search behaviour of the unemployed and the matching process is identical for the five types of labour (low-skilled with minimum income, other low-skilled, technically skilled, economically skilled and service orientated skilled), no index is used in section 4.1 and 4.2 to denote different types of labour.

[38] If a variable is presented without time index, it relates to period t.

$$Uv_t = \log(T - ts) + p \frac{Ev_{t+1}}{1+r} + (1-p) \frac{Uv_{t+1}}{1+r} , \tag{4.3}$$

$$Uc_t = \log(b/pc) + p \frac{Ec_{t+1}}{1+r} + (1-p) \frac{Uc_{t+1}}{1+r} . \tag{4.4}$$

T denotes total available time in period t, p the probability of moving into employment, Ev_t (Ec_t) the utility from leisure (consumption) of an employed worker during the planning period from period t onwards, r the discount rate, and b and pc the net unemployment benefit and consumption price in period t. It is assumed that the rate at which the unemployed worker moves into employment (p) is positively related to his search intensity s and negatively to his reservation wage (wr):

$$p = (s/\bar{s})\, \bar{p}\, f(wr/\overline{wr}), \qquad f' < 0, \tag{4.5}$$

where $\bar{s}$ is the average search intensity of all unemployed persons, $\bar{p}$ the average probability to find a job of all unemployed persons and $\overline{wr}$ the average reservation wage.

Assuming that employed workers also have some probability to change state and become unemployed, for instance because of demand shifts on the goods market, the utility of an employed worker during his planning period can be defined in a similar way:

$$Ev_t = \log(T - l_o) + q \frac{Uv_{t+1}}{1+r} + (1-q) \frac{Ev_{t+1}}{1+r} , \tag{4.6}$$

$$Ec_t = \log(wn/pc) + q \frac{Uc_{t+1}}{1+r} + (1-q) \frac{Ec_{t+1}}{1+r} . \tag{4.7}$$

Ev_t (Ec_t) denotes the utility of an employed worker from leisure (consumption) over his planning period from period t onwards, l_o the official working time in period t, q the rate at which employed workers become unemployed, and wn the perceived net wage rate in period t. It is assumed that job quits follow a Poisson process with rate q, which is exogenous for the model. Furthermore, we abstract from savings and assume that all labour income is consumed.

If we further assume that the unemployed person expects future real unemployment benefits and real wages to grow at constant rate g, equations (4.3) and (4.4) can be rewritten in the following reduced form[39]:

$$Uv_t = \frac{1+r}{r}\left(\frac{(r+q)\ \log(T-ts)\ +\ p\ \log(T-l_o)}{r+p+q}\right), \tag{4.8}$$

$$Uc_t = \frac{1+r}{r}\left(\frac{(r+q)\ \log(b/pc)\ +\ p\ \log(wn/pc)}{r+p+q}\right) + (1+r)^2\ g/r^2\ . \tag{4.9}$$

After substitution of equations (4.8) and (4.9) into equation (4.2) and defining rp as the replacement ratio (b/wn), utility can be expressed as a function of search intensity, reservation wage and all exogenous variables in (4.5), (4.8) and (4.9). Analogous to Chapter 2, in which the minimum productivity standard is assumed to be exogenous in the intertemporal model of firm behaviour and determined by a separate decision rule in order to avoid too complex derivations, the equation for optimal search intensity is also derived under the assumption that the reservation wage is exogenous.[40] After some rewriting, this gives:

[39] We only present the basic assumptions of the model and the main results. For the derivations of the main results from the basic assumptions, see Graafland (1991b).

[40] The complexity of a simultaneous model for search intensity and reservation wage is illustrated by the fact that Pissarides (1990) does not present an integrated model for search intensity and reservation wage, but, instead, develops two separate models in which each of these variables is analyzed without reference to the other one.

$$s = \left(\frac{1}{\zeta} \frac{p}{r+p+q} \frac{T-s^{\zeta}}{T-l_o} (-\eta \log rp - \log \frac{T-s^{\zeta}}{T-l_o}) \right)^{1/\zeta} , \qquad (4.10)$$

where p is equal to $\bar{p}$, since $s=\bar{s}$ and wr = $\overline{wr}$ for a representative unemployed worker. It can easily be shown that equation (4.10) implies that search intensity is positively related to the probability to have a job in the next period (p) and negatively related to the lay-off rate (q), the discount rate (r) and the replacement ratio (rp) (see Graafland, 1991b). A rise in the probability to move into employment will increase the search intensity of the unemployed, because this raises the marginal revenue of search activities. A rise in the lay-off rate has an opposite effect. The net value of finding a job will decline and so the unemployed worker will be less motivated to spend time searching. The negative influence of the discount rate stresses that searching is a way of investing in the future, since current leisure is traded for future income. As the discount rate is higher, the unemployed worker will attach less value to future income and so it will be optimal to substitute leisure for search time. Finally, the replacement ratio also has a negative influence on search intensity of the unemployed. Just as in the case of an increase in the lay-off rate, an increase in the replacement ratio reduces the net value of a job, because the surplus of net wage income over net benefit income will be lower.

The reservation wage of the unemployed

The reservation wage is defined as the wage rate, at which the utility of accepting a job equals the utility of looking for another job. The total utility of an employed person is specified as:

$$E_t = Ev_t + \eta \ Ec_t \ . \qquad (4.11)$$

The reduced form equation of utility from leisure and consumption if starting with a job in period t at the reservation wage wr can be derived as:

$$Ev_t = \frac{1+r}{r} \left(\frac{q \log(T-s^{\zeta}) + (r+p) \log(T-l_o)}{r+p+q} \right), \tag{4.12}$$

$$Ec(wr)_t = \frac{1+r}{r} \left(\frac{q \log(b/pc) + (r+p) \log(wn/pc)}{r+p+q} \right) + (1+r)^2 g/r^2 + \frac{(1+r) \log(wr/wn)}{r+q}, \tag{4.13}$$

where wn is the average net wage rate. Substitution of equations (4.12) and (4.13) into equation (4.11) and equations (4.8) and (4.9) into equation (4.2) and setting U_t equal to E_t gives after some rewriting the following equation for the reservation wage:

$$\log wr = \frac{p \log wn + (r+q) \log b}{r+p+q} + \frac{(r+q) \log((T-s^{\zeta})/(T-l_o))}{\eta(r+p+q)}. \tag{4.14}$$

The net reservation wage is related to a weighted average of the average net wage rate and the net unemployment benefit. The weight of the average wage rate depends on the probability to find a job. The higher p, the higher the probability that an unemployed worker will find a job with an expected wage equal to the average wage rate, and the less probably jobs with relative low wage levels will be accepted. This reflects the influence of the labour market situation on reservation wages. In addition, the reservation wage is positively influenced by the ratio between the number of leisure hours of an unemployed person and an employed person.

Because of perfect substitution between individual workers of the same type of labour and the resulting proportionality of individual wages to (match-specific) individual productivity, the minimum productivity standard implied by the reservation wage of the unemployed can be defined as:

$$hu = wr\ hg\ /\ wn, \tag{4.15}$$

where *hg* denotes the average productivity of filled job-worker combinations.

As already noted in Chapter 2, it is assumed that the productivity of individual job-worker combinations follows a lognormal distribution. The share of contacts that is acceptable for unemployed workers can then analogously be formulated as the share of contacts acceptable for employers derived in Chapter 2:

$$fu = 1 - G((\log hu)/sd + 0.5\,sd)\ , \tag{4.16}$$

where *sd* denotes the standard deviation of the lognormal distribution of the productivity index. Equation (4.16) expresses that the share of contacts acceptable for the unemployed worker is inversely related to the minimum productivity standard implied by his reservation wage. This implies that a rise in unemployment benefit will make it more difficult for employers to fill vacancies.

4.2 The matching process

The matching function describes the number of vacancies filled from contacts between employers offering a job and unemployed workers seeking a job per type of labour:

$$m = co\ fm\ , \tag{4.17}$$

where *co* denotes the number of contacts between employers and unemployed persons, and *fm* the fraction of contacts that lead to successful matchings. The number of contacts is assumed to be specified by a Cobb-Douglas function (Blanchard and Diamond, 1989):

$$co = \Theta\ v^{\theta}\ (s\ u)^{1-\theta}, \qquad 0<\theta<1\ . \tag{4.18}$$

In (4.18) v denotes the number of vacancies, s search intensity of the unemployed[41], u unemployment, and Θ a scaling parameter, which measures the mismatch from differences between vacancies and unemployment in terms of skill, work experience and location (Jackman and Roper, 1987). The contact-function is assumed to exhibit constant returns to scale, because in a growing economy it is the only assumption that can assure a constant unemployment rate along the balanced-growth path (Pissarides, 1990). There are also empirical reasons for assuming constant returns (Pissarides, 1986). The job vacancies and unemployed workers are contacted at any point in time and randomly selected from the pool of vacancies and unemployed workers. The process that changes unfilled vacancies into filled vacancies and unemployed workers into employed workers is Poisson with rates m/v and m/u respectively. The average vacancy duration and unemployment duration are v/m and u/m respectively. The average probability to move from unemployment into employment within one period can be derived as:

$$\bar{p} = 1 - \exp(-m/u) \ . \tag{4.19}$$

Because of the choosiness of both employers and unemployed workers only a part of all contacts will result in matchings. The share of contacts not leading to an agreement will depend on the acceptance rates of the employers and the unemployed. At the micro-economic level the job match can be refused either by the employer or by the unemployed person. Because of heterogeneity in reservation wages of unemployed persons and marginal productivity of firms at the microeconomic level, the macro acceptance rate is assumed to be a CES-weighted average of the share of contacts acceptable for employers (*fe*) and unemployed workers (*fu*):

[41] We abstract from modelling search intensity of employers. Pissarides (1990) finds that if the firm can use its vacancy rate as an instrument for attracting workers, the optimum level of advertising is independent of market variables and it only depends on the properties of the cost function. Furthermore, the specification of the matching function abstracts from differences between short-term and long-term unemployed. In this way, hysteresis in unemployment because of duration effects is excluded (Budd *et al.* 1987; Jackman *et al.*, 1989; Layard and Nickell, 1987).

$$fm = \left(fe^{-\lambda} + fu^{-\lambda}\right)^{-1/\lambda} \qquad \lambda > 0 \ . \tag{4.20}$$

Equation (4.20) implies that the influence from the share of contacts acceptable for employers will be relatively high if the acceptance rate of employers is relatively low compared to the acceptance rate of the unemployed and vice versa. The average macro minimum productivity standard is approximated by the inverse of equation (4.16) with *fu* replaced by *fm*:

$$hm = \exp(sd\ G^{-1}(1-fm) - 0.5\ sd^2) \ . \tag{4.21}$$

where G^{-1} denotes the inverse of the cumulative distribution function of the productivity index. The macro minimum productivity standard is used in the equation of the average productivity of accepted new employees (*hn*) which is defined as the expected productivity of all job matches with productivity larger than *hm* (see equation (2.28) in Chapter 2).

4.3 Contractual wage formation

In the Netherlands collective bargaining is the predominant mode of wage formation. Wage bargains mostly take place at the industry level[42]. Generally, only wages are subject to the bargaining process, employment being set by individual firms. Therefore, the wage bargain can be described by a right-to-manage model[43] (Nickell and Andrews, 1983; Hoel and Nymoen,

[42] Calmfors and Driffill (1987) note that in this situation real wages might be higher than in case of either corporatistic wage bargaining or wage bargaining at the micro level of the firm.

[43] McDonald and Solow (1981) and Malcomson (1987) argue that the wage-employment solutions of the right to manage model are inefficient and generate underemployment. As Manning (1987) stresses, efficiency will only be achieved if all issues, which affect the utility of the agents are subjects of bargaining. Empirical research on the relevance of this so-called efficient bargain model against the right-to-manage model provides no decisive verdict (Farber, 1986).

1988). Wage contracts generally apply to periods of only one or two years, which is much shorter than the typical duration of employment relations between employers and employees. Since intertemporal considerations may therefore be less important in wage formation than, for example, in firm behaviour and because intertemporal models for wage bargaining, like for example Kidd and Oswald (1987), are rare in the literature because of their complexity, we use a static model to describe the wage formation process. In general, the outcome of collective (gross) wage growth applies to all types of labour in The Netherlands. Hence, it is assumed that the collective (gross) wage rates of the various types of labour are proportionally related to the development of the average collective (gross) wage corrected for changes in the productivity index per type of labour.

The outcome of the bargaining process is assumed to be given by the first-order condition of the generalized Nash solution (Nash, 1950, 1953; Binmore *et al.*, 1986):

$$(1 - \mu)\ ge_{\hat{w}}/ge + \mu\ gu_{\hat{w}}/gu = 0\ . \tag{4.22}$$

In (4.22) ge denotes the gain of the employers' organisation, gu the union gain, $\hat{w}$ the contractual wage rate, $ge_{\hat{w}}$ and $gu_{\hat{w}}$ denote the marginal employers' gain and marginal union gain with respect to the collective wage, and μ the relative bargaining power of the union.

The gain function of the employers' organisation

The gain of the employers' organisation is defined as real profits of all firms within the industry at the bargained wage minus real profits obtained if no contract is concluded. It is assumed that the consequence of not reaching an agreement is that all workers leave the industry and search for jobs in other industries. The threat point of the employers' organisation is therefore assumed to be equal to profits received if all labour positions must be filled by new employees. The gain function of the employers' organisation can then be modelled as:

$$ge = y_i - pl\ l_i/py_i - (y_n - pl_n\ l_n/py_n)\ , \tag{4.23}$$

where y_i (py_i), l_i and pl denote industry value added (price), industry employment and the average wage costs per employee and y_n (py_n), pl_n and l_n denote threat point value added (price) and threat point wage costs per employee and employment. Abstracting from incidental wage formation, average wage costs are defined as the collective wage rate, including average search costs per employee:

$$pl = \hat{w}\ (1 + \gamma vq)\ , \tag{4.24}$$

where vq denotes the ratio between the number of industry vacancies and employment. It is assumed that the bargaining parties consider the vacancy rate to be exogenous. The threat point wage rate is defined as the wage in other industries plus search costs if all employees have to be acquired through the costly search process:

$$pl_n = w^*\ (1 + \gamma v/m)\ , \tag{4.25}$$

where w^* is the expected contractual wage in other industries.

The gain function of the union

The union gain function is specified by the following Stone-Geary function (Oswald, 1985):

$$gu = l_i^{1-\nu}(\hat{w}(1-\tau)/pc - wf/pc)^{\nu}, \qquad 0<\nu<1\ . \tag{4.26}$$

In (4.26) τ denotes the rate of income taxes and social premiums and wf the threat point wage of individual workers. The parameter ν captures the relative importance of wages and employment to the union. If ν is one, union utility is independent of employment, like in an extreme insider-outsider model in which unions ignore the interests of outsiders[44].

The threat point wage is partly related to income from outside opportunities if no wage agreement is obtained and workers have to look for a job in other industries, and partly to macro labour productivity ($\bar{h}$) valued by the consumer price. The latter plays an important role in wage negotiations in The Netherlands and can be interpreted as an indicator for a fair wage:

$$wf = \phi\ wu + (1-\phi)\bar{h}pc\ . \tag{4.27}$$

The income from outside opportunities (wu) is defined as:

$$wu = (1-qu)w^{*}(1-\tau) + qu\ rp\ w^{*}(1-\tau)\ . \tag{4.28}$$

If workers have to look for jobs elsewhere, they will spend some time unemployed before finding a job. While unemployed, the worker receives an unemployment benefit that equals the net replacement ratio (rp) times the average wage (which is set equal to the expected contractual wage in other industries w^*) times one minus the average rate of taxation and social premiums (τ). While employed in another industry, the worker receives the expected wage rate in other industries. The latter is related to the lagged macro contractual wage rate.

The variable qu denotes the proportion of time spent unemployed in the period of the wage contract and depends on excess labour supply and search intensity of the unemployed. This proportion is related to the ratio between the number of matchings and unemployment (see appendix 2 in Graafland, 1991b):

$$qu = (u/m)\ (1\ -\ \exp(-m/u))\ . \tag{4.29}$$

[44] For models that explicitly describe the role of insiders in wage bargaining, see Blanchflower *et al.* (1989), Carruth and Oswald (1987), Graafland (1992a), Lindbeck and Snower (1987, 1988), Nickell and Wadhwani (1990), and Solow (1985).

The perceived firms' reactions on the wage outcome

To take account of wage effects on employment and profits, both the workers and the employers use a simple, short-term version of the model of the firm. In this model the industry consists of *n* identical firms and is characterized by monopolistic competition. Demand for value added of an individual firm (y) depends on value added of the industry (y_i) and the value added price of the firm (py) compared to the value added price of the industry (py_i):

$$y = \frac{1}{n} y_i (py/py_i)^{-\delta_1}, \qquad \delta_1 > 1 . \tag{4.30}$$

The short-run production function of the firm relates value added of the firm to employment of the firm (l) and the index of labour augmenting technical progress (el):

$$y = A\,(l\ el)^{\delta_2}, \qquad \delta_2 < 1 . \tag{4.31}$$

In the short term capital is constant and returns to scale are decreasing. Capital is included in the autonomous factor A. It is assumed that replacing all current workers by new employees entails an extra loss in human capital resulting in a lower level of the autonomous factor, because dismissing all current workers would hamper the gradual transfer of human capital from incumbent workers to new employees:[45]

$$y_n = A_n\,(l_n\ el)^{\delta_2}, \qquad with\ \ A_n = \delta_4\, A, \qquad \delta_4 < 1 . \tag{4.32}$$

Profit maximization of the individual firm, constrained by (4.30) and (4.31), leads to the following condition:

[45] In this respect the simple model of perceived firm behaviour is not contradictory to the model of actual producer behaviour in Chapter 2, where the existing work force is gradually replaced by new employees, so that the extra loss in productivity does not occur.

$$pl\,l = \frac{\delta_1 - 1}{\delta_1}\,\delta_2\,py\,y\,. \tag{4.33}$$

Substitution of (4.33) into the production function and rewriting for *py* gives the price equation for the individual firm:

$$py = \frac{pl}{el}\,\frac{\delta_1}{\delta_1 - 1}\,\frac{1}{\delta_2}\,y^{1/\delta_2 - 1}\,A^{-1/\delta_2}\,. \tag{4.34}$$

In the demand equation of the industry, the value added of the industry (y_i) depends positively on some exogenous demand (y_a) and negatively to the value added price of the industry (py_i) compared to the exogenous value added price of competitive industries (py_a):

$$y_i = y_a(py_i/py_a)^{-\delta_3}\,, \qquad 1<\delta_1<\delta_3\,. \tag{4.35}$$

In accordance with Section 2.1, competition among industries is less severe than among individual firms within an industry. Since all firms in the industry are assumed to be identical and have to pay the same wage, the value added price of the industry is equal to the value added price of the firm, and value added of the firm is equal to value added of the industry divided by the number of firms:

$$\begin{aligned} py &= py_i\,, \\ y &= y_i/n\,. \end{aligned} \tag{4.36}$$

The value added price of the industry can be derived from (4.34), (4.35) and (4.36):

$$py_i = \left[\left(\frac{pl}{el} \frac{\delta_1}{\delta_1 - 1} \frac{1}{\delta_2} \right)^{\delta_2} \left(\frac{y_a}{n} \right)^{1-\delta_2} py_a^{\delta_3(1-\delta_2)} A^{-1} \right]^{\frac{1}{(\delta_2 + (1-\delta_2)\delta_3)}} . \tag{4.37}$$

Total employment of the industry follows from the inverted production function (4.31) and from (4.36):

$$l_i = \frac{n}{el} \left(\frac{y_i}{n\ A} \right)^{1/\delta_2} . \tag{4.38}$$

The workers and the employers derive the influence of wages on the value added price of the industry by means of the price equation (4.37). Similarly, the threat point value added price can be derived from equation (4.37) after substituting pl by pl_n and A by A_n. The value added price and threat point value added price determine industry demand and threat point industry demand according to the demand equation (4.35). Effects on employment and threat point employment follow from the employment equation (4.38).

The workers' marginal utility of wages can be derived from the above equations as:

$$\frac{\partial gu}{\partial \hat{w}} = \frac{\nu\ gu(1-\tau_{\hat{w}})}{\hat{w}(1-\tau) - wf} - \frac{(1-\nu)\delta_3\ gu}{(\delta_3(1-\delta_2) + \delta_2)\hat{w}} , \tag{4.39}$$

where $\tau_{\hat{w}}$ denotes the marginal rate of taxes and social security premiums on labour income. The first term in the right hand side of (4.39) reflects the marginal utility of a rising wage rate for the employed workers. The second term reflects the negative marginal utility associated with the loss of employment, because of the wage increase.

The employers' marginal utility of wages can be derived as:

$$\frac{\partial ge}{\partial \hat{w}} = \frac{-\delta_2\delta_3}{\delta_2 + (1-\delta_2)\delta_3}(1-\delta_2(\delta_1-1)/\delta_1)y/\hat{w} \ . \tag{4.40}$$

The negative influence of wages on utility of the employers is stronger if competition with other industries is stronger (δ_3) and if the scale parameter (δ_2) in the short term production function is higher.

The wage outcome and characteristics of the wage model

The wage outcome can be derived by combining equations (4.22) – (4.28), (4.39) and (4.40). Using equations (4.39) and (4.40) we first derive the wage elasticities of workers utility:

$$\frac{\hat{w}}{gu}\frac{\partial gu}{\partial \hat{w}} = \frac{\nu\hat{w}(1-\tau_{\hat{w}})}{\hat{w}(1-\tau) - wf} - \frac{(1-\nu)\delta_3}{\delta_3(1-\delta_2) + \delta_2} \ , \tag{4.41}$$

and of employers utility (assuming $w^* = \hat{w}$):

$$\frac{\hat{w}}{ge}\frac{\partial ge}{\partial \hat{w}} = \frac{-\delta_2\delta_3}{\delta_2 + (1-\delta_2)\delta_3} \Big/ \left[1-\left(\frac{1+\gamma v/m}{1+\gamma vq}\right)^{\frac{-\delta_2\delta_3}{\delta_2+(1-\delta_2)\delta_3}}\right] . \tag{4.42}$$

Substitution into the first order condition (4.22) gives, after some rewriting:

$$w = \frac{wf}{(1-\tau) - \zeta(1-\tau_{\hat{w}})} \ ,$$

$$\text{with} \quad \zeta = \frac{\nu(\delta_2 + (1-\delta_2)\delta_3)}{(1-\nu)\delta_3 + (1-\mu)\delta_2\delta_3/\left(\mu-\mu\left(\frac{1+\gamma v/m}{1+\gamma vq}\right)^{\frac{-\delta_2\delta_3}{\delta_2+(1-\delta_2)\delta_3}}\right)} \ . \tag{4.43}$$

From equation (4.43) it can be seen that the wage outcome is a mark-up over the fall back income of workers. Hence, wages depend positively (negatively) on all variables that enter the fall back income of workers with a positive (negative) sign. Furthermore, the mark-up is negatively related to the marginal tax and premium rate and positively to the average tax and premium rate and the ratio between threat point search costs ($\gamma\ v/m$) and search costs for additional employees only ($\gamma\ vq$). The influence of the exogenous variables on the wage outcome is summarized by Table 4.1.

The influence of the consumer price (pc) and labour productivity (y/l) on wages is positive, provided that $\phi < 1$. For $\phi = 1$ the fall back income of workers in (4.27) does not depend on the consumer price and consequently utility of workers in (4.26) depends multiplicatively on the consumer price. Hence the consumer price will not influence the wage elasticity of union utility and wages are independent of the consumer price, if $\phi = 1$.

A higher average tax and premium rate of employees (τ) (at a constant marginal tax and premium rate) lowers workers utility and leads to wage demands to compensate for the loss of utility. A higher marginal tax and premium rate of employees ($\tau_{\hat{w}}$) (at a constant average tax and premium rate) reduces workers marginal utility of wages and lowers the wage rate. With a higher marginal tax and premium rate, a one percent higher gross wage rate yields less net income. Hence the bargaining parties are better off when they reduce the wage rate and increase employment. (Hersoug, 1984; Hersoug *et al.*, 1986)

A higher replacement ratio (rp) and expected macro wage rate (w^*) raise the fall back utility of workers and increase wage demands. A rise in the unemployment rate has an opposite effect on the fall back utility of workers by increasing the time spent unemployed before finding a job in another industry (qu) and reduces the wage outcome.

Table 4.1 Signs of first order derivatives of the wage bargaining model

pc	$\bar{h}$	τ	$\tau_{\hat{w}}$	rp	w^*	qu	v/m
+/0	+/0	+	–	+	+	–	+

In order to illustrate the implications of the wage bargaining model for equilibrium unemployment, equation (4.43) is rewritten in a reduced form equation for the proportion of time spent unemployed (qu) by taking into consideration the following notions. Firstly, at the macro level the contractual wage of the representative industry ($\hat{w}$) is equal to the average macro contractual wage rate (w^*). Secondly, using equations (4.24) and (4.33) macro labour productivity is defined:

$$\bar{h} = \frac{\hat{w}(1+\gamma vq)\delta_1}{py(\delta_1-1)\delta_2} \,. \tag{4.44}$$

Substitution of equations (4.27), (4.28) and (4.44) in equation (4.43) gives the following reduced form equation for qu:

$$qu = \left[\frac{1-\phi}{\phi}\left(\frac{1+\gamma vq}{1-\tau}\,\frac{\delta_1\; pc}{py(\delta_1-1)\delta_2} - 1\right) + \frac{\zeta\;(1-\tau_{\hat{w}})}{\phi\;(1-\tau)}\right] / \;(1-rp) \,. \tag{4.45}$$

Since the proportion of time spent unemployed is monotonically increasing with the unemployment rate, equation (4.45) implies that the rate of equilibrium unemployment is negatively related to the marginal tax and premium rate and positively related to the average rate of income taxes and social security premiums, the replacement ratio, and the ratio between consumer prices and producer prices (which includes the influence of indirect taxes), and the ratio of search costs to wages. The latter variable reflects the influence of the efficiency of the matching process and is influenced by the replacement ratios of different groups of labour and the level of minimum wage scales.

4.4 Calibration

In this section the calibration of the models for search behaviour of unemployed, the matching process between vacancies and unemployed, and contractual wage formation is considered.

The search strategy of the unemployed

Table 4.2 presents the specification and calibration of the model for search behaviour by the unemployed. The parameters measuring the effectiveness of search time (ζ) and the weight of consumption in the utility function (η) are set in such a way that the mark-up of the reservation wage over net benefit income and the influence of unemployment benefits on unemployment duration are in line with empirical research. The mark-up of the reservation wage over net benefit income is based on a study of Antonides and Van Raaij (1990)[46] and equals 1.25 on average. The elasticity of the replacement ratio on average unemployment duration, through the effects of search intensity and reservation wage on the number of matchings, is equal to 0.5 for all types of labour.[47] Although the magnitude of this elasticity is modest, it is high in light of micro-econometric estimates of benefit-elasticities of unemployment duration. Almost all micro-econometric investigations for the Netherlands hardly find any influence of replacement ratios on unemployment duration (for a review, see Groot and Jehoel-Gijsbers, 1990). Only Van den Berg, (1990) and Groot and Jehoel-Gijsbers (1990) estimate some significant

[46] Using panel data Antonides and Van Raaij (1990) find that the mark-up of reservation wage over benefit income equals 30% for single persons, 23% for breadwinners in households without children and 2% for breadwinners with children (both with a non-participating partner).

[47] Micro econometric research shows that the unemployed accept almost all jobs, once they receive a job offer from an employer (See Gorter *et al.*, 1993; Van den Berg, 1990). However, this does not exclude the possibility that unemployed workers screen jobs on beforehand on basis of the expected wage, before actively applying for a job. This implies that this analysis may underestimate the elasticity.

Table 4.2 Specification and calibration of search model of the unemployed

type of labour	minimum	other low	technical	economical	medical
parameters					
ζ	10.	10.	10.	10.	10.
η	2.0	2.0	2.0	2.0	2.0
exogenous variables					
rp	0.67	0.57	0.52	0.51	0.50
$\bar{p}$	0.48	0.70	0.74	0.66	0.60
endogenous variables					
s	0.59	0.65	0.67	0.66	0.66
hu	0.96	0.78	0.74	0.71	0.70
fu	0.58	0.81	0.81	0.84	0.85

elasticities, which vary between 0.4 and 0.6 and are more or less in line with the calibrated elasticities.

The most relevant exogenous variable in the search model of the unemployed is the replacement ratio (*rp*). The value of the replacement ratio is based on a detailed description of the unemployment benefit structure in the Netherlands. The average unemployment benefit is a weighted average of the net social assistance benefit received from the government and the unemployment insurance benefit received from the social security fund. The net social assistance benefit from the government is equal for low and high-skilled labour. Since the wage rate of the low-skilled is lower than the wage rate of high-skilled labour, this implies that the net replacement ratio of low-skilled unemployed persons receiving government assistance is higher than the net replacement ratio of high-skilled unemployed persons. The unemployment benefit paid by the social security fund is proportionally related to the wage income earned before the person became unemployed, hence the net replacement ratio for this type of benefit is equal for different types of labour. On average the replacement ratio of the low-skilled unemployed is therefore higher than for the other types of labour. Another important explanatory variable is the probability to find a job (*p*). This probability is based on data on average unemployment duration per type of labour from Ministry of Social Affairs and Employment (1989). Since the average unemployment duration is highest for the low-skilled unemployed, their probability to find a job is lower. Both the low probability to find a job and the relatively high replacement ratio cause search intensity (s) of low-skilled labour to be relatively low compared with the other types of labour. The minimum productivity standard by the unemployed is relatively high for the low-skilled unemployed and so their acceptance rate is relatively low.

The matching function

Table 4.3 presents the specification and calibration of the matching model. The weight of the number of vacancies in the matching-function (θ) is based on estimation results of Van Ours (1991) and equals 0.6. The scaling parameter (Θ) is computed in such a way that the average unemployment duration per type of labour, which is related to the ratio between the number of matchings and unemployment, is in accordance with data of Ministry of Social Affairs and Employment (1989). For the low-skilled unemployed the average unemployment duration equals 13 months (18 months for the first income group and 10 months for the second income group) and for the high-skilled unemployed 11 months (9 months for technical, 11 months for economical and 13 months for service oriented skilled labour). The parameter of the CES-function that defines the average acceptance rate (λ) is set to 5.

In Table 4.3 the average macro acceptance rate (*fm*) for low-skilled labour with minimum income appears to be substantially lower than the acceptance rate of the unemployed (*fu*) in this group. This is explained by the fact that for this group the matching of vacancies and unemployed is more hampered by minimum wage legislation than by the system of unemployment benefits. For the other types of labour the average acceptance rate (*fm*) is almost equal to the acceptance rate of the unemployed (*fu*). This is explained by the fact that the reservation wage of these types of unemployed workers well exceeds the minimum wage level, since it is partly related to the unemployment insurance benefit from the social security funds equalling 70% of the previously earned wage, which is relatively high. Hence the acceptance rate of employers based on the minimum wage level, is hardly relevant for the matching process of high-skilled labour, the average acceptance rate being

Table 4.3 Specification and calibration of matching model

type of labour	minimum	other low	technical	economical	medical
parameters					
Θ	9.9	7.3	4.8	3.1	5.8
θ	0.6	0.6	0.6	0.6	0.6
λ	5.	5.	5.	5.	5.
exogenous variables					
u^a	166	203	48	34	61
v^a	14	22	12	12	6
fe	0.37	0.95	0.96	0.97	0.95
fu	0.58	0.81	0.81	0.84	0.85
endogenous variables					
m^a	110	243	64	37	57
$\bar{z}$	7.8	11.1	5.3	3.1	9.5
$\bar{p}$	0.48	0.70	0.74	0.66	0.60
hm	1.04	0.83	0.79	0.77	0.78
fm	0.38	0.81	0.81	0.84	0.85

[a] thousands of labour years

almost fully determined by the acceptance rate of the unemployed. This implies that minimum wage legislation has almost no influence on the matching process of these groups.

Contractual wage formation

The calibration of the contractual wage model is partly determined by the values of the parameters in other submodels. For example, the search cost parameter (γ) follows from the model of the firm outlined in Chapter 2, whereas the parameters reflecting the degree of competition between industries (δ_3) and between individual firms (δ_1) are set in line with the allocation model for the exposed sector in Chapter 2. The production function parameter (δ_2) and the value of the parameter representing the bargaining power of the union (μ) follow from the restrictions that the calibrated labour income share and contractual wage must be in accordance with the actual macro labour income share and contractual wage in 1985.

Table 4.4 Estimation results for contractual wage equation: 1967-1991[a]

$$\Delta\log((w(1-\tau)/pc) = \underset{(4.11)}{0.38}\ \Delta\log(py(1-\tau)/pc) + \underset{(7.29)}{0.74}\ \Delta\log(\bar{h})_{-1} + \underset{(1.79)}{0.14}\ \Delta\log((1-\tau_w)/(1-\tau))_{-1/4} -$$

$$\underset{(2.56)}{0.66}\ \Delta ur_{-1} + \underset{(2.35)}{0.17}\ \Delta\log(rp_{-1}) - \underset{(3.18)}{0.01}$$

Statistics: R^2=0.96, SE=0.91, DW=1.96

[a] T-values are presented between parentheses. The estimation method is OLS. Labour productivity has a distributed lag with mean a lag of one year.

Special attention has been paid to the calibration of the other parameters in the model for contractual wage formation (ν, ϕ, δ_4) because the values of these parameters appeared to be crucial for the simulation results of MIMIC with respect to the influence of the direct and indirect tax rates and the replacement ratio. For this purpose the parameters are set in such a way that the simulation results of changes in consumption price, tax variables and replacement ratio are similar to simulation results obtained if the model for contractual wage formation is replaced by an estimated macro contractual wage equation for The Netherlands.

The estimation result for the macro contractual wage equation is reported in Table 4.4. The explanatory variables of the estimated wage equation include all relevant exogenous variables presented in Table 4.1 except for the influence of search costs on the wage outcome. This effect may be captured by the influence of the proportion of time being unemployed, which is proxied by the unemployment rate (*ur*). In addition, the value added price is included as explanatory variable. In this way the structure of the estimated wage growth equation is similar to that of the contractual wage equation in the empirical FKSEC model of the Central Planning Bureau (1992a). There are three differences. Firstly, the FKSEC wage growth equation shows a small (insignificant) negative influence from the level of the unemployment rate on wage growth (the so-called Phillips curve effect), which has been deleted from the wage growth equation in Table 4.4. Secondly, in the wage growth equation in the FKSEC model social premiums paid by employers are shifted

Table 4.5 Calibrated parameters and simulation results of the wage model

Calibrated parameters	$\mu = 0.55$	$\nu = 0.5$	$\delta_1 = 8.0$	$\delta_3 = 2.0$
	$\gamma = 0.75$	$\phi = 0.5$	$\delta_2 = .85$	$\delta_4 = 0.8$

Simulation results due to 1% change in	consumer price (*pc*)	average tax rate (τ)[a]	marginal tax rate (τ_w)[a]	replacement ratio (*rp*)[b]
		percentage change in wage rate		
Calibrated model	0.49	0.60	−0.09	0.20
Estimated model	0.50	0.63	−0.12	0.22

[a] Simulated reduction in the complement of the tax rate of 1%.
[b] Simulated increases in replacement ratio and ratio between minimum and average wage rate of 1%.

forward into higher wage costs for 80%, whereas income taxes and social premiums paid by employees are shifted forward for 30%. In the wage growth equation in Table 4.4 the forward shifting effect is uniform for different components of the rate of income taxes and social premiums and restricted to the coefficient of the consumer price. The data easily accepted both restrictions. The estimated value equals 0.62. Thirdly, the FKSEC contractual wage growth equation contains no estimate of the influence of the marginal tax rate on wages. If this variable is added as explanatory variable, a small negative coefficient is found, which is in line with the predicted sign of the first order derivative in Table 4.1.[48] Finally, it is noted that the estimated values of the coefficients of consumer price, value added price, labour productivity and replacement ratio are in line with those in the FKSEC contractual wage growth equation.[49]

The simulation results with the calibrated wage model and the estimated wage equation are presented in Table 4.5. The simulation results apply to an

[48] A negative coefficient for the marginal tax rate is also found by Graafland (1991) and Gelauff (1992).

[49] Positive influences of consumer price, value added price, labour productivity and replacement ratio on wages are also found by Graafland (1992a,b) and Lever (1991). In a detailed disaggregated empirical analysis of wage formation in 22 Dutch industries similar effects were estimated (Graafland and Verbruggen, 1992).

economic situation in which the rate of equilibrium unemployment is equal to the average unemployment rate during the estimation period of the estimated wage equation (about 7% of the working population). The simulation results of the calibrated wage model mimic the simulation results with the estimated wage equation very well. Note that in the calibrated model the coefficient of the consumer price is almost equal to the sum of the coefficients of the complements of the average and marginal tax rate. This implies that a reduction in indirect taxes has a similar effect on wage growth (through the consumer price) as a reduction in income taxes. Furthermore, in both simulated and calibrated model the negative influence of the marginal tax rate is relatively small compared to the positive influence of the average tax rate. This means that if marginal and average direct tax rates move more or less proportionally, a positive influence of taxes on wages is obtained. If an increase in marginal tax rates is compensated by an increase in tax allowances in such a way that the average tax rate remains unchanged, the contractual wage will fall. With respect to the last column it is noted that this reflects the simulation result of a combined reduction in replacement ratio and minimum wage. The reason is that the influence of the replacement ratio in the estimated contractual wage growth equation may also stand for the influence of the ratio between the minimum wage and average wage, because during the estimation period government assistance has fully been related to the net minimum wage.

5 The public sector

The public sector consists of the government, the social security funds and the pension funds. Section 5.1 briefly discusses the structure and modelling of the components of the accounts for the public sector. Section 5.2 contains a detailed representation of the system of taxes and social security premiums in The Netherlands. By documenting the different tax instruments of the government and their relation to social security premiums this section provides a background for the simulations in Part II. Because in general 1992 is the reference year for the simulations in Part II, the system for the year 1992 will be described in Section 5.2.

5.1 Modelling of the public sector

In the Netherlands total public sector expenditures amount to 80% of net national product in the year of calibration 1985. Table 5.1 presents the main components of public expenditures and public revenues subdivided into accounts for the government, social security funds and pension funds. In MIMIC the goods transactions and labour transactions of pension funds and social security funds are aggregated with the analogous transactions of the government. Therefore, the accounts for social security funds and pension funds only comprise premiums received, interest received, transfers received from other agents like the government, benefits provided, and the financial surpluses of these funds.

In Table 5.1 four components of government revenue are distinguished: taxes on household income, indirect taxes, profit taxes, and non-tax revenues, which constitute 13%, 17%, 4% and 8% of total public revenues respectively.

For each of the classes of the income distributions of breadwinners in families and single persons, income tax payments are computed by applying the statutory tax rates to the relevant tax base. The tax base consists of wage income or benefits from social security or from pension funds plus the part of non-wage income that is subject to taxation (compare the budget constraint in (3.2)). The income tax payments by working partners are derived by means of the statutory tax code in the labour supply model taking into account the distribution of working hours resulting from heterogenous relative preferences for leisure versus consumption (see (3.24)). Likewise, marginal tax rates for breadwinners, single persons and partners are derived from the statutory tax rates and the income and working hours distributions respectively. To prevent so-called 'bracket creep' and steadily rising tax incidence, in simulations with MIMIC future border values of the tax brackets of the statutory tax code are indexed by the wage rate.

Indirect taxes are differentiated into value added taxes and other indirect taxes minus price subsidies like excise duties, import duties and taxes on factors of production. Indirect tax receipts are also computed by multiplying average tax rates by relevant tax bases. The tax base is output for each of the five types of goods: export goods, private consumption goods, government consumption goods, investment in equipment and investment in buildings. Because of the large share of value added taxes on consumption in indirect tax receipts, consumption is subdivided according to value added tax rate so as to have the statutory value added tax rates available for simulation experiments. Indirect tax rates feed back into output prices (see (2.41)).

In the model profit taxes are classified into taxes on non-wage income from exploitation of natural gas and taxes on profits of firms. Taxes on natural gas revenues are based on non-wage income of the mining sector, which mainly consists of natural gas exploitation. The tax base for the second component is net non-wage income of firms minus interest payments of firms.

Non-tax revenues from natural gas exploitation pertain to the share of the government in the after tax profits from natural gas exploitation, and are also treated separately. Among others, the remaining part of non-tax revenue consists of profits from government owned enterprises. These revenues are computed as a fixed percentage of after tax non-wage income of firms minus interests payments and investments.

Government expenditures consist of wages, government consumption of goods and services, public investment, transfers, and interest payments on government debt. The total wage sum is the largest expenditure category on the account for the government. The government wage rate is linked to the private sector wage rate and government employment is exogenous. The

Table 5.1 Public sector revenues and expenditures as a percentage of public sector total in 1985

	Revenues		Expenditures
	Government		
Income taxes	13.4	Wages public sector employees	15.7
Indirect taxes	16.8	Non-wage consumption	7.1
Profit taxes	4.4	Net investment	2.8
Non-tax revenues	8.4	Price subsidies	4.2
Government deficit	8.4	Transfers to households	
		– income replacing benefits	5.2
		– other	4.5
		Transfers to social security	0.9
		Transfers to firms and abroad	3.1
		Interest on government debt	7.8
Subtotal	*51.4*	*Subtotal*	*51.4*
	Social security funds		
Premiums employee insurance	12.0	Disability benefits, employees	2.4
		Unemployment benefits	0.9
		Sickness benefits	2.7
		Early retirement benefits	0.3
		Health care benefits	5.1
Premiums national insurance	18.5	Family allowances	2.5
		Disability benefits, national	4.0
		Special health care benefits	3.7
		Old age benefits	7.7
Transfers from government	0.9	Administration costs	0.8
		Financial surplus	1.2
Subtotal	*31.4*	*Subtotal*	*31.4*
	Pension funds		
Premiums	6.5	Benefits	5.9
Interest received	10.7	Financial surplus	11.3
Subtotal	*17.2*	*Subtotal*	*17.2*
Total public sector	100.	Total public sector	100.

volumes of non-wage government consumption and public investment are exogenous too.

The second largest expenditure category on the government budget is total transfers. This category only concerns transfers financed through the budget of the government, *viz.* by taxation. If transfers through the social security funds are also taken into account, the total of transfers to households well exceeds the wage sum of the government, as Table 5.1 shows. An important part of government transfers to households consists of income replacing benefits, which are mainly social assistance benefits. The quantity component of social assistance benefits to the unemployed is related to the number of unemployed people. A large share of the remaining part of social assistance benefits is received by single parent households. Hence, the quantity component of this category depends on the number of single parent households.

Institutionally the net social assistance benefit rate is linked to the net minimum wage rate. This system of net-net linking has been incorporated in the model. The gross minimum wage rate is related to the gross contractual wage rate. Net minimum wages are derived from gross minimum wages and the relevant parts of the system of taxes and social security premiums. Social assistance benefits equal 100% of net minimum wages for breadwinners, 90% for single parent households and 70% for single persons.

Other transfers to households consist among other things of payments to partly offset high rents for low income households, of contributions to the costs of nursing people at home, and of scholarships. Quantity components of other transfers to households are related to the number of households concerned and price components of transfers follow wages. Transfers to social security funds and firms are modelled as a fixed percentage of national product. The last item of government expenditure in Table 5.1 are interest payments on government debt, which in MIMIC equal total debt times a distributed lag of the long term interest rate.

The social security system can be subdivided into two main categories, *viz.* employee insurances and national insurances. Employee insurances only apply to working people and cover a part of the risks of income loss from getting disabled, unemployed or sick. Generally, benefits of employee insurances depend on previously earned wages. In 1985 employee insurances constituted about one third of the total social security system (see Table 5.1). The other two third consists of national insurances, which provide basic benefits to which the entire population is entitled. These are classified into family allowances, disability benefits, financing of special health care costs, and basic benefits to the elderly.

In MIMIC the quantity components of the social security transfers are related to the number of households concerned and the price components are indexed by the wage rate. For some components, like for instance family allowances, this is in contrast to the actual indexation on the consumer price index. However, to keep long run real family allowances related to welfare instead of holding them constant, wage indexation is necessary. The computation of social security premiums is comparable to that of the income taxes. The statutory premium system is used, which is explained in detail in the next section. The only difference is that in simulations future premium rates are not exogenous, but are set in such a way that for each social fund premiums plus transfers from the government to that fund cover benefits.

In the Netherlands, a large part of savings by households consist of premiums paid to pension funds. According to Table 5.1 the financial surplus of the pension funds amounted to 11% of total public sector revenues in 1985. In MIMIC a model of pension fund behaviour is included, which is a simplified version of the Bolhuis and Vossers (1986) model. Two categories of pension funds are modelled, *viz.* government pension funds and pension funds for employees in the enterprises sector. Most of the employees in the public sector are affiliated with the government pension fund, which, having a total financial wealth of 126.7 billion guilders in 1985, is only somewhat smaller than the total of the pension funds for the enterprises sector (145.9 billion).

The core of the pension model consists of an equation for the actuarial pension premium rate, which equilibrates the actuarial balance of the pension fund. The actuarial pension premium rates as a percentage of the total wage bill can be computed from:

$$pa = (\gamma_1 B + \gamma_2 L - V) / (\gamma_3 L), \tag{5.1}$$

where pa is the actuarial premium rate, B are total pension payments, L is the wage bill, and V denotes current financial wealth of the pension fund. The numerator of (5.1) defines the difference between financial wealth that pension funds require to meet their future obligations, and current wealth. Required wealth consists of two parts. The first part concerns the wealth needed to pay the present and discounted future benefits to present-day pensioners. This component of required wealth is related to the current pension payments by means of the coefficient γ_1. The value of γ_1 is about nine, which indicates that nine times the current pension payments are needed to obtain the discounted future benefits for present-day pensioners. The second part of required wealth is needed to pay future claims of persons who at present are working and pay pension premiums. This component is related to the wage bill. A value of γ_2 of about four means that four times the wage bill is required for this purpose. The denominator of (5.1) gives the discounted value of the premium base for all present and future premiums received by the pension fund, under the assumption of a constant premium rate. When the actuarial balance of the pension fund is in equilibrium, the discounted value of premiums to be received must equal the difference between required and current financial wealth. Thus the actuarial premium rate can be computed from (5.1). In MIMIC the annual pension premium rate is gradually adjusted to the actuarial premium rates[50].

5.2 The 1992 system of income taxes and social security premiums

In this section we document the different tax instruments of the government and their relation to social security premiums. The purpose is to give some insight in the Dutch system of taxation and social security and to provide a background for the simulations in Part II.

[50] More information on the pension model can be found in Gelauff (1992).

For a single person with a gross wage of 50000 guilders a year, Table 5.2 illustrates the 1992 system of social security premium rates and taxes, which determines the steps from total wage costs for employers to net income of an employee. In the upper part of the table the main concepts are defined. The premium sums are derived starting from gross wages. Adding the social security premiums paid by employers to gross wages yields the total wage costs for employers. Subtracting social security premiums payed by employees and income taxes from gross wages leads to net income received by employees.

In the lower part of the table, the system of premiums and taxes is described in greater detail. Firstly, pension premiums are computed. In practice many different pension systems exist, which are too detailed to include in the model. Therefore, pension premiums are derived from multiplying gross wages by the average premium rate for employers and the average marginal premium rate for employees, taking into account an average franchise. Because generally employers pay pension premiums over the total wage sum, the franchise is only relevant for premiums paid by employees. Subtracting the pension premiums paid by employees (*f*1485) from gross wages yields the premium base for employee insurances (*f*48515). Premiums under the Disablement Insurance Act[51] are completely paid by employees and have a franchise of *f*98 a day and upper limit of *f*283 a day. On an annual basis this yields the interval given in the table. From the premium rate in this interval, the premium amounts of *f*2855 can be derived. The upper limit of premiums for unemployment insurance and sickness benefits also equals *f*283 per day, but there is no franchise.

The upper limit of the premium interval for the Health Insurance Act[52] is lower than the premium base in our specific example. Hence these pre-

[51] The Disablement Insurance Act provides a supplementary benefit for employees in excess of the base amount provided by the General Disablement Benefits Act. Thus the total disability benefit is a percentage of previously earned wages.

[52] Benefits under the Sickness Benefits Act compensate for loss of income during sickness, while the Health Insurance Act is an insurance for medical expenses.

Table 5.2 Derivation of net income and wage costs from gross wages by means of the 1992 system of social security premiums and taxes[a]

	Income interval		Premium/tax rate (%)		Income, or premium / tax base	Premiums / taxes	
	Lower	Upper	Employer	Employee		Employer	Employee
Wage costs					63.817		
Premiums employers						13.817	
Gross wages					50.000		
Premiums employees							12.043
Income taxes							6.844
Net income					31.113		
Premium and tax system							
Gross wages					50.000		
Pension premiums							
– employers	0.0	∞	4.90			2.450	
– employees	27.841	∞		6.70			1.485
Employee insurance					48.515		
– disability	25.676	73.884		12.50			2.855
– unemployment	0.0	73.884	1.25	1.25		0.606	0.606
– sickness	0.0	73.884	6.45	0.95		3.129	0.461
– health care	0.0	46.636	5.15	1.20		2.402	0.560
(nominal premium)							0.198
Transfer to employees	1.518	71.500	11.50	–11.50	46.995	5.230	–5.230
Income taxes and national social insurances					52.225		
Basic allowance					5.225		
Labour costs allowance					1.518		
Bracket 1							
– special health care	0.0	42.966		7.30			3.137
(nominal premium)							0.130
– other nat. insurances	0.0	42.966		18.25			7.841
– income taxes	0.0	42.966		13.00			5.586
Bracket 2[b]	42.966	85.930		50.00			1.258
Bracket 3[b]	85.930	∞		60.00			

[a] All amounts are in thousands of guilders

[b] Income taxes only

miums equal the maximum of 5.15% of *f*46636 for employers and 1.2% of *f*46636 plus a nominal premium amount of *f*198 for employees. Insurance under the Health Insurance Act is only provided for persons with an income below a certain threshold, which exceeds the upper limit of the premium interval. Higher paid persons have to insure their health expenses privately. To preclude a discontinuity in the net income at the threshold, premiums paid under the Health Insurance Act are not deductible for national social insurance premiums and income taxes. Hence, the premium base after payment of premiums for employee insurances (*f*46955) equals the premium base for employee insurances (*f*48515) minus premiums paid by employees under the Disablement Insurance Act (*f*2855), the Unemployment Insurance Act (*f*606), and the Sickness Benefits Act (*f*461), plus health care premiums paid by employers (*f*2402).

Since the 1990 income tax reform in The Netherlands a transfer of premiums from employers to employees exists in the tax and premium system. The transfer has been introduced to compensate employees for the fact that since 1990 they have to pay all national insurance premiums, while before 1990 the premium rate was divided over employees and employers. According to Table 5.2 the transfer equals 11.5% of the premium base after payment of employee insurance premiums, adjusted for a franchise and with an upper limit of *f*71500.

The transfer of premiums from employees to employers raises the base amount for income taxes and national social insurances, in our example by *f*5230 to *f*52225. Since 1990 national social insurance premiums are integrated in the first bracket of the income tax system. Before applying the tax code various allowances and deductions have to be subtracted. In our example only the basic allowance of *f*5225, which is doubled for a single income earner in a family, and the allowance of *f*1518 for costs associated with work (like transport) are taken into account. In the model, various important deductions like interest paid on mortgages are also included.

The current tax system consists of three tax brackets, with marginal rates rising from 38.55% to 60%. The 38.55% rate in the first bracket consists of a 25.55 %-points national social insurance premium rate and a 13 %-points

Figure 5.1 Marginal rate of taxation and premiums in 1992

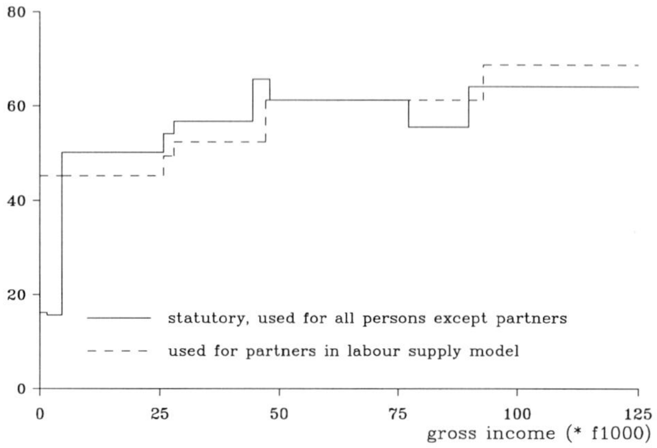

income taxes rate. In Table 5.2 national social security premiums are further subdivided into premiums under the General Act on Exceptional Medical Expenses and other premiums, because aged people incomes are exempt from the latter category of premiums. Moreover, there exists a nominal premium amount for special health care. In our example taxable income falls in the second tax bracket. Summation of the premiums and taxes in the two right columns of the lower part of Table 5.2 yields total premiums and taxes in the upper part, from which wage costs and net income can be derived. Finally, in the model net income is increased by income components not subject to social premiums and taxes, like benefits under the General Family Allowance Act.

The marginal rate of taxes and social security premiums corresponding to the 1992 system is depicted by the solid line in Figure 5.1. These rates are applied for each class of the income distribution of breadwinners and single persons. For very low incomes only the pension premium rate and the employee insurance rates, excluding premiums under the Disablement Insurance Act, are relevant. If taxable incomes exceed the zero tax bracket amount, income tax and national social security premium rates add to the marginal rate. Furthermore there is a rise of the marginal rate at the lower border of the premium interval for Disablement Insurance premiums. Marginal rates fall at the upper border of the Health Insurance premiums and at the upper border of other employee insurance premiums.

The schedule of marginal rates in Figure 5.1 is somewhat theoretical in the sense that various tax deductions are not taken into account. Deductions like interest paid on mortgages, gifts to charitable institutions and costs associated with working can substantially shift the marginal rate schedule and are relevant for the person in the household who earns most. In MIMIC these deductions are included in the derivation of net incomes of breadwinners and single persons.

For partners only the standard allowances mentioned in Table 5.2 apply. Moreover, the marginal tax schedule used for partners in the labour supply model differs from the statutory one in three further respects (see the dotted line in Figure 5.1). Firstly, as has been explained in Chapter 3, any kinks at a partner income equal to the basic allowance due to the system of transfer of the basic allowance to the breadwinner, are ignored. Secondly, for partners we abstract from health insurance premiums in the labour supply model. Incorporating health insurance premiums, we would have to adjust the premium rates under the Health Insurance Act for the fact that the household would save private health insurance premiums for the partner once a partner decides to work and enters the Health Insurance system. Moreover the benefit regimes differ between private insurance systems and the Health Insurance Act system. For instance, dental care is not insured in most private systems. To avoid these complications health care premiums have been omitted completely. Thirdly, for partners no fall in marginal rates has been taken into consideration at a gross income corresponding to the maximum of the employee insurance premium intervals. In this way a simplified marginal schedule has been constructed, which is used in the labour supply model for high incomes of partners. Since a small number of partners work for a large number of hours and since on average partners have lower incomes compared to breadwinners, these upper limits would hardly be relevant in the labour supply model. The increase of complexity of the labour supply model, if all kinds of possible cases associated with falling marginal rates would have to be distinguished, does not outweigh the small improvement in precision which would result. Moreover, we emphasize that these simplifications only apply to partners, who constitute about 10% of the total number of income earners in MIMIC. For all other income earners the actual statutory tax and premium rates are used.

6 Links between model blocks

Having presented the separate model blocks of MIMIC in the previous chapters, this chapter will deal with the links between them. For this purpose we will survey the set of model variables and distinguish between the variables which are exogenous in the complete model and the variables which are exogenous in submodels only. In this way we will also encounter links which are lacking in the previous chapters and which are necessary to understand the interactions between the different model blocks.

Following the classification in the previous chapters, five model blocks are distinguished: firm behaviour (Chapter 2), household behaviour (Chapter 3), matchings including search intensity of the unemployed (Sections 4.1 and 4.2), wage bargaining (Section 4.3) and the public sector (Chapter 5).

6.1 The model of the firm

Table 6.1 provides an overview of the input variables in the model of the firm. The first part presents those variables that are exogenous to the complete model. In the model of the firm, foreign prices like import prices and competitive export prices form, together with the volume of world trade, important exogenous determinants of the price and output of goods supplied by the firm sector. Another exogenous demand component is the volume of non-wage public expenditure. A second category of exogenous variables concern institutional parameters, like the indirect tax rates and the profit tax rate and the share of non-tax government revenue in the profits of enterprises. Furthermore, the interest rate is directly related to the exogenous foreign interest rate and influences output prices through the user cost of capital. Finally, the standard working time of a full time job and the ratio between the gross minimum wage and the average gross wage are exogenous.

The second part and third part of Table 6.1 present the input variables for the model of the firm that are determined in other model blocks and the distribution model that transforms one of these variables into categories fitting in the model of the firm. First, the model of the firm is linked to the house-

Table 6.1 Input variables of the model of the firm

exogenous variables		
import prices		indirect tax rates
competitive export prices		profit tax rate
world trade		non-tax revenue rate
volume non-wage public expenditure		interest rate
standard working time		minimum wage as a ratio of average wage
input variables from other model blocks		*source*
macro private consumption		household model
contractual wage rate		wage model
average vacancy duration[a]		matching model
average min.prod. standard[a]		matching model
distribution model	*from*	*to*
contractual wage	macro	per sector and per educational level

[a] per educational level

hold model via the macro private consumption, which is another category of the demand for goods besides the exogenous foreign demand of goods and non-wage government expenditure. A second input variable is the contractual wage, which is determined by the wage bargaining model. Since the wage bargaining model only generates the contractual wage outcome for the whole enterprise sector, a distribution model is used which translates the macro contractual wage rate into sectoral contractual wage rates per educational category by means of fixed ratios which are input for the incidental wage setting by firms. A third set of input variables relate to the average vacancy duration and the minimum productivity standard, which are determined in the matching model and influence the search costs of firms and the average productivity of new employees selected by firms.

6.2 The household model

Table 6.2 presents an overview of the exogenous variables and other input variables in the household model. Exogenous variables like population per type of household and labour supply of breadwinners and single persons are

Table 6.2 Input variables of the household model

exogenous variables		
population[a]		statutory benefit rate of:[a]
labour supply breadwinners[a]		– unemployment insurance
persons/labour years ratio breadwinners[a]		– unemployment assistance
labour supply single persons		– disability benefits
persons/labour years ratio single persons		– children's allowance
number of disabled persons[a]		– other transfers
savings rate		statutory income tax parameters
interest rate		standard working time
input variables from other model blocks		*source*
consumption price		model of the firm
employment[c]		model of the firm
profit income		model of the firm
wage rate[c]		model of the firm
unemployment[a]		matching model
– receiving insurance		
– receiving assistance		
social security premium rates		public sector
distribution models	*from*	*to*
wage	per educational level	per type of household
profit income	macro	per type of household
wage income	per type of household	per type of household and income class
profit income	per type of household	per type of household and income class
unemployment insurance	per type of household	per type of household and income class
unemployment assistance	per type of household	per type of household and income class
disability benefit	per type of household	per type of household and income class
other income[d]	macro	per type of household and income class
labour supply	per type of household	per educational level
replacement ratio	per type of household	per educational level

[a] per type of household
[b] per type of household and income class
[c] per educational level
[d] like children's allowances, net interest payments, other income transfers, etc.

direct inputs for the household model. Also the number of disabled persons (as a percentage of population in the age of 15 to 65 year) is exogenous in MIMIC. Another important set of exogenous variables relate to the benefit rates of all social security benefits distinguished in MIMIC, which are institutionally determined. Together with the relevant income component to which benefits are linked and the number of benefit recipients these variables determine total benefits transferred from the public sector to each type of household. Per income class, the statutory income tax system transforms the gross income distribution into a net income distribution and determines the flow of income taxes from households to the public sector. The exogenous savings rate per income class divides net income into net savings and net private consumption. Aggregation over the different income classes and the various types of households yields the macro totals. Analogously, average and marginal rates of taxation and social security premiums per type of household are determined as a weighted average over the various income classes. A second weighting procedure over different types of households leads to macro average and marginal tax and premium rates which are inputs in the model of contractual wage formation. Finally, the standard working time of full time jobs affects the labour supply of partners through the number of working hours of breadwinners.

The second and third part of Table 6.2 report the input variables from other model blocks and the distribution models used to transform these variables into proper input variables for the household model. Input variables from the model of the firm are consumer price, wage rate per educational level[53], macro profit income and employment per educational level. The wage per educational level is aggregated into a wage for low-skilled and high-skilled labour. These two aggregated wage rates are distributed over different type of households using the following distribution model:

$$w_i = wq_i \; w \tag{6.1}$$

$$wq_i = wq_{i_{-1}} \; lq \tag{6.2}$$

[53] Including the public sector wage rate, which is directly related to the private sector wage rate.

$$lq = \frac{\sum l_i}{\sum (wq_{i_{-1}} \, l_i)} \tag{6.3}$$

where w_i and l_i denote the wage rate and employment per type of household and w the average wage rate of low-skilled labour respectively high-skilled labour). This distribution model guarantees that the aggregate of the wage sum per type of household equals the macro wage sum. In a similar way the macro profit income is distributed over different types of households. Furthermore, employment per educational level has to be transferred into employment per type of household. This is done by a distribution model for unemployment in the matching model (see below), which transforms unemployment for high-skilled and low-skilled labour into unemployment per type of household. Finally, social premiums are set in the model of the public sector by the balancing rules of the social security funds (see Chapter 5).

Next, the household model contains exogenous distribution parameters that divide all types of incomes received by households over different income classes as described in Chapter 3. Furthermore, a distribution model is required for labour supply, that translates the outcomes of the household model (which only distinguishes between labour supply of high-skilled and low-skilled labour) into labour supply for all types of schooling distinguished in the model of the firm and the matching model. For this purpose labour supply of low-skilled labour and high-skilled labour is firstly aggregated over all households and secondly exogenously divided over labour supply of minimum skilled labour and other low-skilled labour respectively labour supply of technically, economically and service-oriented skilled labour.

Finally, from the net income of the households receiving unemployment insurance or unemployment assistance and the net income of employed workers replacement ratios can be derived per type of household and per type of benefit. In order to transform these replacement ratios per type of household into replacement ratios per educational level, which are needed as input for the matching model, we also modelled for each type of household the net average wage per educational level using the gross average wage per educational level and the tax- and social premium parameters for that specific gross wage level. Using macro weights of the number of unemployed per type of household, aggregated replacement ratios per educational level can then be constructed.

6.3 The matching model

In Table 6.3 the input variables and distribution model in the matching model are reported. The only exogenous variable is the standard working time, which influences the search intensity of the unemployed. Input variables from the model of the firm are employment, vacancies and the acceptance rate of employers per educational level. Confrontation of employment per educational level with labour supply per educational level from the household model, both measured in labour years, gives unemployment per educational level in labour years. Together with vacancies per educational level this determines the number of matchings. Assuming that the persons/labour years ratio of low-

Table 6.3 Input variables of the matching model

exogenous variables		
standard working time		government employment
input variables from other model blocks		*source*
employment[a]		model of the firm
vacancies[a]		model of the firm
acceptance rate employers[a]		model of the firm
replacement ratio[a]		household model
– unemployment insurance		
– unemployment assistance		
labour supply[a]		household model
persons/labour years ratio		household model
distribution model	*from*	*to*
unemployment	per educational level	per type of household

[a] per educational level

skilled and high-skilled unemployment equals the persons/labour years ratio of low-skilled and high-skilled labour supply, unemployment in labour years can be transformed in unemployment measured in persons for low-skilled and high-skilled labour. In order to divide total low-skilled and high-skilled unemployment over different household types, the following distribution model is used:

$$ur_i = uq_i \; u \; ls_i \; / \; ls \tag{6.4}$$

$$uq_i = uq_{i_{-1}} \; lsq \tag{6.5}$$

$$lsq = \frac{\sum ls_i}{\sum (uq_{i_{-1}} \; ls_i)} \tag{6.6}$$

where ur_i and ls_i denote the unemployment rate and labour supply per type of household, u denotes total unemployment of low-skilled respectively high-skilled labour and ls total low-skilled respectively high-skilled labour supply. This distribution model meets two conditions: Firstly, it assures that the aggregate of unemployment per type of household is equal to macro unemployment. And secondly, total low-skilled and high-skilled unemployment is distributed in such a way that unemployment per type of household is proportional to labour supply per type of household.

6.4 The wage model

In the wage model all input variables come from other model blocks. Input variables from the model of the firm are consumption price, labour productivity, employment and vacancies. Labour productivity and consumption price determine the threat point of employees in the wage bargaining process,

Table 6.4 Input variables of the wage model

input variables from other model blocks	*source*
consumption price	model of the firm
labour productivity	model of the firm
employment	model of the firm
vacancies	model of the firm
average tax and social premium rate	household model
marginal tax and social premium rate	household model
matchings	matching model
unemployment	matching model
average replacement ratio[a]	matching model

[a] per educational level

whereas the vacancy rate influences the threat point of the employers. Input variables from the household model are the macro average and marginal tax and social security premium rate for employees. Input variables from the matching model are the macro number of matchings and unemployed workers and the average replacement ratio, which both affect the threat point of employees. The latter variable is derived from the replacement ratio per educational level weighted by unemployment per educational level measured in labour years.

6.5 The public sector model

Exogenous variables in the public sector block are the interest rate, determining interest payments by the government, and government employment per educational level. The public sector wage rate per educational level is related to the private sector wage rate per educational level generated by the model of the firm. Other input variables from the model of the firm are all collective charges related to the output and profit of firms and nominal non-wage government outlays. Input variables from the household model are income taxes and social premiums paid by households and social benefits received by households from the government and the social security funds.

Table 6.5 Input variables of the public sector model

exogenous variables	
interest rate	government employment[a]
input variables from other model blocks	*source*
wage rate[a]	model of the firm
indirect taxes	model of the firm
profit taxes	model of the firm
non-tax revenues	model of the firm
non-wage government outlays	model of the firm
income taxes	household model
social premiums	household model
social benefits	household model

[a] per educational level

PART II

POLICY SIMULATIONS

7 The base projection

For the simulation results of MIMIC, as presented in Chapters 8 up to and including 12, a base projection is constructed running from the calibration year 1985 to 2017. The starting year for the simulation results is 1993. The presented results from counterfactual simulations relate to 2002 in case of relatively small institutional changes (Chapter 7 and 8) and to 2017 in case of major institutional reforms (Chapter 9 up to and including 12), which are often proposed to be implemented more gradually. In order to link the base path to the actual situation in 1992, most institutional variables are set equal to actual data for the period 1985-1992. For the period 1993-2017 the institutional system is maintained in its 1992 form (see Chapter 5). This means that statutory tax rates and benefit rates are constant during this period, whereas the value of various allowances, franchises and borders of tax brackets are updated with nominal wage growth. Social security premiums are set in such a way as to cover benefits.

The projected values of other exogenous variables, for example with respect to foreign demand, foreign prices, and population growth per type of household are based on the long-term study of the Central Planning Bureau for the Dutch economy (Central Planning Bureau, 1992b). In this way the projection path captures some future trends for the Dutch economy which are relevant for the simulation analysis without pretending to give an accurate prediction of the economic development in the next 25 years. Three examples may illustrate the relevance of this approach. Firstly, Chapter 10 contains simulations on reduction of the welfare state by lowering social security benefit rates. The economic effects of reducing disability benefits depend on base-line assumptions about the number of people in the disability benefit schemes. Secondly, individualization of the social security system, analyzed in Chapter 11, primarily affects the labour supply decision of partners in different types of households. Hence, long-term simulation results depend on exogenous scenario assumptions about the number of two-person households compared to one-person households and about autonomous changes in participation rates of partners through time. Thirdly, introduction of a negative

Table 7.1 Projection of population growth during 1985-2017

	population[a]	working population	disabled persons
	percentage growth rate per year		
Old age pensions	1.6	–	–
Students	0.6	–	–
Single parents	–0.2	0.2	0.6
– high-skilled	1.4	1.4	2.6
– low-skilled	–1.5	–1.5	–0.3
Single persons	0.9	1.0	1.2
– high-skilled	2.2	2.2	3.2
– low-skilled	–0.3	–0.3	0.7
Breadwinners in households[b]	0.3	0.6	0.5
(with low-skilled partner)			
– high-skilled	–0.5	–0.5	0.8
– low-skilled	–2.7	–2.7	–1.5
(with high-skilled partner)			
– high-skilled	2.6	2.6	3.9
– low-skilled	0.3	0.3	1.7
Total	0.6	–	1.0

[a] Excluding the population aged 0-14 year.
[b] The population growth rate of partners is equal to the population growth rate of breadwinners. The growth in working population of partners is endogenously determined. The growth in the number of disabled partners is 1.4% per year higher than of disabled breadwinners.

income tax in a mini welfare state (Chapter 12) is seen to strongly increase low-skilled employment by raising search activity of low-skilled unemployed. Again long-term baseline values of the total labour supply of low-skilled people are relevant for the simulation results. These examples clarify why the simulation results relate to 2017 in case of major institutional reforms, with a more dominant influence of long-term scenario assumptions compared to simulations on small adjustments in institutions.

An overview of the most relevant exogenous variables will be given in Section 7.1. Section 7.2 deals with the outcomes of the base projection.

7.1 Projected development of exogenous variables

Table 7.1 presents the projected population growth over the projection period per type of household. The total population grows about 0.5% per year. The number of old-age pensioners increases relatively more, reflecting the ageing of population. In addition, the share of single persons slightly increases, whereas the share of single parents and families show a steady fall. The share of students is constant. The upgrading of the working population during the past is assumed to continue in the future, raising the share of high-skilled labour for all types of households. From the second column it can be seen that the working population of single parents, single persons and breadwinners of households rises with the population, hence labour market participation rates for these groups are constant. With respect to the relative number of disabled persons, there are two opposite forces in work. On the one hand the share of disabled persons rises because it is highest among relatively old workers. Therefore, with the ageing of population the flow into disability schemes per type of education increases. On the other hand, since the pool of disabled persons consist mainly of low-skilled workers, the relative number of disabled persons falls with the upgrading of the labour force. The total share of disabled persons only rises slightly over the projection period.

Table 7.2 Other exogenous base projections: 1985-2017

	percentage growth rate per year		
Competitive export price	1.7	World trade	5.6
Import price		Government consumption	3.1
– energy	4.0	Government investments	
– intermediaries	1.4	– buildings	2.6
– consumption	1.6	– machines	4.4
– investments	1.7	Government employment	0.7
Standard working time	–0.25		
	level in 2017		
Value added tax rate		Profit tax rate	35.0
– luxury goods	19.0	Foreign interest rate	6.3
– normal goods	5.0		

Table 7.2 presents some other important exogenous projections. Competitive export prices and import prices show a modest growth rate of about 2% per year, reflecting a stable international situation with little inflationary tendencies. Similarly, the foreign interest rate relevant for the Netherlands is set on a modest value of 6.3%. The growth rate of world trade is equal to that over the last 30 years and equals 5.6%. Non-wage government outlays rise by 3% per year on average, whereas government employment is assumed to rise with total population. Finally, the value added tax rates and profit tax rate reflect current values. Income tax rates and social security premium rates have been presented in Section 5.2.

7.2 Selected outcomes of base projection

Table 7.3 summarizes the macro outcomes of the base projection. Export prices rise with competitive export prices and the balance of payments hardly changes. The participation rate of partners increases from 38% in 1985 to 55% in 2017. This is partly caused by the relative increase of the number of high-skilled partners, who have a higher participation rate on average. For another part the rise in partner labour supply is simulated by an autonomous shift in labour supply parameters, which is assumed to reflect the cultural tendency to more labour market participation by partners. Furthermore, the rate of unemployment shows a fall from 10 %-points in 1985 to 7 %-points in 2017. The fall in unemployment follows from a reduction in the net replacement ratio and the average tax rate effected during the period 1985-1992. Finally, there is a strong reduction in the budget deficit from 7% to 2% of net national income.

Looking to the sectoral employment shares reported in Table 7.4, it appears that the relevance of the exposed sector for total employment is reduced in the future, whereas the employment shares of the other (more labour intensive) sectors increase. The main explanation for these trends lies in the relative high rate of autonomous labour augmenting technical progress in the exposed sector (see Chapter 2). This can be seen from the rise in the relative output share of the exposed sector. Since the high rate of technologi-

Table 7.3 Macroeconomic outcomes of base projection: 1985-2017

yearly growth rate		level	1985	2017
Prices		*Ratio's*		
Wage rate	5.5	Unemployment rate	10	7
Capital costs	2.1	Participation rate partners[a]	38	55
Production price	2.6	Labour income share	69	72
Export price	1.8	Taxes[b]	27	33
Consumption price	2.8	Social premiums[b]	24	20
		Average tax rate[c]	48	46
Volumes		Marginal tax rate[c]	62	59
Private consumption	3.4	Net replacement ratio[d]	60	57
Investment	4.2	Budget deficit[b]	7	2
Export	5.0	Balance of payments[b]	5	4
Import	5.2			
Private production	3.6			
Private employment	0.8			
Labour supply (persons)	0.7			
Labour supply (hours)	0.7			

[a] Number of participating partners as a percentage of total number of partners (excluding disabled partners)
[b] As a percentage of net national income
[c] Per person, averaged over the working population
[d] Average ratio between net unemployment benefit and net wage

cal progress reduces the costs per unit product, output prices of the exposed sector rise less than output prices of the labour intensive sectors. As a result, the nominal production shares of the various sectors remain more or less constant.

Table 7.4 Employment and output shares per sector

	employment share		output shares	
	1985	2017	1985	2017
Exposed	39	32	47	69
Sheltered	36	38	31	19
Construction	9	11	8	8
Medical	15	19	13	11
Total	100	100	100	100

In Table 7.5 the development of unemployment and employment per type of labour is reported. The unemployment rates per type of labour are rather constant and inversely related to the level of education. The overall unemployment rate falls, however, because the relative share of low-skilled labour diminishes over time. The employment share of low-skilled workers is halved during the simulation period, whereas the employment shares of high-skilled workers rise with about 50%. Furthermore, the average vacancy rate is almost constant. For the low-skilled with minimum income the vacancy rate falls, mainly because of an increase in the average acceptance rate. The rise in acceptance rate follows from a fall in the replacement ratio and the ratio between the official minimum wage and the average wage rate during 1985-1992. For the economically and service-oriented skilled workers the vacancy rate rises a little bit: as unemployment decreases for these groups it takes longer before a suitable candidate is found and so the vacancy duration and average vacancy rate increases.

Table 7.5 Unemployment, vacancies, acceptance rates and employment per type of labour

types of education	1985	2017	1985	2017
	unemployment rate		employment shares	
Minimum	21	23	15	8
Other low skilled	12	12	35	18
Technically skilled	5	5	21	31
Economically skilled	4	3	15	22
Service oriented	6	5	14	21
Total	10	7	100	100
	vacancy rate		acceptance rate	
Minimum	2.4	1.0	0.34	0.48
Other low skilled	1.6	1.2	0.79	0.81
Technically skilled	1.5	1.5	0.80	0.83
Economically skilled	2.0	2.5	0.81	0.83
Service oriented	1.1	1.5	0.80	0.82
Total	1.7	1.6	0.67	0.77

Table 7.6 presents the development of labour participation by partners per type of household. The relative share of partners with an unemployed breadwinner decreases over time because of the reduction in unemployment. For each group the participation rate increases substantially, except for partners with a breadwinner receiving government assistance. For this group any partner income is subtracted from the unemployment benefit of the breadwinner, which makes working unattractive. As long as this institutional rule is maintained, there will be no stimulus to labour market participation by the partner.

Table 7.7 gives insight in the development of the relative number of unemployment benefit recipients over time. The most significant change between 1985 and 2017 concerns the rise in the relative share of unemployed partners, which is caused by the overall rise in partner labour supply. Since partners have no right on government assistance, this suppresses the average replacement ratio for government assistance. The average replacement ratio for unemployment benefits from the social security funds is not affected by the relative rise of unemployed partners, because in this case the replacement

Table 7.6 Labour market participation of partners per type of household

	1985	2017	1985	2017
	share in potential working population		participation rate	
With children, breadwinner with				
– wage income	57	59	36	54
– unemployment insurance benefit	2	1	29	48
– government assistance	2	1	0	0
– disability benefit	6	5	33	43
No children, breadwinner with				
– wage income	25	24	60	68
– unemployment insurance benefit	1	0	47	60
– government assistance	1	1	0	0
– disability benefit	6	8	45	54
Total	100	100	38	55

Table 7.7 Shares of different types of unemployment benefit recipients and replacement ratios

	1985	2017	1985	2017
	share of recipients		replacement ratio	
Government assistance				
– single persons	62	60	50	49
– single parents	6	6	71	69
– breadwinners	22	18	59	60
– partners	10	16	0	0
Total	100	100	48	44
Unemployment insurance benefit				
– single persons	30	34	75	70
– single parents	11	9	75	73
– breadwinners	42	33	71	75
– partners	16	25	72	72
Total	100	100	72	73

ratios are more or less similar for different types of persons. The overall replacement ratio falls with about 3 %-points as can be seen from Table 7.3, partly because of the fall in the average replacement ratio of government assistance. For another part the fall in the overall replacement ratio follows from a rise in the relative share of unemployed receiving government assistance instead of social security benefits.

8 Income tax instruments

Simulation experiments in this chapter are related to the income tax system, because this is an important instrument of government policy and because there are various ways to change income tax parameters. Since we want to refer to current policy options, the simulation results are based on the 1992 income tax system as explained in Chapter 5.

In Section 8.1 single parameters of the 1992 income tax system, like the tax rate in a specific tax bracket or a border value of a tax bracket, and the value added tax rate are changed in such a way as to cause an identical ex post effect on the government budget. The purpose of these results is to compare the relative importance of the different tax parameters in affecting the labour market and to provide a set of basic results, which can be used to devise and interpret more complicated policy measures.

The simulations in Section 8.2 relate to recent Dutch policy discussions about replacement of the basic allowance by a tax credit. Because the basic allowance must be deducted from taxable income before applying the income tax rates, its effect on net income depends on the marginal tax rate of the tax payer. The net value of the basic allowance rises with the marginal tax rate and is highest for people with high incomes. A tax credit is an amount that a tax payer is allowed to subtract from the amount of taxes due. Hence, the tax credit is independent of the marginal tax rate of the tax payer.

Section 8.3 deals with the question whether the model can reveal Laffer curve characteristics for the Dutch economy. According to the literature[54], a Laffer curve is obtained if supply side reactions from higher tax rates reduce the tax base and eventually lower tax receipts. One of the mechanisms underlying the shrinking tax base is falling labour supply, because higher marginal tax rates curb the incentives to work and cause a shift towards the informal sector. To examine the consequences of ever rising tax rates, MIMIC is used to generate a Laffer-type curve for The Netherlands. In contrast to the

[54] Estimates of the Laffer curve can be found in *e.g.* Stuart (1981), Fullerton (1982), Van Ravestein and Vijlbrief (1988).

mechanisms described in the literature, the shape of this curve is not caused by a shrinking tax base but by ever increasing government expenditure due to large wage increases and rising unemployment.

8.1 Simulations on single tax parameters

As Table 5.2 shows, the current income tax system in The Netherlands consists of three tax rates and two border values between the three tax brackets. For these five and two additional income tax parameters we computed the required change that generated ex-post identical effects on the budget of the government. The additional income tax parameters relate to the zero tax bracket amounts. Two ways of changing the zero tax bracket amounts have been chosen. The first one is a general rise in the basic allowance, which equals *f*5225 in 1992. In correspondence to the statutory tax code, the zero tax bracket amount of sole wage-earners has been taken equal to twice the basic allowance in this case. Secondly, the supplementary allowance for workers has been raised, to analyze the consequences of a change in the wedge on income from working compared to benefit income. Moreover, a budgetary equivalent decrease in the value added tax rate has been included in the comparison.

To finance the tax reduction, the government is assumed to reduce its non-wage consumption by 0.2 %-points of net national product. This is equivalent to 1 billion guilders in 1992. Subsequently, taxes are lowered so that an ex-post balanced budget for the government is obtained at the end of the simulation period.[55] Thus, effects of the tax reduction on the government budget through behaviourial reactions of economic agents are completely taken into account. For instance, if lower tax rates imply a fall in unem-

[55] As a referee noted, a second condition for budget-neutrality is that the public debt may not change either. Experiments with simulations in which the public deficit is unchanged relative to the base projection in each period of the simulation in order to meet this requirement showed, however, that the simulation results hardly changed. As the additional requirement of public debt neutrality generated other complications, we further abstained from this condition.

ployment and consequently lead to lower unemployment assistance payments for the government, the additional financial capacity of the government has been used to further decrease tax rates. Some of the tax instruments also directly affect the budget of the social security funds. Examples are the border value of the first tax bracket and the basic allowances, which also apply to national social insurance premiums since these are integrated in the first tax bracket. The influence of tax reductions on the budget of the social security funds via these direct effects and via indirect behaviourial reactions is taken into account by setting social security premium rates so as to balance the budgets of the funds.

The main economic outcomes of the eight simulations on tax reduction are presented in Table 8.1. Table 8.2 contains the changes in real disposable incomes averaged over the different types of breadwinners[56] and single persons distinguished in the household sector of MIMIC. This table gives an impression of the consequences of the various ways of tax reduction for purchasing power of different categories of people. According to the first row of Table 8.1, lowering the tax rate in the first tax bracket by 0.6 %-points is equivalent in ex-post budgetary impact to a fall in the tax rate in the second tax bracket by 3.1 %-points and of the tax rate in the third tax bracket by 7.4 %-points. Of course, the fall in the upper tax rate considerably exceeds the fall in the lower tax rate because only a small part of total taxable income is subject to the upper tax rate. The same argument applies to the border values of the tax brackets. Ex-post a higher border value of the lower bracket by *f*1600, yields an identical effect on the budget as a rise in the border value of the second tax bracket by *f*45800. The equivalent increase in the basic allowance, the allowance for workers, and the equivalent fall in the VAT rate are seen to be *f*270, *f*2100 and 0.8 %-point respectively.

[56] Note that the table only contains real disposable incomes of breadwinners. Those of families are not included, because effects may differ substantially between families with participating and with non-participating partners.

Table 8.1 Main economic outcomes of eight ways of tax reduction combined with a reduction of government expenditure by 0.2% NNP

	Income tax rates			border values		allowances		VAT
	1	2	3	1	2	basic	wages	rate
Level in 1992	13.0	50.0	60.0	42966	85930	5225	1518	17.5
Change	−0.6	−3.1	−7.4	1600	45800	270	2100	−0.8
	1	2	3	4	5	6	7	8
Prices				*percentage changes*[a]				
Wage rate	−0.63	−0.26	−0.11	−0.41	−0.07	0.16	−1.26	−0.17
– minimum	−0.66	−0.25	−0.11	−0.42	−0.07	0.18	−1.53	−0.19
– other low skilled	−0.60	−0.25	−0.12	−0.39	−0.08	0.15	−1.24	−0.18
– high skilled	−0.64	−0.28	−0.11	−0.42	−0.07	0.18	−1.21	−0.17
Production price	−0.43	−0.14	−0.03	−0.25	−0.02	0.09	−0.49	−0.21
Consumption price	−0.28	−0.09	−0.02	−0.16	−0.01	0.06	−0.31	−0.45
Volumes								
Private consumption	0.33	0.20	0.17	0.25	0.17	0.16	0.17	0.31
Investment	0.07	0.00	−0.05	0.03	−0.04	−0.06	−0.17	0.21
Exports	0.23	0.07	0.02	0.13	0.01	−0.05	0.28	0.10
Imports	−0.03	−0.04	−0.04	−0.03	−0.03	−0.02	−0.15	0.01
Private production	0.26	0.06	−0.02	0.14	−0.03	−0.09	0.22	0.15
Private employment	0.36	0.13	0.02	0.22	−0.01	−0.18	0.65	0.11
– minimum	0.64	0.22	0.10	0.39	0.05	−0.25	2.13	0.19
– other low skilled	0.46	0.14	0.07	0.28	0.03	−0.17	1.10	0.14
– high skilled	0.27	0.11	−0.02	0.17	−0.03	−0.18	0.22	0.08
Labour supply persons	0.12	−0.08	−0.06	0.00	−0.06	−0.15	−0.11	0.01
Labour supply hours	0.13	0.01	−0.07	0.06	−0.07	−0.15	−0.31	0.01
Ratios				*absolute changes*[a]				
Unemployment rate	−0.16	−0.09	−0.08	−0.12	−0.06	0.00	−0.81	−0.08
– minimum	−0.39	−0.20	−0.14	−0.27	−0.09	0.06	−1.85	−0.14
– other low skilled	−0.27	−0.16	−0.12	−0.20	−0.08	0.00	−1.14	−0.12
– high skilled	−0.09	−0.05	−0.06	−0.07	−0.04	−0.01	−0.51	−0.05
Inactivity ratio	−0.43	−0.20	−0.11	−0.29	−0.06	0.12	−1.37	−0.16
Replacement ratio	−0.09	−0.23	−0.14	−0.17	−0.08	0.31	−1.50	0.02
Average tax rate	−0.42	−0.30	−0.24	−0.36	−0.20	−0.07	−1.26	−0.02
Marginal tax rate	−0.32	−1.03	−0.79	−0.75	−0.68	0.06	−0.36	−0.02
Total taxes[b]	−0.28	−0.21	−0.19	−0.24	−0.18	−0.13	−0.50	−0.17
Social sec. premiums[b]	−0.12	−0.05	−0.03	−0.07	−0.02	0.06	−0.45	0.02
Public expenditures[b]	−0.40	−0.27	−0.22	−0.31	−0.20	−0.08	−0.95	−0.14
Public deficit[b]	0.00	0.00	0.00	0.00	0.00	0.00	0.00	0.00

[a] Cumulated differences between simulation and base projection

[b] As a percentage of net national product

Table 8.2 Average real disposable income with eight ways of tax reduction combined with a reduction of government expenditure by 0.2% NNP

	Income tax rates			border values		allowances		VAT
	1	2	3	1	2	basic	wages	rate
Level in 1992	13.0	50.0	60.0	42966	85930	5225	1518	17.5
Change	−0.6	−3.1	−7.4	1600	45800	270	2100	−0.8
	1	2	3	4	5	6	7	8
				percentage changes[a]				
Breadwinners								
– employed	0.36	0.43	0.35	0.37	0.35	0.25	0.91	0.31
– unemployment insurance	0.50	0.22	0.27	0.38	0.32	0.32	−1.27	0.31
– social assistance	0.34	−0.12	−0.07	0.06	−0.05	0.67	−1.31	0.29
– disability benefit	0.41	−0.09	−0.09	0.12	−0.06	0.55	−1.71	0.28
Single persons								
– employed	0.42	0.47	0.44	0.48	0.26	0.12	1.15	0.30
– unemployment insurance	0.55	0.09	0.24	0.27	0.33	0.15	−1.82	0.29
– social assistance	0.34	−0.14	−0.08	0.05	−0.06	0.72	−1.47	0.30
– disability benefit	0.51	−0.11	−0.10	0.15	−0.07	0.28	−1.86	0.29
Aged persons	0.24	0.19	0.21	0.19	0.35	0.45	−1.66	0.25

[a] Cumulated differences between simulation and base projection

Lower tax rate first bracket

In the first column of Table 8.1, the lower tax rate in the first bracket is seen to increase labour supply. Because many partners in families work part-time and because partner wages are lower than breadwinner wages, on the margin the income of most of the partners is subject to the tax rate of the first tax bracket. The substitution effect, due to the lower marginal tax rate of these partners, increases labour supply. In contrast, the tax reduction also increases the net income of breadwinners and hence decreases labour supply through the income effect. Since the substitution effect dominates, labour supply rises. The tax reduction affects wage formation through two main channels. Firstly, the rise in labour supply strengthens the bargaining power of employers and lowers wages. Secondly, the tax reduction lowers the average tax and premium rate of workers, which also reduces wage demands. Lower wage costs enable a fall in prices, which improves the competitive position of Dutch firms with respect to foreign competitors. Hence, exports rise. Also private consumption increases because of the tax reduction. These two effects dominate the fall in demand due to the reduction in non-wage government consumption. By consequence, production and employment increase. The rise in employment exceeds the rise in labour supply so that unemployment falls.

In column one of Table 8.2 average real disposable incomes of all categories are seen to rise because of the fall in the tax rate in the first bracket. People receiving an unemployment insurance benefit gain most from the lower tax rate because almost their entire income falls in the first bracket. A substantial part of income of working people is subject to the tax rates of the second and third bracket. Therefore, on average they gain less compared to the unemployed. The increase in average real disposable incomes of unemployed people receiving social assistance benefits is lower than that of people receiving unemployment insurance benefits. The reason is that the basic allowance constitutes a larger share of the lower social assistance benefit and therefore a smaller share of this benefit gains from the lower tax rate. This effect is strengthened because all breadwinners receiving social assistance benefits have twice the basic allowance, since none of their partners participates, in contrast to partners of breadwinners receiving unemployment insurance benefits. Hence the average zero tax bracket amount of breadwinners receiving social assistance benefits also in absolute terms exceeds the average zero tax bracket amount of breadwinners receiving unemployment insurance benefits.

Lower tax rate second bracket

A reduction in the tax rate of the first bracket is almost three times as effective in raising employment than utilizing the same amount of money for a lower tax rate in the second bracket. The main reason for this difference stems from the labour supply reaction. Because of part-time work and lower wages, only a small number of partner incomes are affected by the tax rate of the second bracket. Hence, on the one hand the rise in labour supply due to the substitution effect from a lower tax rate in the second bracket is relatively small. On the other hand, the opposite income effect of breadwinners is relatively large, since a larger part of breadwinner incomes is subject to this tax rate. This explains why, in the second column of Table 8.1, the labour supply effect from a reduction in the tax rate of the second bracket is less than the labour supply effect from a reduction in the tax rate in the first bracket. Consequently wage moderation due to rising labour supply is less substantial.

In contrast to the average worker, column two of Table 8.2 indicates that on average unemployed and disabled people do not gain from this way of tax reduction. The small decrease in their average real disposable benefit incomes is explained by the fact that these benefits are indexed to falling gross wages. For the relatively low benefit incomes there is no tax reduction to offset the fall in gross benefits. The same applies to the low wage incomes so that replacement ratios for minimum incomes do not change. However, replacement ratios of unemployed people previously earning incomes exceeding the first bracket decrease because of the lower tax rate. Hence, the average replacement ratio falls, which stimulates wage moderation.

In the model the fall in wages is tempered by the relatively large fall in the marginal tax and premium rate associated with the falling tax rate in the second bracket. In this case the lower marginal tax and premium rate makes it less worthwhile to moderate wages in order to create additional employment, since the price in terms of loss of net additional income is higher. Less wage moderation also limits the positive feedback of the tax reduction on the government budget. There is less scope for tax reduction, which is apparent from the change in the weighted average tax and premium rate in Table 8.1. Because the effects of the smaller fall in the average tax and premium rate, of the larger fall in the marginal tax and premium rate, and of the smaller increase in labour supply more than offset the effects of the fall in the replacement ratio, wage moderation in column two is less than in column one. By consequence reducing the tax rate in the second bracket is less effective in raising employment than reducing the tax rate in the first bracket.

Lower tax rate third bracket

Labour supply measured in hours decreases in column three of Table 8.1 because the income effect through breadwinner incomes is no longer offset by a substitution effect via partner incomes. Very few partners earn an income that is liable to the tax rate of the third bracket. The fall in the replacement ratio is less than in column two because a smaller part of previous wages of the unemployed depends on the third bracket tax rate. Wage moderation and employment growth are modest. Positive feedbacks on the government budget are smaller, restricting the scope for tax reduction. However, because wage moderation is also modest, the changes in average real disposable incomes are largely comparable with the simulation of a fall in the tax rate of the second bracket (compare column two and three of Table 8.2).

Higher upper border first bracket

A higher upper border of the first bracket raises labour supply measured in hours because some of the partners no longer face a 50% tax rate in the second bracket but a 38.5% rate in the first bracket. Moreover, this instrument lengthens the income trajectory over which national social insurance premiums are due. Recall from Table 5.2 that national social insurance premiums constitute two thirds of the first bracket rate (25.5% / 38.5%). With the premium rate balancing the budget of the national social insurance funds, a higher upper border enables a fall in the first bracket social security premium rate by 0.4 %-point. The positive consequences of this reduction of the first bracket rate have been described above. Therefore the economic effects in column one and four of Table 8.1 do not differ very much. Purchasing power effects for minimum incomes in Table 8.2 differ to a greater extent, because minimum incomes do not gain directly from the higher upper border.

Higher upper border second bracket

The economic effects of a higher upper border of the second bracket in column five largely concur with the effects of the reduction of the tax rate in the third bracket in column three and need no further discussion.

Higher basic allowance

A higher basic allowance for income taxes (column six of Table 8.1) has a negative influence on labour supply. For many working partners it generates a negative income effect by way of both the own income and the income of breadwinners. If partners do not participate or work a small number of hours the income effect only operates via the breadwinner income, because in these cases the basic allowance has been transferred to the breadwinner. In both cases the number of labour hours supplied falls. In addition there is a negative feedback on labour supply via the national social insurance premium rate. A higher basic allowance decreases the premium receipts of national social insurance funds and therefore requires a rise in the first bracket premium rate (by 0.3 %-points). In column one this is seen to reduce labour supply.

Column six of Table 8.2 shows that a higher basic allowance works out very favourable on the average real disposable income of people receiving social assistance benefits. The net minimum wage of a sole wage-earner gains twice from the increase in the basic allowance, because of the transferability. Institutionally the social assistance benefits of both breadwinners and single persons are linked to the net minimum wage of a sole wage-earner. Therefore, both net benefits rise with the same substantial percentage[57]. The rise in the net single person benefit exceeds the rise in the net single person wage, since the latter person can subtract the basic allowance from his taxable income only once. By consequence the replacement ratio rises. Moreover, the replacement ratio rises because unemployed persons gain most from the higher basic allowance, which constitutes a larger part of their relatively low incomes compared to workers. The higher replacement ratio strengthens the bargaining position of workers, which slows down wage moderation. In addition, the tightening of the labour market because of declining labour supply, exerts an upward pressure on wages. Higher wages raise wage-related government expenditures and limit the scope for tax reduction. Consequently, with this tax instrument employment falls. The fall in employment equals the fall in labour supply so that on balance unemployment does not change.

[57] In Table 8.2 average real disposable incomes of breadwinners receiving a social assistance benefit always react somewhat less strongly than average real disposable incomes of single persons receiving a social assistance benefit. This is caused by other net income components not subject to taxation, which are larger for breadwinners than for single persons. The most important of these are family allowances for breadwinners with children.

Hence, from a labour market perspective raising the basic allowance is no useful option. It should be noted, however, that slightly positive effects on employment can be obtained if the government is able to prevent the rise in the national social insurance premium rate. Options to achieve this are: a reduction of the tax component of the first bracket rate, raising the upper border of the first bracket, or a transfer from the government to the national social insurance funds. Obviously the rise in the basic allowance will be smaller if government funds will be used for these purposes. Nevertheless, even with this kind of compensation the rise in employment will be so small that increasing the basic allowance remains least effective in terms of employment creation.

Higher supplementary allowance for workers

The system of the supplementary allowance for workers in The Netherlands consists of a reduction of the income tax rate for incomes below a relatively low threshold[58] and a nominal allowance for incomes above the threshold[59]. Moreover the supplementary allowance cannot be transferred to the breadwinner if the partner does not earn an income. Because of these differences between the system of the supplementary allowance for workers and the general basic allowance, labour supply effects in column seven of Table 8.1 differ from the effects of the higher general basic allowance in column six of Table 8.1. The fall in the income tax rate for partners with incomes below the threshold generates a substitution effect, which stimulates labour supply of these partners and causes a positive effect on participation. This is offset by the income effect from higher breadwinner incomes. On balance, the fall in labour supply in persons is less than in the previous simulation. For partners with incomes above the threshold the income effect from the higher nominal

[58] The threshold income in 1992 is roughly three quarters of the upper border of the first income tax bracket.

[59] In the simulation the reduction in the tax rate and the increase in the nominal allowance are adjusted proportionally.

allowance decreases labour supply. Hence, labour supply measured in hours falls.

A second difference compared to the previous simulation is that in this case wage moderation is reinforced by the fall in the replacement ratio, since only workers benefit from the tax reduction. The latter fact is also directly clear from Table 8.2, which shows a relatively large fall of the average real disposable incomes of people depending on social security or social assistance. These gross benefits decline because they are linked to the falling wage rate and there is no tax reduction to offset this effect.

A relatively small part (less than 50%) of the fall in wages manifests itself in the fall in producer prices, because on the long run labour productivity decreases. This is caused by the fall in the reservation wage of the unemployed as a result of the decrease in net benefits compared to net wages. The lower reservation wage implies that more unemployed people, who are less productive at their working place, find a job. On the long run this leads to a decline in the average productivity of workers. The lower productivity feeds back into the producer prices, which follow wage decreases less strongly. The same argument applies to output prices, so that exports and production rise less strongly. However, the increase in employment exceeds the rise in production because of the fall in labour productivity and is largest of all the tax instrument distinguished in Table 8.1. Also the fall in unemployment is largest with this tax instrument. Especially the employment perspectives of workers earning a minimum income improve. This is caused by substitution between this category of labour and other types of labour. The fall in wage costs of low productive labour is strongest owing to lower search cost for employers. Finally, there are large feedback effects on government expenditure caused by the wage moderation, which enables a very strong increase in the supplementary allowance for workers. Analogously to the previous simulation at the same time the national social insurance premium rate rises (by 0.6 %-points) to offset the fall in premium receipts because of the higher allowance.

Lower value added tax rate

A reduction in the VAT rate lowers consumer prices and thus is most effective in reducing inflation (column eight of Table 8.1). Real wages of partners rise, which stimulates labour supply through the substitution effect. In addition there is a relatively strong income effect because real disposable incomes of breadwinners also rise proportionally to the fall in consumer prices. On balance labour supply hardly changes. In the wage bargaining process the fall in consumer prices compared to producer prices generates wage moderation leading to higher employment and less unemployment. The reduction in the VAT rate has an almost identical influence on the average real disposable incomes of all types of persons in households distinguished in Table 8.2. Compared to the reduction in the tax rate of the first bracket, a lower VAT rate is a less effective instrument to improve employment because there are no positive effects on labour supply and because the replacement ratio does not fall.

In conclusion, the above simulation results indicate that raising the supplementary allowance for workers is most effective in creating employment opportunities. The fall of the replacement ratio generates a downward pressure on wages which improves competitiveness and raises employment. Associated with these favourable results is a relatively large fall of real disposable income of people dependent on social security or social assistance benefits. The second most effective instrument to raise employment is a reduction of the tax rate in the first bracket, followed by a higher upper border of the first bracket. Moreover, with these instruments average real disposable income increases for all categories of persons distinguished. Increasing the basic allowance raises average real disposable income for most of the people depending on minimum social assistance benefits, but has a negative influence on employment if the required increase of the social insurance premium rate in the first bracket is taken into account. Reducing value added taxes is most effective in reducing inflation.

8.2 Replacing the basic allowance by a tax credit

In political discussions on the tax system proposals have been put forward to replace the basic allowance by a tax credit. Because the basic allowance must be deducted from taxable income before applying the income tax rates, its effect on net income depends on the marginal tax rate of the tax payer. For instance, the net value of the 1992 basic allowance of *f*5225 equals *f*2014 for people with a first bracket marginal tax rate of 38.55% and *f*3135 for people with a third bracket marginal tax rate of 60%. A tax credit is an amount that a tax payer is allowed to subtract from the amount of taxes due. Hence, the tax credit is independent of the marginal tax rate of the tax payer, which makes it an attractive instrument to contribute to the levelling of net incomes. In accordance with the proposals by political parties, in the simulations of this section the basic tax credit is set at *f*2014 so that its value is neutral for people with taxable incomes falling in the first tax bracket. It is assumed that, analogously to the basic allowance, the tax credit can be transferred from partner to breadwinner if the amount of taxes to be paid by the partner is less than the tax credit amount[60].

Also for aged people a tax credit of *f*2014 is used. Because aged households do not pay all national social insurance premiums their first bracket tax rate equals 20.5% instead of 38.55%. Hence, the tax credit of *f*2014 exceeds the amount of *f*1071 which would apply according to the first bracket rate of aged persons. However, the latter amount would imply a relatively large fall of net income for aged people with marginal tax rates of the second and third bracket. Moreover, institutionally the net income of aged people receiving

[60] Because the first bracket rate is a combination of a tax rate and a national social insurance premium rate, the basic allowance applies to both tax receipts of the government and premiums received by the national social insurance funds. Since the tax credit is deductible from the total amount of taxes and premiums to be paid it is not straightforward which part of the total amount of tax credits has to be supplied by the government and which part by the social insurance funds. To solve this difficulty, in these simulations national social insurance premium rates remain unchanged and financial deficits of the social funds are supplied for by the government while financial surpluses of the funds are transferred to the government.

Table 8.3 Main economic outcomes of replacing the basic allowance by a tax credit

Budgetary neutral by		family allowance and tax rate first bracket	tax rate first bracket
Prices		*percentage changes*[a]	
Wage rate	0.3	0.5	0.0
– minimum	0.3	0.5	–0.1
– other low skilled	0.3	0.5	–0.1
– high skilled	0.4	0.6	0.0
Production price	0.1	0.3	–0.1
Consumption price	0.1	0.2	–0.1
Volumes			
Private consumption	–0.6	–0.1	0.1
Investment	–0.2	–0.1	0.0
Exports	–0.1	–0.2	0.1
Imports	–0.2	0.0	0.0
Private production	–0.3	–0.2	0.1
Private employment	–0.5	–0.4	0.0
– minimum	–0.7	–0.6	0.1
– other low skilled	–0.5	–0.4	0.1
– high skilled	–0.4	–0.3	0.0
Labour supply persons	0.1	0.1	0.3
Labour supply hours	–0.1	–0.1	0.0
Ratios		*absolute changes*[a]	
Unemployment rate	0.3	0.2	0.0
– minimum	0.5	0.4	0.0
– other low skilled	0.4	0.3	0.0
– high skilled	0.2	0.1	0.0
Inactivity ratio	0.6	0.5	0.0
Replacement ratio	0.4	0.5	0.4
Average tax rate	0.6	0.5	0.1
Marginal tax rate	1.6	1.5	1.3
Public deficit[b]	–0.3	0.0	0.0

[a] Cumulated differences between simulation and base projection
[b] As a percentage of net national product

only a benefit under the General Old Age Pension Act is linked to net minimum wages. Since almost all of the aged people with marginal tax rates in the first bracket receive a benefit under the General Old Age Pension Act, their net income does not depend on the specific tax credit for aged people, but on the tax credit that is relevant for the minimum wage rate. Therefore, the tax credit of aged people is taken equal to that of other income recipients.

The first column of Table 8.3 and Table 8.4 present the simulation results of the replacement of the basic allowance by a tax credit of *f*2014, without

Table 8.4 Average real disposable income with replacing the basic allowance by a tax credit

Budgetary neutral by		family allowance and tax rate first bracket	tax rate first bracket
		percentage changes[a]	
Breadwinners			
– employed with children	–1.1	0.0	–0.4
– employed, no children	–1.1	–0.8	–0.4
– unemployment insurance	–1.2	–0.1	–0.2
– social assistance	0.1	1.3	1.1
– disability benefit	–0.1	0.8	0.9
Single persons			
– employed	–0.8	–0.5	–0.1
– unemployment insurance	–0.2	0.2	0.8
– social assistance	0.2	0.6	1.1
– disability benefit	0.0	0.4	1.0
Aged persons	–0.4	–0.1	0.2

[a] Cumulated differences between simulation and base projection

any measures to balance the budget of the government[61]. As explained above, for people with incomes falling in the second and third bracket this way of introducing a tax credit implies a loss of net income. Therefore, average real disposable incomes of employed people and of people with an unemployment insurance benefit are seen to fall in Table 8.4. Because they are linked to the rising wage rate (see below), minimum social assistance benefits increase slightly. These benefits are indifferent to the introduction of the tax credit because they fall in the first tax bracket.

Moreover, the abolition of the basic allowance means that implicitly the borders of the tax brackets shift. For single persons and double wage-earners the basic allowance of *f*5225 is cancelled so that the borders of the tax brackets are reached at taxable incomes which are *f*5225 lower. For sole wage-earners the shift is twice as large because of the transferability of the basic allowance. Because of these shifts, the marginal tax rate rises for incomes on a substantial trajectory below the current borders of the tax

[61] Balanced budget effects are postponed to later simulations to be able to explain the effects of the introduction of the tax credit without any complicating additional impulses.

brackets. This also explains the relatively large increase in the weighted marginal tax and premium rate in Table 8.3.

The loss of net income of breadwinners with incomes in the second and third bracket stimulates their partners to increase labour supply. In the first column of Table 8.3 labour supply measured in persons is seen to rise. However, a number of partners encounter the consequences of the implicit shift of the borders and the associated significant increase in their marginal tax rates. These partners, who work a substantial number of hours, will reduce their supply of labour. Because the latter effect dominates, on balance labour supply measured in hours declines.

Three reasons account for the rise in wages. Firstly, the fall in labour supply tightens the labour market, which exerts an upward pressure on wages. Secondly, employees aim at shifting forward the higher average tax and premium rate into higher wages. Thirdly, the replacement ratio rises because net wages above the first bracket fall while net minimum benefits are not affected by the introduction of the tax credit. Higher wages lead to higher output prices, loss of competitiveness, falling production and employment and rising unemployment. As a consequence of the higher average tax incidence the government budget deficit falls.

Of course the additional financial capacity of the government can be used in various ways. In column two of Table 8.3 a combination has been selected consisting of a rise of family allowances by 20% and a decrease of the tax rate in the first bracket by 0.2 %-point. This combination has been selected to keep the average real disposable income of working breadwinners with children unchanged (see Table 8.4) and to arrive at ex post budgetary neutrality for the government. The increase of real disposable incomes raises consumption compared to column one, which stimulates production. Therefore the fall in employment is less than in column one and unemployment rises less strongly.

The increase in unemployment vanishes if the financial capacity of the government is used completely to reduce the tax rate in the first bracket by 0.8 %-point. The falling average tax and premium rate compared to column two causes wage moderation, which raises employment. Moreover, the lower tax rate stimulates labour supply, which also exerts a negative pressure on wages. The economic consequences of this way of introducing the tax credit are seen to be modest.

In conclusion, budgetary neutral replacement of the basic allowance by a tax credit generates slightly negative to neutral consequences for the labour market and a shift of purchasing power from employed people to people depending on minimum benefits.

8.3 The 'Laffer' curve

The economic implications of ever rising tax rates have been analyzed by stepwise raising the tax rates in the three tax brackets. Analogously to the simulations in Section 8.1, the extra tax revenues for the government are used to increase non-wage consumption in such a way that the government budget remains balanced.

The consequences for tax revenues and government expenditure are depicted in Figure 8.1. The horizontal axis indicates the increase in the tax rates in percentage points and the vertical axis depicts the change of tax

Figure 8.1 Change in tax revenues and components of government expenditure (%-NNP) with rising statutory income tax rates

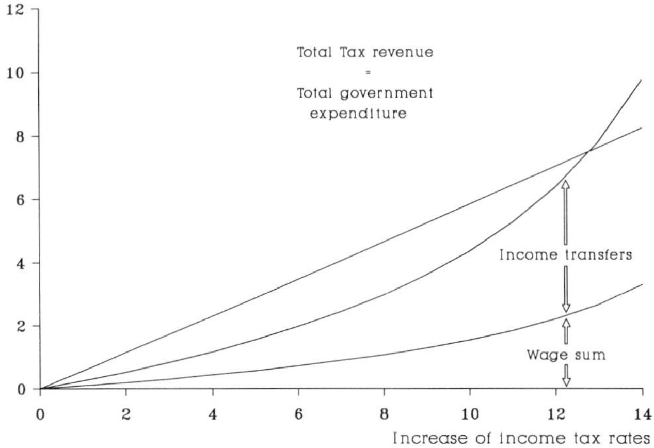

Figure 8.2 Change of weighted average and marginal tax rates (%-points) and wage rate (%) with rising statutory income tax rates

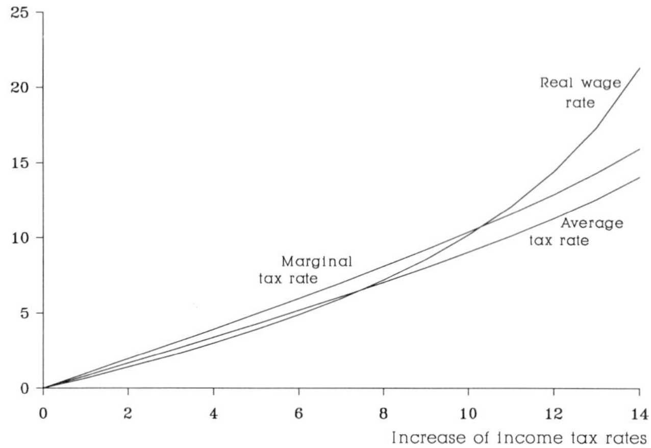

revenues (in percents of net national product) as the difference between the simulation with higher tax rates and the base projection of MIMIC. Because of the balanced budget constraint, the change in tax revenues as a percentage of net national product equals the change in government expenditure in Figure 8.1. In contrast to the curvature of the original Laffer-curve, the figure shows that ever increasing tax rates do not cause a fall in tax revenues. The basic explanation for this divergence lies in the forward shifting of higher taxes into higher wages. The wage curve in Figure 8.2 even rises exponentially, because the intensity of the wage reaction depends on the level of the tax rates in MIMIC[62]. The strong increase in wages precludes the shrinking of the tax base in Figure 8.1. Moreover, the rise in wages dampens the negative labour supply effects from higher marginal tax rates[63]. As can be seen from

[62] See equation (4.43) in Section 4.3. If the average and marginal tax rates approach a value of one (hundred percent) wages approach infinity.

[63] Another reason for the relatively modest fall of labour supply is the exogeneity of labour supply of breadwinners and single persons in MIMIC. With very large increases of tax rates adverse labour supply reactions of breadwinners and single persons will become quantitatively more important even with relatively low labour supply elasticities.

Figure 8.3 Change of labour market variables with rising statutory income tax rates

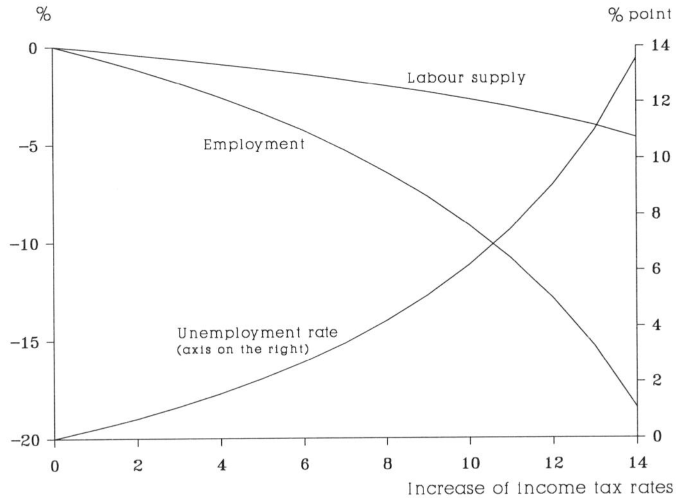

Figure 8.3, the fall in labour supply is not very large if tax rates increase.

Although the rise of the wage rate prevents the tax base from falling, it has other negative consequences for the economy. Higher wages imply cost increases and rising domestic prices, which impair the competitive position of domestic firms and lead to falling exports (see Figure 8.4). Lower demand generates a fall in production and employment, leading to a large rise in unemployment. This is depicted in Figure 8.3. On the government budget the net revenues from higher taxes are crowded out by a strong increase in wage-related expenditure of the government. On the one hand wage-related expenditure consists of wage costs of government officials, on the other hand it concerns income transfers, which are indexed by the wage rate. Income transfers also rise because higher unemployment raises the number of people applying for unemployment assistance benefits.

Figure 8.5 presents the change in non-wage government consumption associated with the rising tax rate under a balanced budget. The curve resembles the Laffer curve. Although the mechanisms underlying it are rather different, the policy implications are the same. Hence, the curve in Figure 8.5 can be called a Laffer-type curve. Non-wage government consumption is seen

Figure 8.4 Percentage change of consumption, exports and production with rising statutory income tax rates

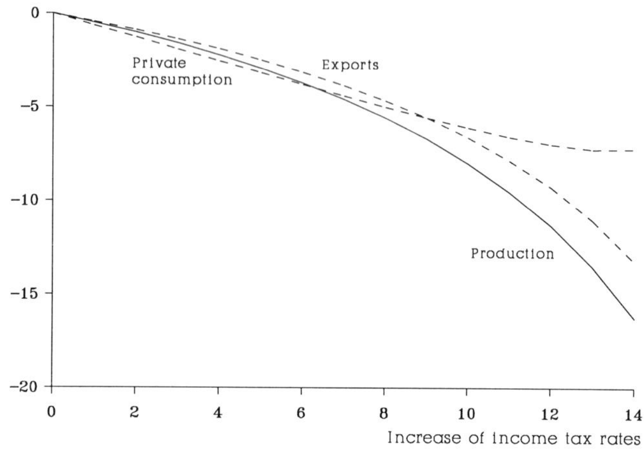

to increase with higher tax rates until the three tax rates have been raised by 9 %-points. Increasing the tax rates from that point onwards implies a relative fall in non-wage government consumption. If the increase of the tax rates exceeds 13 %-points the government even has to cut back on non-wage

Figure 8.5 Percentage change of non-wage government consumption with rising statutory income tax rates under a balanced budget

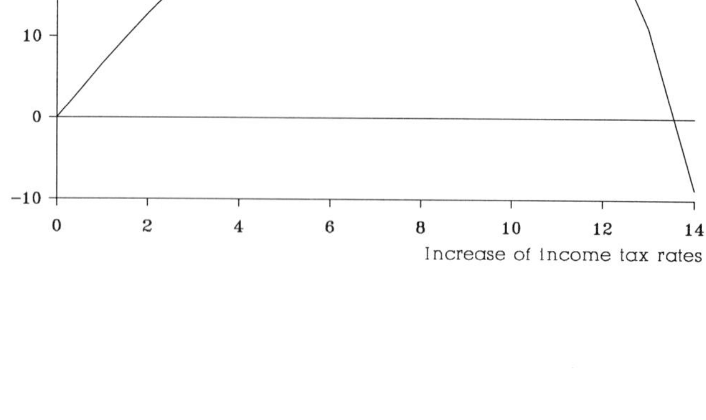

consumption to keep the budget balanced. Then the Laffer-type curve in Figure 8.5 crosses the horizontal axis. However, we should note that the specific shape of this Laffer-type curve depends on the way the tax revenues for the government are spent. For instance, if tax proceeds are used to raise social assistance benefits, the replacement ratio will rise which will affect wage formation and influences the shape of the curve.

In summary, these simulations with stepwise increasing tax rates show net revenues of higher taxes for the government to rise in an ever smaller degree and eventually to go down. In contrast to the main mechanisms behind the original Laffer curve, in MIMIC the shape of the curve is not caused by a shrinking tax base but by ever increasing government expenditure due to large wage increases and rising unemployment.

9 Reform of the income tax system

After the analysis of specific income tax instruments in the previous chapter, this chapter is concerned with reforms of the income tax system. System reforms consist of much more comprehensive changes in the structure of taxation, than merely changing a single instrument like the tax rate in a specific bracket. In the recent past two income tax reforms have been relevant for The Netherlands. The first one has actually been implemented in 1990. It has become known as the 'Oort' reform after the chairman of the committee that prepared a report on the income tax reform, Oort (1986). In this reform the tax system has been simplified, amongst others by reducing the number of tax brackets from nine to three, the tax base has been broadened and marginal tax rates have been reduced. Section 9.2 analyses the economic consequences of the 1990 income tax reform.

In Section 9.3 we discuss proposals for further income tax reform by the second Committee for Tax Reform (Stevens, 1991). These are meant to reduce income tax rates, to broaden the tax base and to simplify the taxation procedure. One of the targets of the reform is to increase labour supply and the simulation results will indicate to what extent this can be achieved. The Stevens proposals have not actually been implemented (see Social Economic Council, 1992 for a discussion on this issue).

Before turning to the two system reforms, Section 9.1 contains a short introductory discussion of the international trend towards income tax reform.

9.1 Income tax reform in OECD countries

With respect to the income tax system the second half of the nineteen eighties may be called the years of reform. In many OECD countries sometimes substantial changes were brought about in the income tax and social security premium system. A well-known example is the 1986 tax reform in the United States, which did not only concern income taxes but had a much wider scope. The top corporate income tax rate was lowered from 46% to 34% together with the elimination of the investment tax credit. The top personal income tax

Figure 9.1 Decrease in number of income tax brackets and top income tax rates in OECD countries over 1986 – 1990

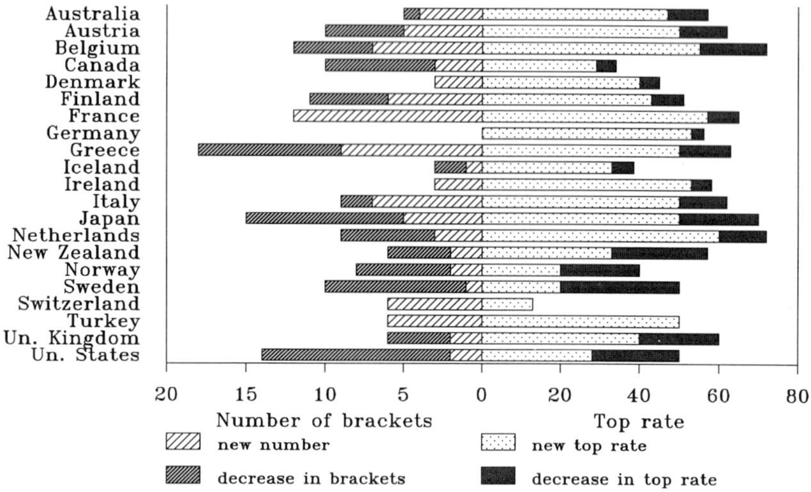

rate was reduced from 50% to 28% and standard income tax allowances were raised.

The United States was by far not the only country in which income tax reforms took place. Figure 9.1, which is based on OECD (1991b), visualizes that between 1986 and 1990 in 17 out of 23 countries the number of tax brackets were reduced. Only in Luxembourg the number increased from 21 to 24 and in Denmark, France, Ireland, Switzerland and Turkey no changes occurred[64]. Figure 9.1 also shows the often substantial decline of the top income tax rate in this period. For instance, in Japan, New Zealand, Norway, Sweden, The United Kingdom and The United States the decline equals 20 percentage points or more. Only in Switzerland and Turkey the top marginal income tax rates have not been lowered. For Switzerland this is not remarkable because it already had a very low upper tax rate of 13%.

[64] Germany is not included because the income tax system does not consist of brackets but is based on a formula. Figures for Sweden refer to 1991 instead of 1990.

As stated in Chapter 1 applied general equilibrium models have frequently been used to analyze the economic consequences of tax reform. For instance, Henderson (1991) reviews the simulation results of six different applied general equilibrium models on the 1986 Tax Reform Act in the United States. Turning to The Netherlands, in the next two sections the 1990 income tax reform and the 1991 proposals for further income tax reform by the Committee for Tax Reform are assessed using simulation results of MIMIC. In these simulations the focus will be largely on the labour market consequences of the reforms, which is not addressed extensively in other model exercises on income tax reform.

9.2 The 1990 income tax reform in The Netherlands

The 1990 income tax reform in The Netherlands has been directed at broadening the tax base, at lowering marginal rates of taxation and social security premiums and at simplifying the tax system. The relevant parts of the tax systems before and after the reform are presented in Table 9.1[65]. In this section a simulation is presented which contains the three major characteristics of the tax reform[66]. Firstly, the number of tax brackets is reduced from nine to three. Secondly, the national social insurance premiums are integrated into the first tax bracket and are no longer tax deductible. To prevent this to cause a fall in net income, the base for national social insurance premiums and income taxes is increased by 10.4% with a maximum of *f*6952. This is implemented in the system by imposing a 10.4% rate on employers and transferring the associated amount to employees. In this way employees are compensated for the fact that after the tax reform they have to pay all

[65] The complete after reform system of taxes and social security premiums has been described Section 5.2.

[66] A few other aspects of the reform, especially the reduction of tax-deductible expenses, are not incorporated in the simulation. In this section the simulation with the 1990 system is compared to a base projection in which the before 1990 system is used throughout the simulation period.

Table 9.1 The income tax and national social insurance premium system before and after the 1990 tax reform

	Income interval (* *f*1000)		Nat. social insurance premium rate	Income tax rate
Before tax reform: 1989 system[a]				
National social insurance	0.0	65.900	23.4	
Income taxes				
– bracket 1	0.0	9.681		14.0
– bracket 2	9.681	17.127		24.0
– bracket 3	17.127	31.636		32.0
– bracket 4	31.636	44.658		42.0
– bracket 5	44.658	65.248		51.0
– bracket 6	65.248	91.676		60.0
– bracket 7	91.676	121.224		66.0
– bracket 8	121.224	230.314		69.0
– bracket 9	230.314	∞		72.0
After tax reform: 1990 system				
Bracket 1	0.0	42.123	22.1	13.0
Bracket 2	42.123	84.245		50.0
Bracket 3	84.245	∞		60.0

[a] In the simulations the 1990 tax system before the tax reform consists of the 1989 tax rates and the 1989 income levels adjusted for inflation in 1990 according to the indexation rules in the model.

national social insurance premiums, while before the reform these premiums were shared by employees and employers. Aged households will also pay a part of the national social insurance premiums, for which they are financially compensated as far as their benefit under the General Old Age Pension Act is concerned. The integration of national social insurance premiums in the tax system implies a reduction of the maximum income subject to national social insurance premiums from *f*65900 in 1989 to *f*42123 in 1990. Thirdly, tax rates and zero tax bracket amounts are altered. The basic allowance is lowered from *f*7415 in 1989 to *f*4568 and a substantial additional allowance for single persons of half of the basic allowance (*f*3708 in 1989) is cancelled. The maximum marginal tax rate falls from 72% to 60%.

Figure 9.2 illustrates that the new tax system has resulted in a combined marginal tax and premium rate with a simplified appearance compared to the before reform tax system. The after tax reform marginal tax and premium

Figure 9.2 Marginal tax and premium rate before and after 1990 income tax reform

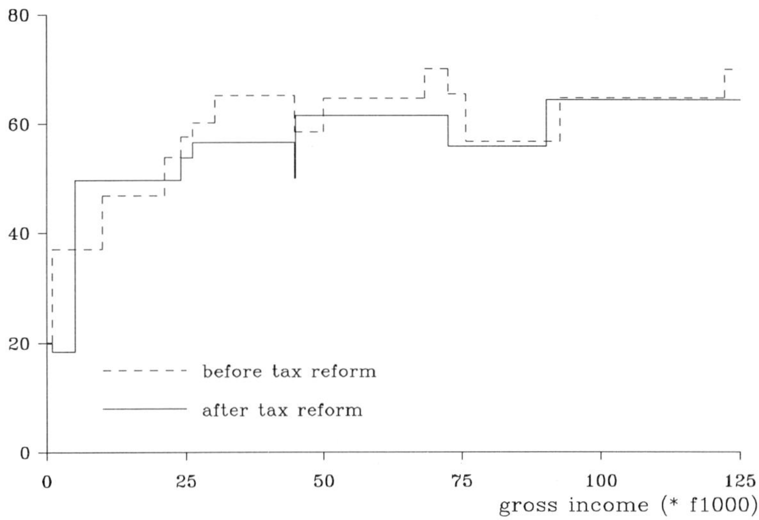

rate, represented by the solid line in Figure 9.2, starts at almost 20% which equals the combined pension premium and employee insurance premium rates without a franchise (see Section 5.2 for more details). Soon the curve jumps upward when the basic allowance is exceeded and the tax and premium rate of the first bracket is added. Small steps in the curve occur when the franchises of pension premiums and the employee insurance premiums are exhausted. Although these premium rates are substantial the increase in the combined rate is modest because the premiums due can be deducted for income taxes and national social insurance premiums. In the tax reform the segment of the gross income trajectory below *f*35000 has been simplified by cancelling a number of tax brackets. On the interval between *f*35000 and *f*75000, generally, the marginal rates of taxation and premiums are lower after the tax reform. Moreover, an upward kink in the before tax reform system slightly below *f*75000 followed by two downward kinks, is absent. It had been caused by the interaction of the lower border of the sixth tax bracket and the upper border of national insurance premiums in the before reform system. Both are absent in the new system, only one downward kink

Table 9.2 Ex ante budgetary consequences of 1990 reform of income taxes and national social insurance premiums (% NNP)

Budget national social insurance funds		*Government budget*	
Social security benefits	0.3	Transfers to national insurance	2.5
Social security premiums	−2.2	Taxes	1.4
Transfers from government	2.5	Public deficit	1.1

remains at the maximum of the premium interval for employee insurances. The final upward jump in the curve coincides with the lower border of the third 60% tax bracket.

The ex ante budgetary effects of the 1990 tax reform can be found in Table 9.2. As part of the tax and premium reform, national social insurance premiums are reduced by 2.2% of net national product. Social security benefits rise by 0.3% of net national product mainly because of the financial compensation of aged persons mentioned above. In order to keep a balanced budget of the national social insurance funds, 2.5% of net national product is transferred from the government to these funds. Tax rates rise compared to the before reform tax system, implying 1.4 %-points higher government tax revenues[67]. Since transfers to the national social insurance funds exceed the additional tax revenues, the public deficit rises by 1.1 %-points. Hence, the reform of the system of income taxes and national social insurance premiums implies a reduction in the average incidence of taxes and premiums.

[67] The reason for these transfers between taxes and premiums is the following. It has been indicated above that aged persons also pay part of the national social insurance premiums as part of the tax reform. This pertains to premiums under the General Act on Exceptional Medical Expenses. Originally, aged persons were meant to pay premiums under the General Disablement Benefits Act as well. However, at the end of 1989 the risk was felt that by consequence elderly people would also become entitled to these benefits, which could have substantial budgetary costs. Therefore, the proposal was cancelled. To keep the tax and premium rate in the first bracket unchanged at the proposed level of 18.4% for the elderly, the tax rate in the first bracket was raised from 7% to 13%. To compensate this tax increase for persons under 65, the premium rates under the General Widows and Orphans Act and the General Disablement Benefits Act (which are not paid by the elderly) were reduced by 6 %-points in total. To even the budgets, the extra tax receipts were transferred to the social security funds.

Table 9.3 Simulation results on 1990 income tax reform

Prices (percentage changes)[a]		*Ratios (absolute changes)*[a]	
Wage rate	0.5	Unemployment rate	–0.4
Production price	0.5	Replacement ratio	0.8
Consumption price	0.3	Average tax rate	–1.3
Volumes (percentage changes)[a]		Marginal tax rate	–3.3
Private consumption	1.2	Labour income share	–0.1
Investment	0.3	Taxes[b]: total	1.8
Exports	–0.2	income tax	1.7
Imports	0.7	Social security premiums[b]	–2.6
Private production	0.3	Public deficit[b]	1.0
Private employment	0.2	Current account[b]	–0.4
Labour supply persons	–1.8		
Labour supply hours	–0.3		

[a] Cumulated effects as differences between simulation and base projection.
[b] As a percentage of net national product.

Table 9.3 contains the simulation results of the 1990 tax reform. The decrease of labour supply measured in persons indicates that participation falls, which occurs because the tax reform increases the tax and premium rate in the first tax bracket and because average tax and premium rates of bread-winners fall. The lower marginal tax and premium rates on a substantial income interval (compare Figure 9.2) increase the number of working hours supplied by partners in this interval. On balance labour supply measured in hours falls by 0.3%.

The increase in the wage rate results from the dominance of three upward influences over one downward influence on the wage outcome. Because of the forward shifting effect the fall in the weighted average tax and premium rate leads to a wage reduction. An upward impact on the wage rate stems from the fall in the weighted marginal rate of taxes and premiums for workers by over 3 %-points, from the fall in labour supply, and from the increase in the replacement ratio. Two effects explain the higher replacement ratio. Firstly, compared to the before 1990 system the supplementary allowance for workers has been lowered. Secondly, cancelling the supplementary allowance for single persons substantially reduces net disposable incomes of working single persons with a low income, while single persons receiving government assistance are compensated, because their net incomes are indexed to the net income of a married sole wage earner receiving minimum wages.

Consumption increases considerably because of higher wages and because the tax reduction raises disposable incomes. The increase in wage costs raises production prices and implies a loss of competitiveness of Dutch firms. Exports slightly fall and imports increase. Production and employment rise moderately to match the demand impulse from the tax reduction. The rise in employment and the decrease in labour supply cause equilibrium unemployment to fall. On the one hand, higher consumption raises government tax revenues compared to the ex ante budgetary effects in Table 9.2. Also unemployment benefits paid by the government fall. On the other hand higher wage rates raise wage-related expenditure of the government. On balance, behaviourial reactions induced by the tax reform somewhat reduce the ex ante rise in the public deficit of 1.1 %-points to 1.0 %-points.

9.3 Further income tax reform: the Stevens proposals

In April 1990 a Committee for Tax Reform was installed by the Dutch government with the intent to advise on the possibilities of further income tax reform after the introduction of the 1990 system. Elements of the tax reform should contain further steps towards reduction in income tax rates, broadening of the tax base and simplification of the taxation procedure. Furthermore, the income effects of the changes in the tax system to be proposed should be small and the operation should be budgetary neutral. The committee was named the Stevens Committee after its chairman.

In July 1991 the report of the Committee was published (Stevens, 1991). The social security and income tax system as proposed by the Committee is summarized in Table 9.4. Broadening of the tax base has been achieved by ending the deductibility of employee insurance premiums for national social insurance premiums and income taxes. Moreover, a common base is created for all social security premiums and income taxes, which simplifies the tax system and makes it more lucid. For the same reasons the franchise of

Table 9.4 Main characteristics of the 1990 income tax and social security premium system and the system proposed by the Stevens Committee

	Income interval (* *f*1000)		Social security premium rate	Income tax rate
1990 system				
Employee insurance				
– Deductible for national social insurance and income taxes				
– Franchise disability insurance *f*92 per day			12.15	
National social insurance and income taxes				
Basic allowance	4.568			
Labour costs allowance	1.015			
Costs deduction benefits	0.481			
Bracket 1	0.0	42.123	22.1	13.0
Bracket 2	42.123	84.245		50.0
Bracket 3	84.245	∞		60.0
Proposal Stevens Committee				
Employee insurance				
– Not deductible for national social insurance and income taxes				
– No franchise disability insurance			5.5	
National social insurance and income taxes				
Basic tax credit	2.175			
Labour costs allowance	1.250			
Costs deduction benefits	0.150			
Bracket 1				
– sub-bracket 1	0.0	46.500	23.3	10.3
– sub-bracket 2	46.500	57.000		33.6
Bracket 2	57.000	∞		55.0
Reduction tax deductions and taxation non-wage income components				

premiums under the Disablement Insurance Act is abolished. A franchise constitutes an administrative burden for employers and narrows the base amount. Without the franchise the marginal premium rate can fall from 12.15% to 5.5%.

The Committee further suggested to replace the basic allowance for national social insurance premiums and income taxes by a tax credit. The proposed tax credit of *f*2175 exceeds a tax credit of *f*1603, which is equivalent to the 1990 basic allowance for incomes in first tax bracket (*f*1603 =

0.351 * ƒ4568). Analogously to the 1990 system of transfer of the basic allowance, the partner is allowed to transfer the tax credit to the breadwinner if (s)he earns less than the income corresponding to the tax credit. Because of the relatively higher tax credit and the lower tax rate in the first bracket (see below), the break-even income rises from ƒ4568 to ƒ2175 / 0.336 = ƒ6473. Both the introduction of the tax credit and the higher tax credit amount relative to the 1990 basic allowance are motivated by the requirement to keep income effects of the new system within small margins. The same motivation applies to the higher (imputed) labour costs allowance of ƒ1250, which is the only element in the proposed system which narrows the tax base. Together with a cutback of the standard costs allowance for persons with social security benefits from ƒ481 to ƒ150, the higher labour costs allowance raises the difference between net wages and net benefits.

In the tariff structure of income taxes and national social insurance premiums the number of tax brackets is reduced from three to two, the upper border of the first bracket is raised from ƒ42123 to ƒ57000, the tax and premium rate in the first bracket is lowered from 35.1% to 33.6% and the upper tax rate is lowered from 60% to 55%. The first tax bracket is split into two sub-brackets to take account of the specific situation of the elderly[68]. For other income recipients the two sub-brackets are irrelevant, since the combined tax and premium rate equals 33.6% in both sub-brackets. As a consequence of the change towards two brackets, employees with gross wages between ƒ56850 and ƒ100000 move from the second bracket of the 1990 system to the upper bracket of the new system. Hence, their marginal tax rate rises from 50% to 55%. Because the proposed system should be budgetary neutral it was not possible to lower marginal tax rates for all incomes, as

[68] Aged persons pay a low national social insurance premium rate of 5.4% in the 1990 system. Applying the new tariff structure for aged persons would lower the marginal tax rate for low income persons from 18.4% (5.4% + 13%) to 15.7% (5.4% + 10.3%) and for another group of aged persons from 50% to 15.7%. To mitigate these effects the national social insurance premium rate for the elderly is raised from 5.4% to 8.1%, which implies that the lowest tax and premium rate does not change, and a sub-bracket is introduced in which only the income tax rate of 33.6% applies.

Figure 9.3 Marginal tax and premium rate corresponding to the proposed tax system of the Stevens Committee

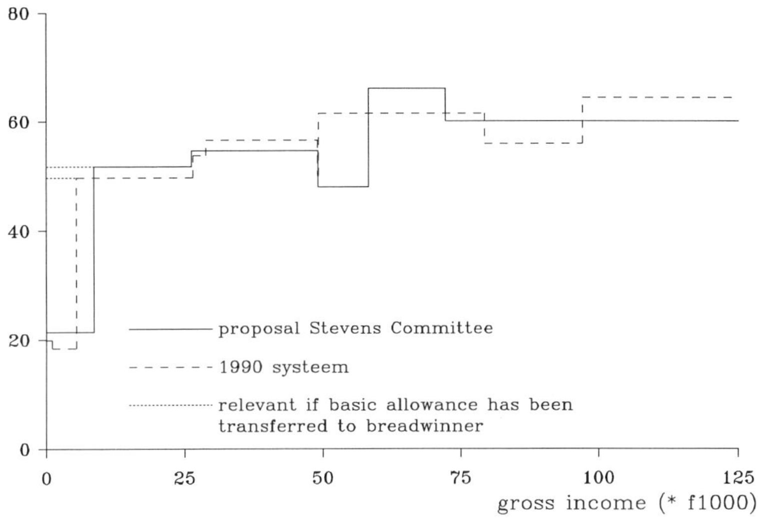

Figure 9.3 shows.

Finally, a number of tax deductions is abolished and taxes on some non-wage income components are increased. Examples of these base broadening recommendations are cancelling of the standard deductibility of cost of commuting, cancelling of the deductibility of interest paid on consumer loans, and increasing the taxation of private use of company owned cars. By reducing the number of deductions the tax system is also simplified.

Implementing the tax system of the Committee in the ex ante version of MIMIC, the proposals indeed turn out to be almost budgetary neutral: ex ante the public deficit rises by 0.1 %-points. The simulation results with the full version of MIMIC in Table 9.5 show that the new tax system generates a fall in labour supply measured in persons, which is caused by the relatively high tax credit and by cancelling the franchise for premiums under the Disablement Insurance Act. For partners with low incomes the transfer of a much higher tax credit compared to the 1990 basic allowance, implies a rise in breadwinner income which discourages labour supply. Hence, participation

Table 9.5 Simulation results on tax system proposed by the Stevens Committee

Prices (percentage changes)[a]		*Ratios (absolute changes)*[a]	
Wage rate	–0.2	Unemployment rate	0.2
Production price	–0.2	Replacement ratio	–0.3
Consumption price	–0.1	Average tax rate	0.1
Volumes (percentage changes)[a]		Marginal tax rate	–2.0
Private consumption	0.1	Labour income share	0.1
Investment	0.2	Total taxes	–1.4
Exports	0.1	Social security premiums[b]	1.3
Imports	0.0	Public deficit[b]	–0.1
Private production	0.2	Current account[b]	–0.0
Private employment	0.2		
Labour supply persons	–0.7		
Labour supply hours	0.4		
– partners with children	–1.4		
– partners without children	6.9		

[a] Cumulated effects as differences between simulation and base projection.
[b] As a percentage of net national product.

and labour supply measured in persons fall for all types of households. Since partners with children work relatively few hours, they are also affected most by having to pay disability premiums in the new system and they benefit relatively less from the reduction in marginal tax rates. Thus for partners with children the increase in the number of hours worked due to lower marginal tax rates is not sufficient to offset the participation effect and labour supply measured in hours falls. In contrast, for partners without children the hours effect dominates the participation effect and labour supply measured in hours rises. On net, total labour supply measured in hours rises.

With respect to wage formation, the increase in labour supply outweighs the fall in the marginal tax and premium rate, leading to a small decrease in wages and consequently a slight increase in employment. Because the labour supply effect exceeds the employment effect, a 0.2 %-points rise in unemployment results. In conclusion, the proposals of the Committee are seen to raise the number of hours worked by partners without children, who already work a substantial number of hours, while participation of partners falls considerably and unemployment slightly rises.

In 1992 the Dutch Social Economic Council was asked by the government to advice on the proposed system (Social Economic Council, 1992). A majority of the Council rejected implementation because the small and sometimes even negative effects (the fall in participation and the increase of unemployment indicated by the simulation results from MIMIC) from the proposals did not outweigh the objections that could be raised against them. Objections primarily concern the cancelling of the deductibility of employee insurance premiums for national social insurance premiums and income taxes. For instance, this would generate a fiscally different treatment of persons insured by employee insurances and others who have to use private insurance. Since the cancelling of the deductibility of employee insurance premiums is the main source of finance for the proposed system, rejecting this element came down to rejecting the complete system.

10 Cutting back the welfare state

A recurring element in political discussions in the Netherlands is the high level of the ratio between the number of benefit recipients and the active working population. During the last thirty years this inactivity ratio has risen from 40% in 1960 to 86% in 1990. The rise in the inactivity ratio has partly been caused by an increase in the number of old-age pensions recipients, but for the other part by a sharp increase in the number of people in disability and unemployment schemes. A third factor that makes the number of benefit recipients relatively high compared to the active working population is the relatively low participation rate of women in the Netherlands. The latter component will be dealt with in Chapter 11.

The simulations in this chapter are directed at policy options to decrease the inactivity ratio by reducing the inflow in disability schemes and unemployment benefit schemes and at the same time stimulating the creation of jobs with a low productivity profile by lowering (official) minimum wages. In order to highlight the relevance of these policies given the international context, Section 10.1 first presents some statistical information on the public sector in the Netherlands in comparison with other countries. Section 10.2 up to and including 10.4 report the simulation results of various policy options. In Section 10.2 the effectivity of a reduction in (official) minimum wages is considered. Section 10.3 deals with reductions in unemployment benefits obtained from social security funds and in the social assistance benefits from the government. Section 10.4 considers the effects of a reduction in disability benefits on the inflow into disability schemes and the consequences for labour supply, collective burden and economic growth. Finally, in Section 10.5 the effects of the introduction of a kind of mini welfare system are investigated, which combines certain aspects of the policy measures of the three preceding sections.

10.1 International comparison of social security systems

Table 10.1 presents an overview of the share of the government sector in GDP in various countries. The share of social security transfers appears to be highest in the Netherlands and lowest in the United States. With respect to other current disbursements (like government investment, non-wage government consumption and the wage sum of government employees) the Netherlands takes an intermediate position. In this case Sweden has the highest figure, whereas again the United States has the lowest position. The relative positions are also reflected by the share of current receipts of the government with Sweden having the highest figure followed by Denmark and Norway and the United States having the lowest share of current government receipts in GDP. The fourth and fifth column present the average and marginal rate of income taxes and social premiums on labour income. For the Netherlands these two figures exceed those of Sweden. This is explained by the fact that in Sweden a larger share of government receipts are levied through consumption taxes instead of taxes on labour income.

Table 10.1 Government expenditures and receipts

	Social security transfers[a]	Other current disbursements government[a]	Current receipts of government[a]	Average tax rate average production worker[b]	Marginal tax rate average production worker[b]
Belgium	22.7	30.4	49.5	44	57
Denmark	18.4	38.1	56.1	47	58
France	21.4	24.8	46.5	46	53
Germany	15.3	27.3	43.4	46	58
Netherlands	26.3	25.4	49.5	51	65
Norway	19.0	31.9	54.9	-	-
Sweden	19.7	39.4	63.9	53	62
United Kingdom	12.2	25.9	40.0	34	40
United States	10.8	23.8	31.8	32	40

[a] as a percentage of GDP in 1990 (for Norway and the US in 1989); source: OECD (1992a).
[b] in 1989; source: Central Planning Bureau (1992b).

Table 10.2 shows that there are basically two causes for the relative high share of social security payments in the Netherlands. Firstly, the standardized unemployment rate is relatively high in the Netherlands. An explanation may be that the replacement ratio, here defined as the ratio between gross benefit and gross earnings of an average production worker, is on average relatively high. Secondly, the Netherlands has a very high number of disability benefit recipients. The size of disability expenditures as a percentage of GDP is almost twice that of the other European countries. Again, part of the explanation of this phenomenon may be that the disability benefit is relatively luxurious in the Netherlands in relation to the previous wage income of the disabled worker. Furthermore, it is noted that the minimum wage level is relatively high in the Netherlands. Only Denmark shows a higher figure. This may also help to explain the relative high unemployment rate for the Netherlands.

Table 10.3 presents some historical statistics with respect to the government sector and the social security system for the Netherlands. It appears that

Table 10.2 Social security, replacement ratio's and minimum wages

	Unemployment rate [a]	Replacement ratio unemployment benefits [b]	Disability expenditures as % of GDP [c]	Replacement ratio disability benefits [d]	Minimum wage as % of average wage cost[e]
Belgium	7.3	43	3.0	60	40.6
Denmark	-	55	2.7	57	54.8
France	8.9	49	2.3	31	36.0
Germany	4.9	49	3.5	31	48.0
Netherlands	7.5	60	6.0	70	52.5
Norway	5.2	43	-	-	-
Sweden	1.5	56	-	-	-
United Kingdom	6.8	31	2.3	35	40.1
United States	5.4	17	-	68	23.1

[a] Standardized rates in 1990; source: OECD (1992a).
[b] Average gross benefit as a percentage of gross 1988 average production worker's earnings; source: OECD (1991a).
[c] in 1988; source: Prins *et al.* (1992)
[d] in 1990; source: OECD (1992b)
[e] in 1990, except for UK; source: Central Planning Bureau

Table 10.3 Historical development of the government sector in the Netherlands[a]

	1960	1973	1982	1990
Social security outlays[b]	11.0	21.4	31.3	29.0
– old-age	6.0	9.0	10.9	10.0
– unemployment	0.3	0.9	4.0	2.6
– disability	1.4	2.8	5.7	5.2
– sickness payments	1.3	2.3	2.4	2.2
– other	2.0	6.3	8.3	8.9
Other government outlays[b]	25.0	26.1	32.7	30.2
Government receipts[b]	34.0	47.0	54.0	52.2
Marginal tax rate[c]	-	46	60	54
Replacement ratio[d]	-	68	75	69
Inactive/active working population	40	51	79	86
– old age	-	35	43	46
– sickness	-	6	6	7
– disability	-	6	15	17
– unemployment[e]	-	3	12	12
– social assistance[f]	-	2	3	4

[a] source: Central Planning Bureau (1992b).
[b] as a percentage of net national income.
[c] of median worker.
[d] ratio between net social assistance and net wage of median worker.
[e] number of recipients of unemployment benefit of social security fund.
[f] including unemployed workers receiving government assistance.

the rise in the share of social security payments started in the sixties and ended in the beginning of the eighties. During the eighties the trend was reversed somewhat, partly because of reductions in benefit levels and partly because of an increasing participation in early retirement schemes, but the absolute share of social insurance transfers remained very high. This is also reflected by the ratio between the inactive population receiving a benefit income and the active working population receiving a wage or other type of income. This ratio still shows an upward trend during the eighties. Furthermore, also the share of other government outlays has risen in the sixties and seventies, but less dramatically than the share of social insurance payments. Similar trends are reflected by the development of the share of government receipts and the average marginal tax rate.

Concluding, the Netherlands is characterized by a very high share of social insurance transfers because of a strong rise in the number of disability and unemployment benefit recipients over the last thirty years. Reasons behind this may be that benefit levels and minimum wage levels are relatively high for the Netherlands compared to other Western countries.

10.2 Minimum wages

Some policy makers in the Netherlands have recognized the fact that the relatively high level of the official minimum wage rate may have adverse effects on employment creation, notably for low-skilled workers. Therefore, various proposals have been made in the past to reduce the minimum wage, ranging from a 10% to a 30% reduction or a complete abolishment of legal minimum wages. This section provides an analysis of the possible influence of various types of minimum wage reduction. The simulation results are presented in Table 10.4 and Table 10.5.

Column one presents the simulation results of a decrease in the official minimum wage rate by 10%. This change has been implemented without a corresponding change in the level of unemployment benefits. As noted in Chapter 2 a fall in the official minimum wage rate only partially diminishes the minimum wage scales in collective agreements determined by unions and employers' organisations: in the exposed, sheltered and non-market sector minimum wage scales fall by only 2.5% whereas the minimum wage scale in the construction sector is even unaffected. This implies that the quantitative effects of the official minimum wage reduction are rather small.

Qualitatively, the reduction in the minimum wage decreases the minimum productivity standard used by employers to screen candidates for vacancies, especially for the low-skilled unemployed with a minimum productivity. As a result, the acceptance rate of employers increases for this group. The ratio between the number of matchings and vacancies increases. This reduces search costs for employers. In addition, the average productivity falls over time as less productive unemployed flow into employment. Together with the fall in the number of vacancies this induces a fall in the incidental wage

Table 10.4 Simulation results of minimum wage reduction: specific outcomes[a]

		reduction official minimum wage rate by 10%	reduction minimum wage scales by 10%	reduction minimum wage scales by 30%
Production and search strategy of firms				
Wage costs	minimum	−0.4	−1.0	−1.1
	other	−0.0	−0.0	0.0
Employment	minimum	1.8	5.1	6.1
	other	0.0	0.1	0.1
Acceptance rate	minimum	12.5	60.8	120.6
	other	0.4	1.2	2.0
Search strategy of unemployed				
Replacement ratio	minimum	0.9	2.6	3.0
	other	−0.1	−0.4	−0.5
Search intensity	minimum	0.1	0.1	0.2
	other	0.0	0.1	0.1
Acceptance rate	minimum	0.0	0.7	1.5
	other	0.1	0.3	0.4
Matching between unemployment and vacancies				
Unemployment[b]	minimum	−7	−21	−25
	other	0	−1	−2
Matchings/vacancies	minimum	7.1	19.9	23.6
	other	0.6	1.6	1.5
Acceptance rate	minimum	8.4	25.4	31.0
	other	0.2	0.7	1.1
Prod.index employees	minimum	−0.9	−2.7	−3.2
	other	−0.1	−0.2	−0.4
Collective wage formation				
Wage outcome		−0.1	−0.3	−0.4
Threat point wage firms		−0.3	−0.7	−0.9
Threat point wage employees		−0.0	−0.1	−0.2

[a] Cumulated percentage changes between simulation and base projection.
[b] Absolute change in thousands of labour years.

Table 10.5 Simulation results of minimum wage reduction: macro outcomes

	reduction official minimum wage rate by 10%	reduction minimum wage scales by 10%	reduction minimum wage scales by 30%
Prices		*percentage changes*[a]	
Wage rate	–0.2	–0.5	–0.6
Production price	–0.0	–0.0	–0.0
Export price	–0.0	–0.0	–0.0
Consumer price	–0.0	–0.0	–0.0
Volumes			
Private consumption	–0.1	–0.2	–0.3
Investments	–0.0	–0.1	–0.1
Exports	0.0	0.0	0.0
Imports	–0.0	–0.1	–0.2
Production	–0.0	–0.1	–0.1
Employment	0.1	0.4	0.5
– exposed	0.2	0.4	0.5
– sheltered	0.2	0.4	0.5
– construction	0.0	0.7	0.9
– non-market	0.1	0.3	0.4
Labour supply (hours)	0.0	0.0	0.0
Ratio's		*absolute changes*[a]	
Unemployment rate[b]	–0.1	–0.3	–0.4
Taxes	–0.0	–0.0	–0.0
Social premiums[b]	–0.0	–0.1	–0.1
Net replacement ratio	–0.1	–0.4	–0.6
Public deficit[b]	–0.1	–0.2	–0.2
Balance of payments[b]	0.0	0.1	0.1

Selected macro outcomes in case of balanced government budget through compensating changes in income tax rates

		percentage changes[a]	
Income tax rates[c]	–0.1	–0.3	–0.4
Wage rate	–0.2	–0.7	–0.8
Private consumption	0.0	0.1	0.1
Value added	0.0	0.1	0.1
Employment	0.2	0.7	0.8
Unemployment rate[c]	–0.1	–0.4	–0.6

[a] Cumulated difference between simulation and base projection.
[b] As a percentage of net national income.
[c] Absolute changes.

component of the low-skilled with a minimum productivity profile. The acceptance rate for the other types of unemployed with a relatively high productivity is hardly affected, because in the initial situation only a very small part of these unemployed were not accepted by employers because of too low productivity relative to the minimum wage rate (see the high acceptance rate for these groups in Chapter 2). For these groups the fall in search costs is therefore negligible and total wage costs per unit of output fall by less than for the low-skilled unemployed with a minimum productivity profile. This causes some substitution from high-skilled labour to low-skilled labour with minimum productivity. Unemployment of low-skilled workers with a minimum productivity falls by 7 thousand persons (1.1 %-points), raising their probability to find a job and stimulating their search intensity. Finally, the fall in search costs for labour also influences collective wage formation by lowering the threat point wage of the employers.

The upper part of Table 10.5 reports the macro economic consequences of these labour market effects. The fall in the average wage rate causes a rather small price reduction, because the decrease in wage costs is partly offset by the lower labour productivity of employees. As a result, the competitive position of Dutch industries hardly improves. Because of the lower spending power of employees, private consumption is reduced. The net effect on total production is slightly negative. However, because of the fall in the average labour productivity employment increases, except in the construction sector where the minimum wages scales are not lowered. The unemployment rate falls by 0.1 %-point. The average replacement ratio also falls slightly. Although the replacement ratio on micro level rises as shown by Table 10.4, the share of the minimum skilled unemployed with the highest replacement ratio in total unemployment falls and this dominates the change in the average replacement ratio. Because public wages are linked to private wages, public outlays fall. This is reflected by the 0.1% reduction in the public deficit. If this fall in the public deficit would be refunded to the private sector by lowering income tax rates, the output effect becomes slightly positive. This is illustrated in the lower part of Table 10.5, which summarizes the macro outcomes if the reduction in minimum wages is combined with a reduction in income tax rates in such a way, that ex-post the public deficit remains unchanged. Lowering the income tax rate partly stimulates wage moderation, which causes an additional fall in production prices. This strengthens the competitive position of Dutch companies, increasing exports. The fall in income tax rates also raises net income of households, which is reflected by the rise in private consumption.

The second column presents the simulation results in the case that minimum wage scales in all sectors would fully adapt to the 10% reduction in the official minimum wage. In that case the effects would be three to four times as strong, and the unemployment rate would fall by 0.3%. In column three a 30% reduction in minimum wage scales is simulated. This further enforces the effects presented in column one and two, but not proportionally. One reason for this non-linearity in simulation results is that the mass of the productivity distribution of the low income group lies between 90% and 120% of the minimum wage rate, which leaves only relatively few potential matches left below 90% of the minimum wage rate. A second explanation is that at lower levels of minimum wages unemployment benefits become more restrictive, thereby reducing the probability of a successful matching from the perspective of the unemployed. This can be seen from the rise in the replacement ratio of the low-skilled unemployed in Table 10.4. As a consequence the rise in the overall acceptance rate is much less than the rise in the acceptance rate from the perspective of the employer. A further reduction in minimum wages at a given level of unemployment benefits will therefore hardly contribute to a further improvement of the labour market situation. This is an illustration of the non-linearity of the simulation results, which is obtained if relative levels of labour market institutions change considerably.

The effects of minimum wage reduction on unemployment reported in Table 10.4 and Table 10.5 can be considered to be rather modest in light of microeconometric research for the Netherlands, that is based on the methodology followed by Meyer and Wise (1983). For example, Van Soest (1989) estimates that a 10% reduction in minimum wage scales leads to a reduction in unemployment of 160 thousand persons in 1984, which is about eight times as large as our result in the second column of Table 10.4. Using three alternative model specifications Van Soest and Kapteyn (1990) find that a 10% reduction in minimum wages causes a positive employment effect which varies between 113 thousand to 182 thousand persons. Finally, Van Opstal (1990) finds that a 10% reduction in minimum wage would reduce unemployment by about 100 thousand persons, whereas unemployment would fall by 230 thousand persons if minimum wage scales would be abolished.

The main explanation for the difference between these microeconometric results and our simulation results is that in the Meyer and Wise methodology the existence of minimum wages is the only possible reason for unemployment. In this type of model a fall in minimum wages below the productivity level of former unemployable workers reduces unemployment by assumption, without explaining why such a change would induce employers to demand more labour and apply these workers. Although the more recent microeconometric studies allow for the possibility that workers may be unemployed for other reasons than their productivity being too low in relation to the minimum wage, the implicit assumption is still present and is likely to generate a bias to large unemployment effects. The second explanation is that our model generates macro feedback effects that diminish the initial positive effects on employment and wages from a reduction in minimum wages. Firstly, the resulting fall in unemployment will induce higher wage claims by employees, which will reduce the fall in wages. Moreover, as more jobs with a low productivity profile are created, average labour productivity will fall, which reduces the potential for positive output effects. Thirdly, the increased willingness of employers to apply workers with a low productivity profile is frustrated by the supply side of the labour market if minimum wages become relatively low compared to reservation wages of the unemployed. A fourth explanation is that the microeconometric surveys relate to the labour market situation in 1985, in which overall unemployment was relatively high, whereas the simulation results refer to a long-term labour market situation (see Chapter 7). The relevance of the overall labour market situation on the micro estimates of minimum wage effects is also confirmed by Van Opstal (1990), who finds no effect at all at an unemployment rate of 5% (in 1979).

10.3 Unemployment benefits

In addition to the relative high level of minimum wages, the labour market in the Netherlands is also characterized by a rather generous unemployment benefit system compared to other countries. Short term unemployed entitled to social insurance receive a gross unemployment benefit which is equal to 70% of their former gross wage income. Because of the progressivity in the income tax system the ratio between the net unemployment benefit and net former wage is even higher. Long term unemployed whose right on unemployment insurance is exhausted receive government assistance which differs per type of household. Social assistance for unemployed breadwinners with a non-participating partner amounts to almost 100% of the net minimum wage, whereas social assistance for one parent families and single persons amounts to 90% respectively 70% of the net minimum wage. Partners in households in which the breadwinner earns wage or benefit income are not entitled to government assistance.

The simulation results of a reduction of unemployment benefits are presented in Table 10.6 and Table 10.7. Column one presents the simulation result of a decrease in the social assistance benefit of 10% for breadwinners, single parent households and single persons. The fall in the replacement ratio reduces the reservation wage of the unemployed and stimulates their search intensity. As a result their minimum productivity standard falls and this causes a rise in their acceptance rate. Note, however, that the macro acceptance rate rises by less, especially for the group with minimum productivity. This is explained by the fact that in the base path the level of the minimum wage rate is more restrictive than the level of social assistance for this group.

Notwithstanding the rise in the acceptance rate, the average vacancy duration and incidental wage components hardly change. The reason is that the reduction in social assistance benefits also decreases collective wage claims by weakening the threat point position of workers in wage bargaining. The decrease in collective wage rates raises labour demand for all types of labour, hence the number of vacancies increases which has a positive influence on vacancy duration. For high-skilled labour the latter effect dominates

Table 10.6 Simulation results of unemployment benefit reduction: specific outcomes[a]

		reduction of social assistance by 10%	reduction of unemployment insurance benefit by 10%
Production and search strategy of firms			
Wage costs	minimum	−1.7	−0.4
	other	−1.0	−0.2
Employment	minimum	2.6	0.5
	other	0.5	0.2
Acceptance rate	minimum	1.4	0.4
	other	0.2	0.0
Search strategy of unemployed			
Replacement ratio	minimum	−8.6	−1.3
	other	−7.4	−2.5
Search intensity	minimum	5.0	0.6
	other	1.8	0.5
Acceptance rate	minimum	40.2	3.1
	other	3.8	1.0
Matching between unemployment and vacancies			
Unemployment[b]	minimum	−10	−2
	other	−26	−6
Matchings/vacancies	minimum	3.9	−0.3
	other	−5.2	−1.9
Acceptance rate	minimum	6.4	0.6
	other	2.5	0.5
Prod.index employees	minimum	−0.7	−0.1
	other	−0.7	−0.1
Collective wage formation			
Wage outcome		−2.3	−0.5
Threat point wage firms		−1.5	−0.3
Threat point wage employees		−2.2	−0.4

[a] Cumulated percentage changes between simulation and base projection.
[b] Absolute change in thousands of labour years.

Table 10.7 Reduction of unemployment benefits: macro outcomes

	reduction of social assistance by 10%	reduction of unemployment insurance benefit by 10%
Prices	*percentage changes*[a]	
Wage rate	−1.9	−0.4
Production price	−0.8	−0.2
Export price	−0.4	−0.1
Consumer price	−0.5	−0.1
Volumes		
Private consumption	−1.4	−0.2
Investments	−0.3	−0.1
Exports	0.4	0.1
Imports	−0.9	−0.2
Production	−0.2	−0.0
Employment	0.8	0.2
– exposed	1.3	0.3
– sheltered	0.8	0.2
– construction	0.4	0.1
– non-market	0.2	0.1
Labour supply (hours)	0.1	0.0
Ratios	*absolute changes*[a]	
Unemployment rate	−0.6	−0.1
Taxes[b]	−0.0	0.0
Social premiums[b]	−0.3	−0.1
Net replacement ratio	−4.7	−1.1
Public deficit[b]	−1.1	−0.2
Balance of payments[b]	0.5	0.1
Selected macro outcomes in case of balanced government budget through compensating changes in income tax rates		
	percentage changes[a]	
Income tax rates[c]	−1.4	−0.2
Wage rate	−2.4	−0.5
Private consumption	0.1	0.0
Value added	0.5	0.1
Employment	1.6	0.3
Unemployment rate[c]	−0.9	−0.2

[a] Cumulated differences between simulation and base projection.
[b] As a percentage of net national income.
[c] Absolute changes.

so that vacancy duration increases for these groups. For low-skilled labour with minimum productivity the influence from the rise in the acceptance rate prevails, so for this group vacancy duration slightly falls. Furthermore, because of the influence of the replacement ratio on collective wage formation, the fall in wage rates is much more homogeneous for different types of labour than in the case of minimum wage reduction. The resulting rise in employment is therefore more evenly spread among high-skilled and low-skilled labour.

The macro consequences of the reduction in wages for economic growth are more favourable than in the case of a proportionate reduction in minimum wage scales (compare Table 10.7 and Table 10.5). This is partly explained by the fact that productivity of employees is less affected, hence production costs per unit fall much more than in the case of a reduction in minimum wages. As a result, production prices are substantially reduced, strengthening the competitiveness of Dutch industries on the goods market. Especially the exposed sector benefits from this increase in competitiveness, whereas employment in the non-market sector hardly increases.

Column two reports the simulation results of a reduction in the level of unemployment insurance benefits. Before considering the simulation results, we will first discuss a possible complication if unemployment insurance benefits would be reduced without changing the level of the social assistance. This complication arises from the existence of the Supplementary Benefits Act, which was established in 1987 with the purpose to provide any person with an income at least equal to the social minimum as defined by the Social Assistance Act. The social minimum of breadwinners is means-tested and so is the supplement. This implies that if unemployment insurance benefits would be reduced without changing the level of the social minimum, the net income of some breadwinners with a unemployment insurance benefit would fall below the social minimum. This would discourage labour supply by their partners, for in order to collect the supplement the partner will have to withdraw from the labour market. In order to prevent this kind of complications in the model simulation, the reduction in unemployment insurance benefit is simulated in a situation in which the level of social assistance has already been reduced by 10% (as in column one).

Column two shows that the effects are qualitatively more or less the same as those in column one, except that the reduction in government assistance especially affects the replacement ratio of low-skilled with a low productivity profile whereas unemployment insurance benefits are more relevant for unemployed with a higher type of education. The reason is that the duration of the benefit from the social security funds is limited, so after the unemployment benefit right is exhausted the unemployed become dependent on government assistance. Since the average unemployment duration of the low-skilled unemployed exceeds that of the high-skilled, the share of low-skilled unemployed people receiving government assistance is larger. The quantitative differences between columns one and two stem from the fact that the share of unemployed persons receiving government assistance is twice as large as the share of unemployed persons receiving an unemployment benefit from the social security fund. Moreover, as unemployed workers look forward over the time they expect to be still unemployed, some of them will expect to shift from a social insurance benefit to a government assistance benefit. This further increases the relative importance of social assistance over social insurance in the average reservation wage of the unemployed.

10.4 Disability benefits

The disability benefit system has become a matter of great concern to Dutch policy makers, because of the large increase in the number of people who are entitled to a disability benefit. Proposals to reduce the growth of disability benefits range from a more stringent acceptance policy to financial penalties for former employers of newly disabled people, and from financial bonuses for employers who employ a disabled person to cuts in benefit levels.

In this section we only consider the latter type of policy, because an assessment of the effectiveness of the other policies demands too specific information about the procedures followed during the screening of candidates applying for a disability benefit. Cuts in benefit levels can only be simulated after making some additional assumptions, since MIMIC contains no description of microeconomic reactions to changes in disability benefits. The first assumption, based on empirical research by Aarts and De Jong (1992), is that a one percent decrease in the ratio between net disability benefit and net wage income leads to a fall in the number of disabled people by two percent. Furthermore, it is assumed that those who are stimulated by the benefit reduction to stay working instead of entering the disability schemes have a relatively low productivity, which is half of that of the other employees. The reduction in the inflow into disability schemes as a result of a less generous benefit system is therefore combined with an autonomous fall in the labour productivity of the work force. A third crucial assumption is that the worsening of the disability benefit rights will be partly compensated by actions of unions and employers' organisations seeking to reinsure the loss in disability rights in new collective arrangements. In light of experiences with benefit reductions by the government in the early nineties, it is assumed that unions succeed in collectively repairing the former benefit levels for 75%.

As in Section 10.3 we abstract from possible complications in the simulation which arise from the Supplementary Benefits Act by using a base path in which the social minimum has been reduced by 10%. The simulation results are reported in Table 10.8 and represent the effects of a reduction in the average disability benefit by 2.5%. The reduction in the disability benefit causes a fall in the number of disabled people by 5%. Because of this reduced inflow into the disability schemes, labour supply increases. The increase in labour supply is enforced by the labour market reaction of partners of those breadwinners who remain dependent on the disability schemes. In order to compensate for the loss in income generated by the benefit reduction these partners increase their labour supply. The total labour supply effect induces wage moderation, which is enhanced by the fall in the rate of social security premiums being partly shifted forward into lower wage claims. Since both the level of the disability benefit and the number of benefit recipients fall, social premiums as a percentage of gross national product are reduced by 0.7 %-points. The reduction in wage costs raises employment and generates a fall in the equilibrium rate of unemployment. Since government outlays, like wages

Table 10.8 Simulation results of reduction in disability benefits by 2.5%

	percentage changes[a]		
Prices		*Volumes*	
Wage rate	−1.8	Consumption	0.3
Production price	−1.1	Exports	0.5
Export price	−0.5	Imports	−0.1
Consumption price	−0.7	Production	0.7
		Employment	1.3
		Labour supply (hours)	0.9
	absolute changes[a]		
Unemployment rate	−0.2	Taxes[c]	−0.3
Inactivity ratio[b]	−1.9	Social premiums[c]	−0.7
Current account[c]	0.0	Public outlays[c]	−0.9

[a] Cumulated effects as differences between simulation results and base projection after 25 periods. The reduction in disability benefit is combined with a reduction in the number of disability recipients by 5%, a fall in autonomous labour productivity in the enterprise sector of 0.37% and a reduction in income tax rates of the first, second and third tax bracket by 0.6% points each.

[b] Defined as the ratio between the number of persons receiving a benefit income and the number of persons receiving wage income.

[c] As a percentage of net national income.

of government employees and unemployment assistance, are linked to private wages and unemployment, the wage moderation also reduces government outlays. This enables a downward adjustment in the income tax rates of the first, second and third tax bracket by 0.6 %-points each. The tax reduction further enforces wage moderation through the forward shifting effect. Since prices are a mark-up over marginal costs, production prices decrease, although less than wages because of the autonomous fall in labour productivity which follows from the reduced outflow of relatively unproductive workers to disability schemes. The reduction in production prices improves the competitiveness of Dutch enterprises, hence exports and production increase. Because of the fall in labour productivity, employment increases by even more. As a result, unemployment falls by 0.2% of the working population and the ratio between inactive and active working population falls by 1.9 %-points.

10.5 Combined effects of reduction of labour market related social benefits and minimum wage

As already noted in the previous sections the social welfare system in the Netherlands is very interrelated. For example, the level of social assistance benefits is institutionally linked to the level of the net minimum wage. This so-called social minimum is again a reference minimum for general old age provisions, national insurance disability benefits and supplements granted by the government. The interrelationships make it very difficult to investigate the effects of separate reductions in one of the institutional arrangements without running into complex considerations with respect to other institutions. The discussion on the Supplementary Benefits Act in Section 10.3 and 10.4 may serve as an example. The main purpose of the previous sections was therefore to highlight the characteristics of the model in simulating the effects of these

Table 10.9 Combined simulation results of reduction in benefits and minimum wage by 10%

	percentage changes[a]		
Prices		*Volumes*	
Wage rate	–4.7	Consumption	0.3
Production price	–2.1	Exports	1.1
Export price	–1.0	Imports	–0.3
Consumption price	–1.3	Production	1.3
		Employment	3.4
		Labour supply (hours)	1.2
	absolute changes[a]		
Unemployment rate	–1.4	Taxes[c]	–1.2
Inactivity ratio[b]	–4.7	Social premiums[c]	–1.5
Current account[c]	0.1	Public outlays[c]	–2.7

[a] Cumulated effects as differences between simulation results and base projection after 25 periods. The simulation result combines a 10% reduction in the official minimum wage (column 1 in Table 10.5) with a 10% reduction in government unemployment assistance (column 1 in Table 10.7), unemployment insurance benefit (column 2 in Table 10.7) and 2,5% in disability benefits (Table 10.8) and a fall in the tax rates of the first, second and third tax bracket by 2.3 %-points each.

[b] Defined as the ratio between the number of persons receiving a benefit income and the number of persons receiving wage income.

[c] As a percentage of net national income.

Table 10.10 Average real disposable income effects for different types of households from overall reduction in benefits and minimum wage by 10%

	percentage changes		
Breadwinners		*Single persons*	
– working with children	1.0	– working	0.9
– working without children	1.0	– unemployment insurance	–7.9
– unemployment insurance	–7.1	– social assistance	–9.1
– social assistance	–8.7	– disability benefit	–1.6
– disability benefit	–1.6	*Aged persons*	–0.7

partial measures. In a more realistic policy approach, these partial measures should, however, ideally be combined in order to preserve the consistency of the total social welfare system.

For this purpose this section analyzes the consequences of an overall 10% reduction in social benefits related to unemployment and disability and in the official minimum wage. Like in Section 10.4 it is assumed that the loss in disability benefit is collectively reinsured for 75%, so that the effective reduction in disability benefit is only 2,5%. The old age provisions are excluded from the reduction in benefits. The simulation results are presented in Table 10.9 and Table 10.10. The effects of the overall reduction in social benefits and minimum wage are more or less equal to the sum of the separate simulation results, as presented in the first column in Table 10.5, columns one and two in Table 10.7 and Table 10.8. It appears that a reduction in the welfare arrangements along these lines will place the Netherlands in a position which is more in line with that in other European countries with respect to most of the indicators in Table 10.1 and Table 10.2. Social security transfers as a percentage of GDP will fall from 26 to 24,5 %-points, which still is substantially higher than in Germany, the UK and the US, but comparable to Belgium and France. Unemployment will be reduced from 7.5 to 6 %-points and reach an intermediate position. The share of disability expenditures falls from 6 to 5% of GDP, which is still relatively high compared to the other countries. This is explained by the fact that, even if reduced by 2,5%, the average replacement ratio for disability benefits remains rather high in the Netherlands compared to other countries. Total current government receipts will fall from 50 to 47% of GDP. The marginal tax rate is reduced from 65 to 62 %-points, which is still rather high. Only in Sweden the marginal tax rate is higher. Finally, labour supply by partners increases by 5% and also becomes more in line with that in other countries (compare Figure 1.2).

Finally, Table 10.10 shows the average real disposable income effects for different types of households. Clearly, the overall reduction in social benefits causes a larger dispersion in the income distribution by lowering the incomes of benefit recipients and raising the incomes of workers. At the same, it must be kept in mind that the number of people receiving a disability or unemployment benefit will be reduced by about 5 respectively 15%. For this group the improvement in income is substantial. Nevertheless, it is difficult to give an overall judgement on the desirability of the simulated mixture of policy measures, because this would necessitate interpersonal welfare comparisons or a social welfare function, which is not included in the model.

11 Individualizing the income tax and social security system

A topical theme in discussions about the social security and tax system is how it fits with the process of creating equal rights, opportunities, and responsibilities for men and women, which is a main target of government emancipation policy (FNV, 1990; Bruyn-Hundt and Gustafsson, 1991a; Grift *et al.*, 1991). A central concept in these discussions is 'individualizing'. Individualizing means assigning individuals rights and duties, which are irrespective of their living situation. Different degrees of individualisation are possible. In a fully individualized tax and social security system individual rights and duties are unrelated to whether the individual lives with a partner and to the income of this partner. In a less extreme individualized social security system, individual rights and duties may not be completely unrelated to the living situation of individuals. For example, because of economies of scale unemployment benefits of individuals who have a common housekeeping with other people may be lower than unemployment benefits of single-person households.

This chapter analyzes the economic consequences of individualisation of income taxes and the unemployment assistance benefit. The first section describes the present degree of individualisation in the Netherlands in relation to that in other OECD countries. Section 11.2 presents an analysis of the consequences of cancelling the marriage relief in the tax system on labour supply of partners in households and its macro-economic implications. Section 11.3 deals with the simulation results of an individualisation of the unemployment assistance system.

11.1 Marriage relief and unemployment benefits in the OECD

Table 11.1 presents an overview of the unit of taxation and the type of unemployment benefit system in the OECD countries. With respect to the tax system, five out of the 24 OECD countries use joint taxation in 1990, in four countries married taxpayers can choose between individual and joint taxation, and in fifteen countries the individual is the unit of taxation (OECD, 1991a). In a system of joint or family taxation, in which the income of spouses is aggregated before applying the tax schedule, labour supply of partners will be discouraged, because partner earnings are taxed by the marginal tax rate of the breadwinner. If the marginal tax rate of the breadwinner exceeds the marginal tax rate of the partner, individualisation will provide an incentive to switch earnings from breadwinner to partner. OECD (1990) presents some evidence on the positive influence of using individual marginal tax rates on female labour supply for data covering 1974-1978. However, labour supply of partners may also be discouraged in countries with individual taxation, since the tax systems of most of these countries are not fully individualized because of the existence of a marriage relief. The marriage relief consists of a tax allowance or a tax credit available to the breadwinner of a couple. Generally, this allowance or credit is lost or reduced if the partner receives an income. In some countries households with a partner earning an income above a certain threshold loose the complete credit or allowance, causing a drop of household income at the threshold income level and curbing labour supply of partners beyond this threshold income. In other countries the fall of net household income is mitigated because the partner is allowed to transfer the unused part

Table 11.1 Unit of taxation and type of unemployment benefit system in OECD

	Unit of taxation	Unemployment benefit		Unit of taxation	Unemployment benefit
Australia	Individual	Assistance	Japan	Individual	Insurance
Austria	Individual	Dual	Luxembourg	Joint	Insurance
Belgium	Individual	Insurance	Netherlands	Individual	Dual
Canada	Individual	Insurance	New Zealand	Individual	Assistance
Denmark	Individual	Insurance	Norway	Optional	Insurance
Finland	Individual	Dual	Portugal	Joint	Dual
France	Joint	Dual	Spain	Optional	Dual
Germany	Optional	Dual	Sweden	Individual	Dual
Greece	Individual	Dual	Switzerland	Joint	Insurance
Iceland	Individual	Insurance	Turkey	Individual	–
Ireland	Joint	Dual	United Kingdom	Individual	Dual
Italy	Individual	Insurance	United States	Optional	Insurance

Source: Unit of taxation OECD (1991a), Unemployment benefit OECD (1988)

of the allowance or credit to the breadwinner. This system is present in nine countries (OECD, 1991a). Yet, the existence of this type of marriage reliefs also discourages labour supply of partners by raising the marginal tax rate on partner income[69]. Only for three OECD countries (New Zealand, Sweden[70] and Turkey) the tax system may be labelled as fully individualized, since there is no marriage relief at all and the individual is taken as the tax unit.

Regarding the unemployment benefit system, many social security benefits have the character of an insurance and hence are on an individualistic or independent basis. An exception is the unemployment assistance benefit, which generally is means-tested. This means that the unemployment assistance benefit of a breadwinner is reduced by the income earned by the partner, which is equivalent to a 100% marginal tax rate on partner income. This disincentive aspect of unemployment benefits is a reason for participation rates of partners of unemployed breadwinners being lower than those of other partners (see the discussion and references in Atkinson and Micklewright, 1991). In 1987 unemployment benefits in ten OECD countries were based on an insurance type scheme, in two countries there existed an assistance type scheme and in eleven countries a dual system was in place consisting of a combination of unemployment insurance and unemployment assistance. Only in Sweden the unemployment assistance benefit is not means-tested and hence is completely individualized. However, in contrast to most of the other countries the benefit in Sweden is of limited duration. Moreover, it is supplemented by very active labour market policies. Persons not entitled to unemployment assistance can apply for social welfare aid, which is means-tested in Sweden (Björklund and Holmlund, 1991, Vijlbrief, 1992).

[69] In the United Kingdom a marriage allowance exists, which is, however, independent of income earned by the partner and hence does not influence partner labour supply.

[70] Information on the tax system in Sweden has been taken from Bruyn–Hundt and Gustafsson (1991b).

11.2 Individualizing the tax system by cancelling the marriage relief

In the current tax system in the Netherlands the complete basic allowance of the partner is transferred to the breadwinner if the partner earns less than the basic allowance. Hence, the income of the partner is subject to the tax and national social insurance premium rate from the first guilder earned onwards. The consequences of cancelling the transferability of allowances between spouses are presented by Figure 11.1, which visualizes the functioning of the model. The horizontal axis depicts the number of hours of leisure of a household, the vertical axis depicts net income. The line segment BE is the budget constraint of the household in the current tax system with marriage relief. Point B reflects net income received by a household with a non-participating partner because of the marriage relief, point E is the point on the budget curve at which taxable income of the partner equals the basic allowance. Because of the transferability of the allowance, the slope of the line segment BE equals the slope of the budget constraint to the left of point E, since in both cases partner income is taxed by the rate of the first tax bracket.

Figure 11.1 Labour supply effects of cancelling the transferability of the basic allowance between spouses

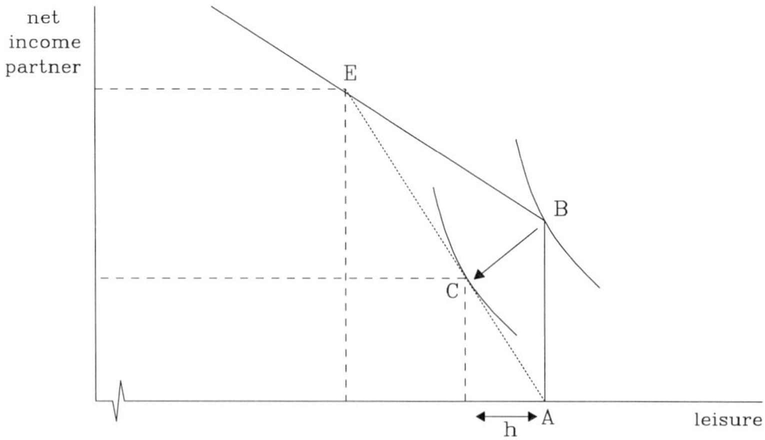

The curved line crossing point B is the indifference curve associated with the utility function of the household, representing the relative preference for leisure and consumption. Maximum utility is reached at the point of tangency of the indifference curve and the budget constraint. In the example of Figure 11.1, utility is maximized if the partner does not participate (point B) under the current tax system. Cancelling the transfer of the basic allowance shifts the budget constraint from the solid line segment BE to the dashed line segment AE with two consequences. Firstly, because partners now have their own zero tax bracket amount, incomes below the basic allowance are no longer subject to the tax and premium rate of the first tax bracket. Hence, for these incomes the marginal tax rate falls considerably, implying a higher marginal wage rate. This generates a positive substitution effect on labour supply of partners. Secondly, the rise in labour supply is strengthened by the loss of net income as a result of the cancelling of the transfer. For households with non-participating partners this is represented by the shift from point B to point A. Compensation for the loss of net income is a second incentive for partners to participate. As a result of these two effects the point of maximum utility shifts from a situation of non-participation in point B to participation in point C in Figure 11.1. However, the number of hours supplied by these partners is relatively small. Cancelling the transfer of the basic allowance only encourages labour supply for jobs with incomes below the income level associated with the basic allowance, which relates to jobs of maximum one day per week[71]. For partners who work a higher number of hours cancelling of the marriage relief does not change their options, since already in the present situation they are not entitled to transfer the basic allowance due to their high income.

Table 11.2 contains the simulation results of abolishing the transferability of the basic allowance. The first three columns differ from the other three columns in the way social assistance is dealt with. In the current social

[71] In the simulation it has been assumed that a sufficient number of jobs with a small number of labour hours will be created without additional costs. Obviously, the results will be different if employers face high costs of creating these jobs.

Table 11.2 Simulation results of abolishment of transfer of basic allowance

Social assistance benefit	decrease			no decrease[b]		
Budgetary neutral through		tax rate first bracket	family allowance		tax rate first bracket	family allowance
	(1)	(2)[c]	(3)[d]	(4)	(5)[e]	(6)[f]
Prices				*percentage changes*[a]		
Wage rate	−5.3	−6.0	−5.7	−0.6	−0.8	−0.4
– minimum low skilled	−5.5	−6.4	−6.1	5.1	4.8	5.3
– other low skilled	−5.2	−6.0	−5.7	−0.9	−1.2	−0.7
– high skilled	−5.4	−6.0	−5.7	−1.3	−1.5	−1.1
Production price	−3.7	−3.8	−3.6	−1.3	−1.4	−1.1
Consumption price	−2.3	−2.4	−2.3	−0.8	−0.9	−0.7
Volumes						
Private consumption	−1.6	1.1	1.0	0.0	0.4	0.3
Investment	0.5	1.2	1.1	0.5	0.6	0.5
Exports	1.8	1.9	1.8	0.6	0.7	0.5
Imports	−1.6	−0.3	−0.3	−0.2	0.0	0.0
Private production	1.3	2.6	2.4	0.7	0.9	0.7
Private employment	2.6	4.1	3.9	−0.1	0.2	−0.1
– minimum low skilled	4.7	7.8	7.4	−10.4	−10.0	−10.4
– other low skilled	3.7	6.1	5.8	0.7	1.2	0.7
– high skilled	2.1	3.1	3.0	0.8	1.0	0.8
Labour supply persons	7.2	7.0	7.0	7.2	7.2	7.2
Labour supply hours	1.7	2.2	2.1	1.1	1.2	1.1
Ratios				*absolute changes*[a]		
Unemployment rate	−0.5	−1.2	−1.1	1.1	1.0	1.1
– minimum low skilled	−1.7	−3.7	−3.5	9.2	9.0	9.2
– other low skilled	−1.1	−2.7	−2.6	1.0	0.7	1.0
– high skilled	−0.2	−0.5	−0.5	0.2	0.1	0.1
Inactivity ratio	−2.2	−4.0	−3.8	1.5	1.2	1.5
Replacement ratio	−4.1	−3.9	−3.9	0.5	0.6	0.6
Average tax rate	−1.0	−3.0	−2.8	0.4	0.1	0.4
Marginal tax rate	−1.1	−2.4	−2.2	−0.1	−0.3	−0.1
Total taxes[g]	0.2	−1.3	−1.1	0.4	0.2	0.4
Social sec. premiums[g]	−1.4	−1.8	−1.8	0.3	0.2	0.3
Public expenditures[g]	−3.2	−3.1	−2.9	0.4	0.4	0.7
Public deficit[g]	−2.0	0.0	0.0	−0.3	0.0	0.0
Current account[g]	0.9	0.1	0.1	0.1	0.0	0.0

[a] Cumulated effects as differences between simulation and base projection after 25 periods.
[b] Simulated by a compensating rise in the official minimum wage by 9%.
[c] Column 1 with a reduction of tax rate of first tax bracket by 3.3% points.
[d] Column 1 with an increase in family allowances by 24% and a reduction of tax rate of first tax bracket by 2.9% points.
[e] Column 4 with a reduction of tax rate of first tax bracket by 0.5% points.
[f] Column 4 with an increase in family allowances by 24% and no reduction of tax rate of first tax bracket.
[g] As a percentage of net national income.

security system net social assistance benefits for breadwinners, single parents and single persons and old age benefits are institutionally related to the net minimum wage of a household in which the partner does not participate on the labour market. Hence, cancelling the transferability of the basic allowance will strongly reduce the net social assistance benefit. In the context of the discussion on individualisation this may be an unintended aspect of abolishment of the marriage relief. Therefore, columns four to six present simulation results in case the gross official minimum wage is raised in such a way that the net minimum wage rate of a breadwinner with a non-participating partner is just compensated for the loss in income from the cancelling of the transferability of the basic allowance.

Column one presents the simulation results in case the abolishment of the transferability of the basic allowance is used for a reduction of the financial deficit of the government. As discussed above, cancelling the transferability stimulates labour supply of partners in small part-time jobs. Labour supply of partners measured in persons rises significantly causing an increase in total labour supply measured in persons by 7%. Because of their preference for small jobs, the rise in total labour supply measured in hours by 1.7% is much smaller. Higher labour supply generates a fall in wages. The wage reduction is enforced by the fall in the average replacement ratio which follows from the overall decrease in social assistance benefits. By consequence, prices fall and the competitiveness of the enterprises sector is strengthened as reflected by the rise in exports. The fall in real wages combined with the loss of net income of households with a non-participating partner and the reduction in social assistance for the unemployed and aged persons generates a fall in private consumption. On balance production rises by 1.3%. Employment rises even more, because lower wage costs induce substitution of capital by labour. As a result unemployment falls by 0.5 %-point. The fall in unemployment is concentrated within the group of low-skilled labour: because of the fall of their reservation wage they raise their acceptance rate reducing search costs for employers. Both because of the positive macro-economic consequences and because of the direct rise in income tax receipts due to the cancelling of the transfer of the basic allowance, the government budget deficit falls by 2.0% of net national income.

In the second column the government uses the additional tax receipts for an ex-post budgetary neutral lowering of the tax rate of the first tax bracket by 3.3 %-points. The tax reduction stimulates labour supply by raising the marginal net wage rate of partners. Note, however, that the participation rate does not increase, because, at an individualized basic allowance, the level of the tax rate of the first tax bracket is irrelevant for an partner considering labour market participation or not. Because breadwinners also profit from the reduction in the tax rate of the first bracket, the participation rate even falls a little bit because of the income effect. The most important change in simulation results follows from the forward shifting effects of the fall in the average tax rate on wages and from the rise in purchasing power of consumers with favourable consequences for both exports and private consumption. Hence, production and employment increase, resulting in an additional fall in unemployment.

In the third column part of the additional tax receipts from the abolishment of the transferability of the basic allowance is used for raising the level of family allowances. The purpose of this measure is to compensate households of which the partner can hardly be expected to actively participate on the labour market because of the responsibility for the care of children. For this purpose family allowances are raised by 24%. Under the condition of ex-post budgetary balance still a fall in the tax rate of the first bracket by 2.9 %-points can be obtained. Raising family allowances instead of reducing the tax rate lowers the increase in the number of hours supplied. This can be explained by the fact that a change in the level of family allowances generates additional income without changing the marginal wage rate. Hence, in contrast to a reduction of the first bracket tax rate, a rise in family allowances only causes negative income effects without compensating positive substitution effects. As a result of the weaker labour supply reaction the decrease in wages is also diminished with the well known consequences for production, employment and unemployment.

In columns four to six the gross minimum wage is raised by 9% in order to achieve income neutrality for people receiving social assistance from the government. Although this hardly changes the labour supply reactions of partners the impact on the other variables is considerable. Firstly, cancelling of the transferability of the basic allowance now slightly raises the replacement ratio which reduces the impulse to wage moderation. Moreover, the rise in the official gross minimum wage for 75% increases the minimum wage scales in collective agreements. This forces employers to reduce the inflow of workers with a minimum productivity, which raises the incidental wage component for this group and worsens their employment perspectives. At the macro level, the extra labour supply generated by the positive participation decision of partners is not fully absorbed in the pool of employed workers, hence unemployment rises. As a result, the macro-economic advantages of the cancelling of the transferability of the basic allowance largely melt away and this measure hardly yields any extra tax receipts for the government because of its unfavourable influence on unemployment. As a result, in this case the government can either reduce the tax rate of the first bracket or increase family allowances but there is no financial room to do both. This explains why the differences between the simulation results in columns four, five and six are much smaller than those between columns one, two and three.

Table 11.3 gives an overview of the consequences for average real disposable income of various types of households. If the net social assistance benefit is reduced along with the abolishment of the marriage relief and the government uses the budgetary surplus for lowering the tax rate of the first bracket (column two), then breadwinners and single people with social assistance benefits experience the greatest loss in real net income. Furthermore, aged persons receive less net income because old age benefits are also partly related to the social assistance benefit. Single persons with a wage income or unemployment or disability benefit experience the highest improvement in net income, because they obtain no income loss from the abolishment of the marriage relief, but profit relatively much from the fall in the first bracket tax rate because single persons have relatively low wages. On average breadwinners with children experience a smaller improvement in net real

Table 11.3 Average real net income effects from abolishment of transfer of basic allowance

Social assistance benefit	decrease			no decrease		
Budgetary neutral through		tax rate first bracket	family allowance		tax rate first bracket	family allowance
	(1)	(2)	(3)	(4)	(5)	(6)
	Percentage changes[a]					
Breadwinners						
–employed with children	–2.8	0.2	0.5	–2.3	–1.9	–1.6
–employed, no children	–2.0	1.1	0.7	–1.7	–1.2	–1.6
–unemployment insurance	–4.2	–0.4	–0.4	–3.0	–2.4	–2.4
–social assistance	–8.1	–4.6	–4.4	0.7	1.2	1.4
–disability benefit	–5.3	–1.5	–1.6	–2.1	–1.5	–1.7
Single persons						
–employed	–0.2	2.9	2.6	0.8	1.2	0.9
–unemployment insurance	–1.3	2.4	2.0	0.8	1.3	0.9
–social assistance	–8.4	–4.8	–5.2	0.7	1.3	0.8
–disability benefit	–0.9	2.7	2.3	3.3	3.9	3.4
Aged persons	–5.8	–3.1	–3.4	0.5	0.9	0.6

[a] Cumulated effects as differences between simulation and base projection after 25 periods.

income than breadwinners without children, because the participation rate of partners is larger for the latter group. If the family allowances are raised, the net income improvement is equal for these groups.

If the official minimum wage is raised in order to compensate households with minimum income or social assistance, the income consequences are quite different. Firstly, all those persons whose income is related to social assistance are better off. On the other hand, because the government cannot allow a large reduction in tax rate or rise in family allowances in this case, people with wage income or a benefit from the social insurance funds are worse off. Single persons still profit from the abolishment of the transferability of the basic allowance, but both breadwinners with children and breadwinners without children experience a fall in net real income.

11.3 Individualizing government assistance

In The Netherlands the unemployment benefit system has a dual character. During the first phase of unemployment, unemployed people receive an individual unemployment benefit from the social funds, which is independent of the income of other household members. The duration of this type of benefit depends on the number of years previously worked by the unemployed person. After this period, the unemployed person receives unemployment assistance from the government. Unemployment assistance is means-tested and is reduced proportionally if other persons in the household raise their income. For households consisting of two adults without any other sources of income, the current unemployment assistance amounts to 100% of the minimum wage rate, for single parents with children 90% of the minimum wage, and 70% for single persons.

Individualisation of the present unemployment assistance system is obtained by abolishing the means-test, so that unemployment assistance becomes independent of the income of other participants in the household and both breadwinner and partner are entitled to a social assistance benefit in case of unemployment. The direct consequence is that the potential number of assistance recipients rises strongly, since, in contrast to the current system, all non-participating partners can potentially apply for a benefit if they can convincingly declare themselves as searching for a job. The economic effects of such a change are uncertain and depend crucially on the number of partners who will be able to collect a benefit without effectively participating on the labour market. In order to highlight the risks involved by individualizing the unemployment assistance system in this way, we simulate two extreme cases, one in which improper use of government assistance can effectively be prohibited, and one in which improper use cannot be prevented and maximum improper use occurs. All simulations are made budgetary neutral for the government by implementing offsetting changes in non-wage government consumption and income tax rates in such a way that each compensates 50% of the change in budget deficit.

Individualizing unemployment assistance without improper use

Columns one and two of Table 11.4 present the simulation results of an individualisation of unemployment assistance if improper use can fully be prohibited. Two cases are simulated. In column one a uniform individualized unemployment assistance right is created, which is equal to 50% of the minimum wage rate. In this case households with two unemployed persons are in the same situation as under the current system since together they receive 100% of the minimum wage rate, but single persons are worse off because they also are entitled to a 50% benefit against 70% in the current system. In the second column an intermediate case is simulated in which the social assistance benefit for individuals with a common household equals 50% of the minimum wage and that of single persons 70%. The higher single person benefit level is motivated by single persons lacking economies of scale of a common housekeeping. Furthermore, it is assumed that in both cases the social minimum defined in the Supplementary Benefit Act is also reduced to 50% of the minimum wage. This implies that the number of supplement recipients will become nihil, so that the Supplementary Benefit Act can actually be abolished.

According to the simulation results in Table 11.4, establishing an independent unemployment assistance system under the assumption of no improper use at all increases labour supply. The rise in labour supply is mainly due to the participation rate of partners of unemployed breadwinners with an unemployment assistance benefit, which increases from 0% to about 80%. Because the unemployment assistance benefit of the breadwinner is no longer means-tested, the effective marginal tax rate of 100% on earnings of partners disappears, which stimulates labour supply of partners. This effect is strengthened by the large fall in the benefit of breadwinners which causes a positive income effect on labour supply.

In addition, there is a small positive labour supply effect from partners of breadwinners whose unemployment or disability benefit from the social security funds fell below the social minimum, and whose income was supplemented by the Supplementary Benefit Act. In the current situation this

Table 11.4 Simulation results of individualisation of social assistance benefit

	no improper use		maximum improper use	
	(1) [b]	(2) [c]	(3) [b]	(4) [c]
Prices		*percentage changes*[a]		
Wage rate	−3.6	−1.4	34.5	39.8
– minimum	−4.2	−1.9	33.5	39.0
– other low skilled	−3.7	−1.4	32.8	38.8
– high skilled	−3.5	−1.4	37.2	42.2
Production price	−1.7	−0.8	28.1	30.8
Consumption price	−1.0	−0.5	17.6	18.9
Volumes				
Private consumption	−0.5	0.1	−5.1	−3.9
Investment	0.3	0.3	−10.3	−11.1
Exports	0.9	0.4	−11.4	−12.5
Imports	−0.2	0.0	−0.6	−0.3
Private production	1.0	0.7	−16.0	−17.4
Private employment	2.3	1.1	−18.4	−20.8
– minimum	6.4	3.0	−20.4	−24.9
– other low skilled	4.0	1.7	−20.7	−25.2
– high skilled	1.5	0.8	−17.6	−19.3
Labour supply persons	0.7	0.7	−24.7	−24.7
Labour supply hours	0.8	0.6	−14.4	−14.5
Ratios		*absolute changes*[a]		
Unemployment rate	−1.1	−0.3	1.4	3.5
– minimum	−4.0	−1.5	3.4	7.7
– other low skilled	−2.4	−0.6	4.1	8.8
– high skilled	−0.5	−0.2	0.6	1.9
Inactivity ratio	−1.5	0.4	74.6	81.6
Replacement ratio	−9.9	−1.9	−10.2	−0.6
Average tax rate	−1.4	−0.5	11.4	12.3
Marginal tax rate	−1.4	−0.5	11.9	12.8
Total taxes[d]	−0.6	−0.2	5.3	5.7
Social sec. premiums[d]	−0.9	−0.4	4.1	5.3
Public expenditures[d]	−1.5	−0.6	9.1	10.9
Public deficit[d]	0.0	0.0	−0.1	0.1
Current account[d]	0.2	0.0	0.4	0.3

[a] Cumulated effects as differences between simulation and base projection after 25 periods. The base projection refers in this case to the simulation in column (1) in Table 11.2 in which the transferability of the basic allowance is abolished.

[b] Unemployment assistance is set equal to 50% of net minimum wage for all types of recipients. In order to achieve ex-post budget-neutrality non-wage government consumption is raised by 8% in column (1) and reduced by 59% in column (3), whereas the tax rates of all tax brackets are lowered by 1.2% points in column (1) and raised by 10% points in column (3).

[c] Unemployment assistance is set equal to 50% of net minimum wage for persons in families (maintaining the 70%-benefit for single persons). Non-wage government consumption is raised by 5% in column (2) and reduced by 88% in column (4), whereas the tax rates of all tax brackets are lowered by 0.3% points in column (2) and raised by 10.4% points in column (4).

[d] As a percentage of net national product.

supplement is also subject to the means-test, so that partners of breadwinners with a supplement also face a 100% marginal rate on income and refrain from participation. According to Smit *et al.* (1991) some 14 thousand breadwinners with an unemployment insurance benefit and some 65 thousand breadwinners with an disability insurance benefit received an income supplement. As the Supplementary Benefit Act is not included in the model, it is assumed that abolishment of the Supplementary Benefit Act causes the participation rate of partners of this group to become equal to that of partners of breadwinners with no supplement in the present situation, which is about 50%. This enforces the positive labour supply reaction of partners of breadwinners with social assistance.

The labour supply effects of the two simulations in column one and two of Table 11.4 hardly differ, because the level of the unemployment assistance benefit hardly influences the labour supply reaction of partners, if improper use is completely absent. The two simulations do differ with respect to the other macro-economic variables. If social assistance is set at an uniform level of 50% of the minimum wage, the average replacement ratio exhibits a larger fall because of the reduction in benefits for single persons. This induces more wage moderation improving competitiveness of Dutch firms and leading to higher production and employment and lower unemployment. Therefore, the unemployment insurance premium rate can be reduced. This lowers the weighted tax and premium rate on income, which further decreases wages.

Individualizing unemployment assistance with maximum improper use

In the third and fourth column of Table 11.4 the consequences of individualizing the unemployment assistance benefit are computed again, but now under the assumption of maximum improper use of the benefit, so that everybody who does not work applies for the benefit. Although this is a rather extreme situation, it is not entirely unrealistic since in the current situation of high unemployment in the Netherlands it is already difficult to control for effective search behaviour of the present assistance recipients. If all partners also become entitled to an unemployment assistance benefit during unemployment, this problem is aggravated. This could lead to a situation in which it would be relatively simple to obtain an unemployment assistance benefit without effectively searching for a job. If such a situation lasts for some time it may also affect the moral of partners working a limited number of hours, because their income is not much higher or even less than that of unemployed people. This will induce withdrawal of partners from the labour market, who will all apply for the unemployment assistance benefit. This is illustrated in Figure 11.2. Starting-point is the case of the previous section, *viz.* without transfer of the basic allowance, represented by the kinked budget constraint running through points A, C, E and F. Establishing a benefit shifts the part of the budget constraint running through points A, C and E to the dashed line segment DE. Point D represents the case of a household with a non-participating partner receiving the benefit. A partner who selected point C previous to the individualisation of the unemployment assistance system, will now earn an income below the net benefit and therefore will choose not to participate effectively any longer. Moreover, also those partners who earned a net income just exceeding the benefit, will stop working, because the difference between net income and net benefit does not offset the loss of leisure. Thus

Figure 11.2 Labour supply effects of individualizing unemployment insurance with maximum improper use.

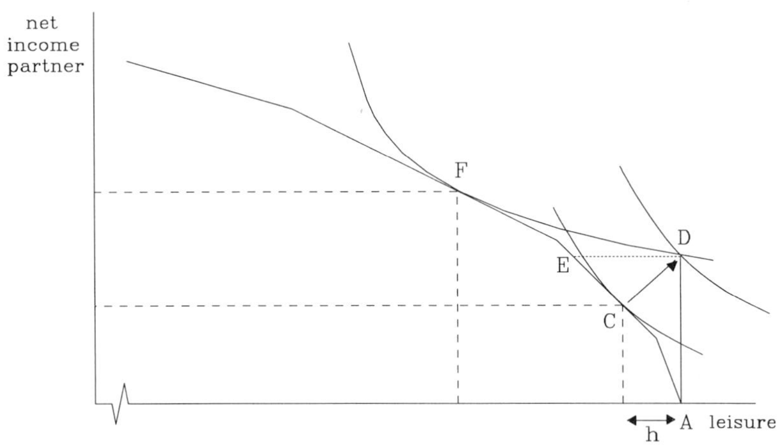

all partners with indifference curves tangent to the budget constraint to the right of point F will withdraw from the labour market. The household with indifference curve crossing point D and tangent in point F will be indifferent between participation and applying for the benefit. Partners with points of tangency to the left of point F will not withdraw, since these households have such a high relative preference for consumption that they prefer a relatively high income above the combination of the benefit and more leisure.

Columns three and four of Table 11.4 indicate that with maximum improper use the picture changes dramatically compared to columns one and two respectively. Three out of every four partners withdraw from the labour market, because the utility of extra income from working falls short of the utility of leisure combined with the benefit received in case they do not work. Because only partners supplying a relatively high number of hours still decide to participate, the effect on labour supply measured in hours is less than the participation effect. Nevertheless, total (macro) labour supply measured in hours falls by about 15%, which generates a large increase in wages with negative consequences for the competitive position of the Dutch economy. Because the unemployment assistance benefit is assumed to be indexed to the wage rate, the benefit level rises with the wage increase, which enforces the negative effects on labour supply. The increase of social assistance benefits for partners must be financed by higher taxes, which manifests itself in a strong increase in marginal and average tax and premium rates. This tendency is enforced by the fact that jobs with a small number of working hours and thus with low marginal and average tax and premium rates vanish and social security premium rates have to be financed by a smaller number of people. This causes a further rise in wages through the forward shifting effect.

Comparing the simulation results in column three with those in column one it follows that in the first case employment falls by 18.5% whereas in the latter case it increases by 2.3%. Although it is very hard to make a final probability judgement on the two cases, the wide range in these outcomes makes clear that the degree of uncertainty in assessing the economic effects of individualisation of social assistance is very large. In any way, the simulation results allow the conclusion that individualisation of social assistance yields unfavourable macroeconomic results if more than about one in eight partners collects social assistance benefits on improper grounds.

12 Introduction of a negative income tax

From the discussion in Chapter 11 it appears that individualisation of the unemployment benefit system entails considerable risks because of possible improper use of the legal right on government assistance. An alternative way of individualizing the social security system without running into this kind of controlling problems is the replacement of current social benefits by a negative income tax, which is independent of marital status and income earned from other sources.

The idea of a negative income tax is not new. On the contrary, it has been under discussion in many appearances for centuries. In 1517, Thomas More already stated that every individual should receive sufficient income to survive. At the end of the eighteenth century, the enlightened rationalist Thomas Paine shaped this idea by suggesting that every citizen should be entitled to a certain income financed by ground rents. The proposals become less utopian and more economically minded in the twentieth century. Although being present in the thirties and fifties in the United States and England, respectively, the discussion strongly revives in the 1960's in the United States, with the ideas of Theobald, Tobin and Friedman proposing a negative income tax. In the 1970's, Friedman's idea gets a hearing in The Netherlands. Here, advocates and opponents of the concept of a negative income tax can be found at both sides of the political spectrum. In 1985, the Scientific Council for Government Policies (WRR, 1985) proposes a partial negative income tax of 5000 guilders a year while maintaining the social security system, except for the minimum wage regulation. However, the Dutch government judges the proposal negatively by pointing at the extra costs and international risks it is likely to involve. More recently, the publication of the long-term scenario study by the Dutch Central Planning Bureau (1992b) breathes new life into the discussion in the summer of 1992. In one of the three scenarios outlined in the report a negative income tax is introduced as an alternative form of income maintenance.

This chapter presents an elaborate analysis of the economic effects of the introduction of a negative income tax. In the following section the chapter starts with a short overview of the pros and cons of a negative income tax found in the literature. Section 12.2 discusses the main results from the NIT experiments in the USA.[72] In Sections 12.3 and 12.4 the simulation results of MIMIC are presented. As an introduction, Section 12.3 describes the effects of a small negative income tax in the context of the present social security system. Section 12.4 deals with a negative income tax in the context of a mini welfare state, in which it serves as an alternative for the whole current social security system. In this context, the negative income tax is set equal to 50% of the net minimum wage. This would entail a strong reduction in net income for various types of benefit recipients. Such a strong reduction in benefit levels might induce reactions of unions seeking to reinsure the risks involved for individual employees with respect to loss in income due to unemployment or disability. Based on experiences the degree of reinsurance of the risks involved with loss in income as a result of disability or unemployment is assumed to be 75%.

12.1 Possible advantages and disadvantages of a negative income tax

Introduction of a negative income tax paid unconditionally to all individuals without means-test, work requirement or marital status is sometimes described in committed literature as the last step in the development of social security from depending on charity or favouritism, via a "claused right" depending on the willingness to work, to an "unclaused" or civil right (De Beer, 1987). Moreover, a negative income tax is suggested to put the current unequal recognition of various kinds of work to an end. According to these views, voluntary workers and housewives among others should have the same right to receive a reasonable income as any other individual working on a paid basis. Although it is beyond the scope of this chapter to go further into these matters, it must be realized that an enormous amount of socio-culturally as well as politically committed literature exists on the phenomenon of a

[72] Sections 12.1 to 12.3 are extracted from the doctoral thesis of N.E.M. de Jager (1993).

negative income tax. Here we concentrate on this issue from an economic point of view.

With respect to the pros and cons of a negative income tax, several advantages can be distinguished. Firstly, the introduction of a negative income tax might improve the operation of the labour market, since it will allow a substantial reduction in the official minimum wage. This would enable employers to create low productivity jobs for workers with a low productivity profile, thereby reducing the high level of unemployment among this type of workers. Especially small scale industry is likely to flourish as small businesses will become profitable at an earlier stage. In addition, the number of small businesses may also rise because potential entrepreneurs and their families are assured of income during the introductory and most uncertain period of their businesses (Nooteboom, 1987). This will encourage them to go into business. Both tendencies will result in decreasing economies of scale.

A second advantage of the introduction of a negative income tax concerns possible improvements in the social security system. The system will become more transparent and more easily manageable since a considerable part of the present social benefits and bureaucracy will be made idle. At the same time, all constraints and obligations imposed on people receiving social assistance will be abrogated so that less inspection is required. Moreover, a negative income tax is thought to diminish competition on an unfair basis by entrepreneurs in the informal sector who make use of people receiving social assistance to lower the labour costs bill, because every individual is free to work while maintaining social assistance. This might make jobs in the informal sector less attractive.

Additionally, women could benefit from the acquired right for they become economically independent from their partners. Especially women who are willing to work but discouraged to do so under the current social security and tax system will likely benefit from it, like partners of unemployed who presently face a 100 percent marginal tax rate. A negative income tax might therefore be advocated on emancipatory grounds (De Beer, 1987; Paulus, 1991). However, this argument is subject to criticism as can be seen below.

Furthermore, it is found in literature (Werkplaats Basisinkomen, 1989) that a negative income tax might stimulate part-time working by diminishing the financial necessity to work a full working week. This might alleviate the unemployment problem as employment may be spread over more people.

Finally, advocates indicate the likeliness of positive effects on the international competitiveness of domestic enterprises as a consequence of more favourable price-fixing through a reduction of wages. When a negative income tax is introduced, the level of gross wages and social assistance benefits can be lower, which decreases labour costs and limits the increase in the collective burden. For these reasons, it can be expected that prices decline and labour demand rises, especially in labour-intensive enterprises (Emmerij, 1985).

The argument most commonly put forward by opponents of a basic subsidy regards the operation of the labour market. They argue that a (partial) disconnection between labour and earnings will reduce the financial incentive to engage in paid regular work. This is argued to affect labour supply negatively in a number of ways.

Firstly, according to the opponents, labour participation of women will stay behind thereby consolidating the existing role patterns between men and women. They argue that a negative income tax will function as a "domestic wage" which women will be satisfied with. The opponents therefore contradict the emancipatory argument mentioned above (see De Beer, 1987). Secondly, the financing of a negative income tax will probably increase taxes which reduces the net wage rate. This could result in a reduction of hours supplied by the individuals working for pay at the present. Moreover, the increase in the marginal tax rate might lead to a flourishing informal sector. In the third place, adolescents might not be induced to strive for good education, which will cause them to be trapped in a dead-end situation at a later stage. Finally, the negative income tax will cause the effort of searching for legally paid work by unemployed to diminish. According to some opponents, this alternative system of income maintenance could therefore entail the danger of leaving a considerable part of low-paid, unattractive jobs vacant (see De Beer, 1987).

The discussion above clarifies that the labour supply reactions induced by the negative income tax play a crucial role in the evaluation of its effects. This was also the central theme of the NIT experiments in the USA. It therefore lies within the scope of this chapter to discuss the findings of empirical tests with a negative income tax in the United States in Section 12.2 before considering the simulation results of MIMIC in Section 12.3 and 12.4.

12.2 Results of NIT experiments in the USA

In the early sixties much interest aroused in the United States regarding the introduction of a negative income tax (NIT) as an alternative scheme of income support to alleviate the existing poverty. The idea behind the negative income tax scheme is the following: income is supplemented whenever it falls below a certain break-even level, with the subsidy increasing to a certain guarantee level when income approaches zero. In case income exceeds the break-even level, no subsidy is received. It therefore represents a means-tested negative income tax: unconditionally in terms of working status and conditionally in terms of income proceeds.

Theoretically, the introduction of a NIT boils down to reducing the net wage rate and simultaneously raising exogenous income for persons whose earnings initially are below the break-even level. The income effect influences hours worked negatively: the individual can "afford" to spend more time on leisure. Moreover, labour supply falls on account of the substitution effect: the tax liability accompanying the income subsidy causes the "opportunity costs" of an hour of leisure to decrease. In addition, some individuals whose income is above the critical income level might also reduce their work effort and hence, their income, to such an extent as to benefit from the NIT scheme.

Prediction of the magnitude of the effects by means of an estimated labour supply function based on non-experimental data provides no unambiguous quantitative judgement. To illustrate, Cain and Watts (1973) estimated that a NIT with a guarantee level of the poverty line and a tax rate of 50 percent would have negative effects on male labour supply ranging from 0 to 53 percent and on female labour supply ranging from 11 to 100 percent.

As a consequence of this unreliable and imprecise knowledge regarding the magnitude of work responses to non-work conditioned income receipts, the United States federal government sponsored four negative income tax experiments between 1968 and 1982. The experiments would make it possible for welfare program designers to gauge the actual costs of such a program once the eligible population adjusts its behaviour. The following briefly describes the characteristics of the experiments and the labour supply reactions.

Description of the four NIT experiments

The four experiments were conducted at diverse sites across the country, with three of them set in urban areas and one in the rural areas of North Carolina and Iowa. Most of the experiments enroled individuals of all racial groups, although the Gary experiment only focused on blacks. Table 12.1 describes the main characteristics of the four experiments.

The New Jersey-Pennsylvania Experiment only enroled husband-wife families for a period of three years. The families were assigned to eight different treatments, with guarantee levels ranging from 50 to 125 percent of the poverty level, and constant tax rates ranging from 30 to 70 percent.

The Rural Experiment focused on non-urban regions and enroled the smallest amount of families. Its results were therefore characterized by a lack of precision (Robins, 1985).

The Gary Experiment only focused on the black population in that region and had a significant number of female-headed families. Moreover, it tested four designs of NIT schemes which were different from the New Jersey and Rural Experiments with regard to the tax rates. The guarantee levels in this experiment amounted to 75 and 100 percent of the poverty income, respectively.

Finally, the Seattle-Denver Experiment was the last and largest of the four NIT experiments. As Robins (1985) states, this experiment differed from the other experiments in a number of respects. Firstly, this experiment enroled the largest number of families (4779) enabling more precise estimates of changes in work effort. Secondly, the guarantee levels were more generous than the

Table 12.1 Characteristics of the NIT experiments

Experiment	Period	Population enroled	Number of families	NIT Plans Tested: G [a]	NIT Plans Tested: tax rate [b]
New Jersey-Pennsylvania	1968-1972	All races, husband-wife families	1357	.50	.30; .50
				.75	.30; .50; .70
				1.00	.50; .70
				1.25	.50
Rural (North Carolina-Iowa)	1970-1972	All races, husband-wife and female-headed families	809	.50	.50
				.75	.30; .50; .70
				1.00	.50
Gary	1971-1974	Black husband-wife and female-headed families	1800	.75	.40; .60
				1.00	.40; .60
Seattle-Denver	1971-1982	All races, husband-wife and female-headed families	4779	.90	.50; .70
					.70 – .025Y
					.80 – .025Y
				1.20	.50; .70
					.70 – .025Y
					.80 – .025Y
				1.30	.50; .70
					.80 – .025Y

[a] G denotes the guarantee level and is measured as a percentage of the poverty level for a family of four in the year of enrolment, which is equal to $10,610 in 1984.
[b] Y is annual income in thousands of U.S. dollars.

Source: Moffitt and Kehrer (1981).

other three experiments with the most generous treatment amounting to 130% of the poverty level. In the third place, the Seattle-Denver Experiment was the only experiment testing treatments of differing lengths (3, 5 and 20 years) and non-constant tax rates.

Although considerable differences existed among the four experiments, they were alike in the fact that they all generally used classical experimental methods. With respect to the NIT-testing, this implies that families belonging to a selected sample of low-income population were randomly assigned to an experimental group and to a statistical control group. Families of the experimental group received NIT support whereas the families of the control group did not. The effect of the NIT was measured by the difference in labour supply of the two groups[73].

The results of the experiments

Very comprehensive surveys of the labour supply results from the NIT experiments are provided by Moffitt and Kehrer (1981), Killingsworth (1983) and Keeley (1981). However, these studies do not provide the reader with a general sense of what was found, in the form of a consensus set of estimates. It was Robins (1985) who presented average labour supply effects together with average structural estimates regarding substitution and income effects.

As the average overall labour supply response is concerned, Table 12.2 presents the main findings. Since the relatively beneficent Seattle-Denver Experiment has a heavy weight in the calculation of the results, these may be viewed as responses to a fairly generous NIT program: averaged across all programs, the weighted average guarantee level is about equal to the poverty level and the weighted average tax rate roughly equals 50 percent. As can be concluded from this table, husbands on average reduced their annual labour

Table 12.2 Average labour supply responses from all experiments with an average guarantee level of 10,610 dollar for a family of four in 1984

Annual hours of work [a]	Absolute change	Percentage change [b]
Husbands	−89	−5
Wives	−117	−21.1
Single female heads	−123	−13.2
Youth	−173	−22.2

[a] Estimates are a weighted average of the total sample results (see Robins, 1985), where the weights are the number of families enroled in each experiment.
[b] Using a weighted average of control group means.

Source: Robins (1985).

73 Among others, Moffitt and Kehrer (1981) indicate that "This design .. attempts to eliminate the bias caused by unobserved variables, for the randomization .. presumably results in identical distributions of unobserved variables within each group".

supply by about the equivalent of two weeks of full-time employment. Wives and single female heads reduced their annual labour supply by about three weeks of full-time employment. Finally, labour supply of youth fell to the largest extent, by about four full-time weeks per year. Considered that women and youth work fewer hours per year than do husbands, their labour supply responses are correspondingly much larger in percentage terms: whereas annual labour supply of husbands declined by 5 percent, labour supply of married women and youth declined by 21.1 and 22.2 percent, respectively. When measuring in hours of work, single female heads reduced their yearly labour supply more than wives, however, this decline corresponds to a much lower figure when measured in percentages.

12.3 The effects of a negative income tax in MIMIC

The fundamental idea of a negative income tax is that every individual from a certain age, whether or not working for pay, is secured of a certain level of income by the government. The negative income tax is implemented by granting a basic income to all individuals in society. As a consequence, non-labour income rises, which, *ceteris paribus*, will result in a reduction of labour supply by reason of the income effect: at any level of income the individual is better off, so that he can "afford" to devote more time to leisure. This is shown in part (a) of Figure 12.1. A negative income tax of *tv* is introduced at the entire income range. The "pure" income effect which by definition is negative, causes utility to rise and labour supply to fall, as can be seen from the movement from point *Q* to *R*.

When explicitly taking the government's need to cover the costs of the income transfers into consideration, income taxes will probably be raised, which will cause the net wage to decline. This is shown in Part (b) of Figure 12.1. The relevant budget curve becomes *tvf'*. Individual *A* whose income is relatively high, will be worse off since his utility falls, whereas individual *B* will profit from the introduction of the negative income tax. Individual *A*'s labour supply increases whereas *B* will work less. The labour

Figure 12.1 Labour supply responses to a negative income tax

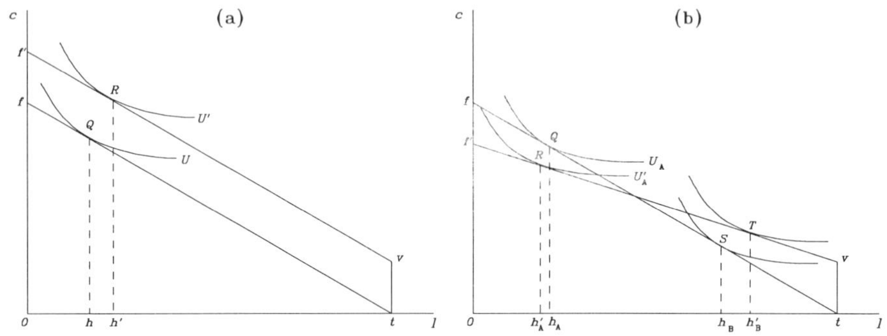

supply effect of the introduction of a negative income tax financed by a higher income tax rate is therefore indeterminate of sign: the income effect of the net wage fall causes labour supply to rise, whereas the substitution effect results in additional negative labour supply effects. It is not known beforehand whether the effect of the rise of non-labour income will dominate the effect on account of the net wage fall.

A negative income tax of 5% of net minimum wage

Before analyzing the more complex case of an introduction of a negative income tax in the context of a mini welfare state, this section presents the simulation results of a more simple variant of a negative income tax of 5 percent of the net minimum wage[74] in the context of an unchanged social security system in order to clarify the economic effects of a negative income tax sec. Except for students and children, it is assumed that all individuals in Dutch society benefit from the negative income tax in addition to their income proceeds. The negative income tax is linked to the net minimum

[74] In 1992, the net minimum wage approximately amounted to *f* 22000 a year, so that the negative income tax in this year would amount to *f* 1100 or alternatively about *f* 90 a month.

Table 12.3 Simulation results of introducing a negative income tax of 5% of the net minimum wage

	no budget neutrality	budget neutrality
Prices	*percentage changes*[a]	
Wage rate	2.3	3.3
– minimum	2.0	3.3
– other low skilled	1.9	3.2
– high skilled	2.6	3.5
Production price	2.4	2.3
Consumption price	1.5	1.5
Volumes		
Private consumption	3.7	–0.9
Investment	0.3	–0.9
Exports	–0.9	–1.1
Imports	2.3	0.1
Private production	0.4	–1.6
Private employment	0.0	–2.3
– minimum	1.6	–3.2
– other low skilled	1.0	–2.8
– high skilled	–0.4	–2.1
Labour supply persons	–0.2	0.1
Labour supply hours	–0.8	–1.5
Ratios	*absolute changes*[a]	
Unemployment rate	–0.8	0.4
– minimum	–2.0	1.3
– other low skilled	–1.8	1.0
– high skilled	–0.4	0.2
Inactivity ratio	–0.9	2.1
Replacement ratio	1.9	2.2
Average tax and social premiums rate[b]	–2.0	1.5
Marginal tax and social premiums rate[b]	0.0	3.8
Total taxes[c]	–0.8	1.6
Social sec. premiums[c]	–0.4	0.3
Public expenditures[c]	2.1	1.9
Public deficit[c]	3.4	0.0
Current account[c]	–1.3	0.1

[a] Cumulated effects as differences between simulation and base projection after 25 periods.
[b] Defined as (collective burden-negative income tax) / labour income.
[c] As a percentage of net national income.

wage. The latter implies that the negative income tax responds to changes in the private wage and income tax. The simulation is run on a base path in which the transferability of the basic allowance is cancelled.

According to the first column of Table 12.3, introducing an unconditioned negative income tax decreases labour supply measured in persons as well as in labour years. Evidently, the negative income tax, in the absence of compensatory measures, entails merely an income effect which accounts for the fall in labour supply. Labour supply measured in labour years falls more than labour supply measured in persons. This can be explained by the fact that since the tax system is individualized, the partner has an own basic allowance below which income is exempted from taxation. Hence, for this income range the marginal wage rate of partners is relatively high, which makes small jobs very attractive. By consequence, labour supply will not fall substantially in this range despite the increased earnings on account of the negative income tax. In comparison, outside this range the marginal return of working an additional hour is relatively lower as a consequence of taxes due, so that there the negative income effect entailed by the negative income tax causes the number of hours supplied to fall.

The fall in labour supply, *ceteris paribus*, tightens the labour market and exerts an upward pressure on wages. In addition, this upward wage pressure is reinforced by the rise in the net replacement ratio: since initially the net replacement ratio is smaller than unity, the replacement ratio rises as a consequence of the increased income receipts for unemployed, despite the fact that the denominator, the net average wage of employed, increases as well through the negative income tax. The higher replacement ratio strengthens the bargaining position of employees and leads to higher wage demands. On the other hand, wages experience a downward pressure through the fall in the average tax rate generated by the negative income tax subsidy. As Table 12.3 indicates, the upward wage pressure exceeds the downward pressure resulting in a wage increase of 2.3 percent.

The wage rise has several consequences. On the one hand, consumption increases through the expanded purchasing power of households. On the other hand, higher wages cause the production price to increase. It can be seen from the table that the increase in the production price exceeds the wage rise. This can be attributed to the fact that, in the search process for employees, enterprises face higher costs, *viz.* advertising charges and costs in terms of foregone production, since it is harder to find workers because of the fall in unemployment. These increased search costs are shifted forward to the consumers through higher output prices. The consumption price index rises as well but to a lower extent because of the mitigating effect of stable import prices in this index. Since the higher production price affects the competitiveness of domestic products, imports rise and exports fall leading to a deterioration of the current account of the balance of payments. Particularly the exposed sector, in which foreign competition is relatively fierce, faces sales difficulties. In the new equilibrium production rises whereas employment does not change. This indicates that the negative effect of the higher labour costs, which encourage enterprises to substitute capital for labour, offsets the positive influence of the moderate production stimulation on labour demand. Since the smaller, part-time jobs remain relatively attractive, the positive influence on employment will likely concern these jobs. Despite the reduced effort of unemployed in finding a job, unemployment falls as a consequence of the fall in labour supply. This causes the inactivity ratio, *i.e.* the ratio between social security benefit recipients and employed, to fall.

As a consequence of the absence of compensatory budgetary measures accompanying the introduction of the negative income tax, the public deficit rises. In the case of budgetary neutrality, the costs of the introduction are fully discounted in equally higher marginal income tax rates in the three tax brackets. This requires an increase in the tax rates of the three tax brackets by 4.6 percent points each.

Introducing a negative income tax under budget neutrality results in a small increase of participation and in a decrease of labour supply measured in hours. Whereas the rise in the marginal income tax rate accounts for the fall in the number of hours supplied, the slight increase of participation can be attributed to the fact that the income of breadwinners is negatively influenced by the tax increase. By consequence of this income effect, some partners will be induced to participate.

In comparison to the previous simulation, the upward wage pressure entailed by the reduction in labour supply is strengthened by the higher tax burden and replacement ratio. On balance, a wage increase of 3.3 percent results. Despite this higher wage rise, the production price increase is about similar to that in the first simulation. This can be explained by the fact that producers now face lower search costs as a consequence of the rise in the unemployment rate[75]. Finally, disposable income of households declines as a consequence of the rise in the average tax rate. This causes private consumption to fall, which leads to a downfall in production.

Summarizing, introducing a negative income tax in addition to the current social security system leads to a reduction in labour supply. Consequently, wages rise and, when implemented under budget neutrality, equilibrium unemployment even shows an upward tendency because of a rise in the tax burden and the replacement ratio.

12.4 A negative income tax in a mini welfare state

As shown in the previous section, introduction of a negative income tax *sec* results in adverse effects on labour market participation and, when taxes are increased to balance the budget, on economic growth. According to Central Planning Bureau (1992b), introduction of a negative income tax might generate more favourable economic effects if combined with a radical reform of the social security system towards a mini welfare system. This section investigates what economic effects may be expected if a negative income tax is considered together with certain elements of a mini welfare state.

The characteristics of the concept of the mini welfare state with negative income tax used in this section are fivefold:

- All people (except children and students) benefit from an individualized negative income tax equal to 50% of the net minimum wage in the base projection;

[75] As a consequence of sectoral differences, the price increase is somewhat larger in the exposed sector. This accounts for the deteriorated export position of domestic firms.

- The social benefits of the social security funds for disability and unemployment are abolished;
- Similarly, social assistance from the government is done away with;
- Social insurance of aged people is reduced in such a way that the rise in net income from the negative income tax is just offset, so that their net income does not change. In a similar way the gross official minimum wage is adapted;
- In order to finance the negative income tax, the basic allowance in the current income tax system is abolished (because all workers receive a negative income tax now). Since the negative income tax is granted on an individual basis, this implicitly implies that the transferability of the basic allowance is also abolished. In addition, instead of raising the tax rates of the current three tax brackets a flat tax rate is introduced in order to prevent very high marginal tax rates for high income groups. The value of the flat tax rate is set in such a way that budgetary neutrality is obtained for the government.

It is assumed that a 1% decrease in disability benefits leads to a 2% decrease in the number of disabled people and that the productivity of disabled people is half that of other employees. The most important assumption concerns the reactions of unions to the reduction in disability and unemployment insurance. Current experiences in efforts to bring down the net disability benefit show that the loss in benefit is reinsured for almost 75% by unions and employers' organisations. Hence the effective reduction in disability benefits will only amount to 25% of the loss in benefit without reinsurance. In order to illustrate the relevance of this assumption, an alternative simulation is also presented in which the degree of reinsurance of disability risks equals 50% instead of 75%. Reductions in unemployment insurance benefits are assumed to be reinsured for only 10%.

In the simulation we abstract from more qualitative effects of a mini welfare state on the inflow into disability schemes. For example, if reinsurance takes place in the private sector and examination procedures are privately organised, this might induce a differentiation of premium rates across different sectors according to the risk of invalidity. As a consequence, large firms might opt for reinsuring the disability risks for their employees by themselves. This will encourage companies to prevent invalidation of workers by providing more intensive social and medical support and offering alternative jobs more suited for potential disabled workers. Central Planning Bureau (1993b) tentatively estimates that this might reduce the inflow into disability schemes by 10%. Furthermore, privatisation of the examination might lead to more stringent conditions required for entering the disability scheme. For example, disability as a consequence of psychological symptoms may be more effectively monitored or even cancelled completely.

Simulation results

The long-term simulation results are presented in Table 12.4 and Table 12.5. The economic effects of this drastic institutional reform are ambiguous. Labour supply shows a large fall because the introduction of the negative income tax decreases labour market participation by partners, as illustrated in Section 12.3. The fall in labour supply generated by the negative income tax is diminished by two opposing developments. Firstly, labour supply of partners of unemployed breadwinners receiving social assistance is stimulated. For this group the 100% marginal tariff caused by the means-test, vanishes since the negative income tax is granted on an individual basis. Secondly, replacement of the wage-related disability benefits by the negative income tax of 50% of the net minimum wage is found to induce an ex-ante decrease in income for disabled people by 32%. With 75% reinsurance the fall in net income for disabled people equals about 8%, inducing a reduction in the inflow in disability schemes by 16%. Hence, from the former 1 million people participating in disability schemes in 2017 according to the base run, 160 thousand people will now recoil from this participation by either preventing to enter the disability schemes or, if already disabled, being more prepared to accept a (less attractive) job for which they are still qualified. Although labour supply of partners falls by 586 thousand persons, total labour supply therefore only decreases by 458 thousand persons.

Table 12.4 Simulation results of introducing negative income tax and mini welfare state

Collective reinsurance	75%	50%
Flat tax rate	53.0	51.5
Prices	*percentage changes*[a]	
Wage rate	1.5	−2.7
– minimum	−8.1	−12.1
– other low skilled	0.1	−4.2
– high skilled	3.9	−0.3
Production price	8.4	6.4
Consumption price	5.8	4.6
Volumes		
Private consumption	1.8	2.2
Investment	−4.5	−4.1
Exports	−3.5	−2.7
Imports	−1.4	−1.6
Private production	−5.7	−4.6
Private employment	−2.9	−0.1
– minimum	16.3	21.9
– other low skilled	3.1	8.2
– high skilled	−6.4	−4.5
Labour supply persons	−6.4	−4.4
Labour supply hours	−6.1	−3.9
Ratios	*absolute changes*[a]	
Unemployment rate	−3.6	−3.7
– minimum	−16.8	−16.9
– other low skilled	−7.1	−7.2
– high skilled	−1.4	−1.4
Inactivity ratio	−4.7	−9.6
Replacement ratio	−26.3	−26.4
Average tax and social premiums rate[b]	−7.5	−9.9
Marginal tax and social premiums rate	2.9	1.4
Total taxes[c]	3.9	3.6
Social sec. premiums[c]	−9.8	−11.2
Public expenditures[c]	−5.7	−7.4
Public deficit[c]	0.0	0.0
Current account[c]	0.3	0.3

[a] Cumulated effects as difference between simulation and base projection after 25 periods.
[b] The average 'tax rate' is defined as (collective burden-basic income) / labour income.
[c] As a percentage of net national income.

Table 12.5 Negative income tax and mini welfare state: effects on replacement ratio, net real income and labour supply

Collective reinsurance	75%	50%
Replacement ratio	*percentage changes*[a]	
Unemployment insurance		
– single persons	–55.7	–55.5
– single parents	–53.7	–53.5
– breadwinners	–60.9	–60.7
– partners	–37.5	–37.9
Social assistance		
– single persons	–38.3	–37.9
– single parents	–53.7	–53.5
– breadwinners	–55.8	–55.6
– partners	0.0	0.0
Net real income		
Breadwinners[b]		
– employed	29.1	30.0
– unemployment insurance	–22.0	–21.3
– social assistance	–8.2	–7.3
– disability benefit	30.4	21.1
Single persons		
– employed	8.1	8.8
– unemployment insurance	–50.9	–50.4
– social assistance	–32.7	–31.9
– disability benefit	–12.4	–21.7
Aged persons	–11.9	–12.0
Labour supply (hours)		
Single persons	1.9	3.9
Single parents	3.4	6.7
Breadwinners	2.6	5.2
Partners	–41.8	–40.2

[a] Cumulated effects as difference between simulation and base projection after 25 periods.
[b] Including negative income tax ascribed to partners of breadwinners.

Although labour supply shows a substantial fall, the fall in employment is more moderate, leading to a substantial decrease in unemployment. This can be explained by the fact that the replacement of social assistance benefits by the negative income tax and the partial reinsurance of the social insurance benefit leads to an enormous fall in the replacement ratio of unemployed workers, both because of a nominator and denominator effect. The nominator effect stems from the fact that the *ex ante* income of unemployed is reduced.

The denominator effect stems from the fact that the negative income tax is independent of other income and therefore not reduced if wage income is received, in contrast to the current unemployment insurance and social assistance benefit. The strong fall in the replacement ratio reduces the reservation wage of the unemployed and raises their search intensity, resulting in lower incidental wages and lower search costs for employees, especially for low-skilled labour. Table 12.4 shows substitution between low-skilled and high-skilled labour to result in a fall in high-skilled employment and a substantial increase of employment for low-skilled people. In addition, the fall in the replacement ratio generates a downward pressure on collective wages by weakening the threat point position of employees in wage bargaining.

The flat income tax rate required to finance the negative income tax equals 53%-points. On average, the marginal tax and premium rate increases by almost 3%-points. The average tax and premium rate falls, however, because collective outlays decline substantially. This is explained by the fall in both the level of benefits and the number of benefit recipients. The latter is expressed by the large fall in the inactivity ratio (defined as the ratio of welfare recipients to employed). As a result, the average burden of income taxes and social premiums minus negative income tax falls by 7.5%-points.

From Table 12.5 it can further be seen that the fall in the collective burden leads to an improvement in the net real income of employed breadwinners and single people, but that the net real incomes of unemployed breadwinners, single and elderly people are deprived. The net income of disabled single people also falls, but less than for unemployed single people, because the loss in disability benefit is reinsured for 75% whereas the loss in unemployment insurance is only reinsured for 10%. The net income of disabled breadwinners even rises, because the reduction in breadwinners' income is compensated by the negative income tax of their partners.

On the whole, total purchasing power rises and private consumption increases by 1.8%. Production falls, however. This can be attributed by the large fall in average labour productivity as a consequence of the shift from high-skilled to low-skilled employment. The higher production prices this elicits weaken the competitive position of domestic firms and reduce exports.

Conversely, together with the fall in the average burden, the favourable rise in the ratio of domestic to foreign prices enables consumption to increase. Moreover, this attributes to the slight improvement of the current account.

If the loss in social insurance benefit is reinsured for 50% instead of 75%, the economic effects appear to be more favourable, as can be seen from the second column in Table 12.4 and Table 12.5. The main reason is that the lower degree of reinsurance causes a larger decrease in net income of disabled people. As a result, the inflow in disability schemes is further reduced so that the number of disabled people falls by another 160 thousand persons. The fall in labour supply is therefore diminished from 6.1% to 3.9% and this generates additional wage moderation. In this case, employment remains unchanged compared to the base projection. However, the production effect is still negative.

Concluding, the economic effects of replacing the current social security system by an individualized mini welfare state with a negative income tax seem ambiguous. On the one hand, it will initiate a strong reduction in unemployment by stimulating the willingness to accept jobs. Especially the employment perspectives of low-skilled people will improve. To this positive quantitative economic effect qualitative effects can be added as mentioned in Section 12.1, like improvement in practicability of the social security system.

On the other hand, the introduction of the negative income tax causes a large fall in labour supply as partners become less inclined to participate on the labour market. The fall in labour supply exceeds the fall in unemployment, hence employment is also reduced. Since the labour productivity of the working population decreases along with the increased inflow of relative unproductive people into the production process, private production shows an even larger fall than employment. Note, however, that the negative effects on labour supply and economic growth will diminish if privatisation of the disability arrangements causes a further reduction in the inflow in disability schemes.

Furthermore, this kind of radical reform will also have negative social consequences by causing a strong financial loss for people who keep completely dependent on a benefit income. This is especially relevant for single persons, whose fall in income is not compensated by a negative income tax of a partner. As the income of employed single people improves, the income distribution for this group will become more dispersed. On the other hand, the reduction in unemployment and disability implies that the number of people dependent on a benefit income is substantially smaller. Hence, there is a substantial number of former benefit recipients, whose income will improve, just because they find a job.

Finally, it can be questioned whether the introduction of a negative income tax is in line with emancipatory goals as it will reduce labour supply of partners in households and therefore consolidate existing role patterns between men and women. As this final conclusion is concerned, it must be noted that this simulation outcome is also due to the assumption of the male chauvinist labour supply model in MIMIC, in which only partners react to changes in income. It might be envisaged, however, that the introduction of the negative income tax will also influence labour supply of breadwinners. In that case, the reduction in labour supply by partners might be partly replaced by a fall in breadwinners labour supply.

13 Evaluation

The purpose of this study is to examine the interrelationship between labour market performance and the system of taxation and social security. The relevance of this issue is indicated by the current situation on the labour market. At the beginning of the 1990's the labour market in The Netherlands is characterized by a high level of unemployment, by low participation rates of women, and by a large number of people receiving a disability benefit. Also, unemployment is largely concentrated within the group of low-skilled persons. As an instrument to analyze the interaction between taxation, social security and the labour market, an applied general equilibrium model for The Netherlands has been developed, called MIMIC (MIcro Macro model to analyze the Institutional Context).

Instruments designed for applied economic analysis are judged by the fact that results should be relevant to current questions of economic policy, by the requirements of economic theory and by the consonance with empirical information. These standards are embodied in the three modelling criteria mentioned in Chapter 1, *viz.* those of relevance, consistency and adequacy. In this chapter we conclude the presentation of the model and its features by investigating the strengths and weaknesses of MIMIC in the light of the three modelling criteria. Section 13.1 will pay attention to the criterion of relevance. It will examine in what way simulation results of MIMIC contribute to policy analyses presented by the Central Planning Bureau to government advisory committees, political parties, unions and employers' organizations. Section 13.2 analyses the structure of MIMIC. The main issues here are the representation of economic theory in the model and the relation to empirical data.

13.1 Policy simulations: relevance

The labour market situation is a matter of concern to many policy makers in The Netherlands. Various instruments are examined to raise employment and to encourage search activity. However, economics does not often allow a free ride. Policy measures that enhance labour market performance pose a price in terms of other targets of economic policy, like the budget of the government or the purchasing power of different types of households. The policy mix applied in practice or proposed in party platforms (see for instance Central Planning Bureau, 1994) is the result of a complicated weighting process between different targets of social and economic policy.

The weighting process is clearly manifest in annual discussions about changes in the tax structure. These changes concern adjustments to several tax instruments within the current tax system. For instance, in 1992 the borders of the tax brackets have not been adjusted for inflation, in contrast to the usual procedure in previous years. Moreover, the basic allowance has been raised in excess of the indexation for inflation. These measures have been motivated by income policy considerations. Net incomes of low paid people benefit from these tax measures compared with high income earners. In this way the loss of purchasing power for low income earners, stemming from amongst others increases in the rate of national social insurance premiums in the first tax bracket, has been countered. According to the simulations in Chapter 8 these adjustments in the tax system will not have been very advantageous to employment. However, the opposite can be said of the final element of the 1992 adjustments in the tax system, which consisted of a considerable increase of the supplementary allowance for working people. By reducing the replacement ratio this measure moderates wage demands and stimulates employment growth.

The simulation results on single tax instruments as presented in Chapter 8 enable policy makers to get insight in the labour market consequences of various adjustments in the tax system. For instance, raising the supplementary allowance for workers appears most effective in creating employment opportunities, but also results in a relatively large fall in average real disposable income of people dependent on social security or social assistance benefits. A lower first bracket tax rate is the second most effective instrument to raise employment and is associated with an increase in average real disposable income for all categories of people. Insight into the labour market consequences of various proposals adds to the information on purchasing power effects for different categories of income earners and benefit recipients and to the budgetary effects, that used to be taken into account by means of detailed accounting schemes of the CPB. Absent from these calculations were the consequences of tax adjustments for behaviour of economic subjects. Neither could these be provided by the empirical macro economic model, since this model lacks sufficient detail both on the number of tax instruments distinguished and on the household sector of the economy. Therefore, by combining a detailed analysis of budgetary effects of various proposals with an economic analysis of labour market and macroeconomic consequences, MIMIC fills a gap in the current model instruments of the CPB. In this way MIMIC can contribute to policy discussions on structural influences of the tax system on labour market performance.

Of course system wide-ranging income tax reforms occur much less frequently than regular adjustments in tax rates, border values and allowances within the current system. MIMIC played no role in discussions about the 1990 income tax reform in the Netherlands, simply because the model was not yet operational at that time. The analysis of the reform in Chapter 9 has mainly served as an ex-post assessment and as a benchmark for the model builders to examine the properties of different versions of the model. However, the model has been used to examine the labour market consequences of the 1991 proposals by the Committee for Tax Reform. The results of Section 9.3 have been forwarded to the working group of the Social Economic Council preparing the report on the tax reform proposals. In the report of the Social Economic Council the simulation results are used to support the assertion that the structural economic benefits of the proposals will not be very large.

Although the complete proposal of the Committee for Tax Reform has not been implemented, elements of the proposal still receive attention. For instance, the Committee highlighted the replacement of the basic allowance by a tax credit. The simulations in Chapter 9 on this issue have been performed at the request of the Ministry of Social Affairs and Employment as a result of questions posed by members of Parliament.

The influence of minimum wage legislation and benefit levels on the labour market is a much debated topic. Employers' organisations and some political parties recommend to lower or abandon minimum wages. Simulation results in Chapter 10 indicate that merely a reduction of minimum wage levels yields a relatively small increase in employment, because reservation wages of the unemployed are hardly affected. Combined with a reduction in unemployment benefit levels the employment effects increase substantially. Also in Chapter 10 the effects of lower disability benefit levels are seen to raise employment. The large number of people receiving a disability benefit make the simulations certainly relevant for the Dutch situation. Various political parties and social institutions apply these results on reduction of minimum wages and benefit levels in devising their policy proposals on these issues, considering the efficiency effects and the income effects of various measures.

To increase participation, proposals have been put forward to individualize the tax and social security system, which can be subdivided into two components, *viz.* individualizing the tax and premium system on the one hand and individualizing the social security benefit system on the other hand. Since 1990 requests have reached the CPB from labour unions and political parties to advise on this subject. Preliminary effects of cancelling the transferability of the basic allowance were presented to the Dutch Scientific Council on Government Policy in 1990. In subsequent discussions especially with experts in the Ministry of Social Affairs and Employment the results were extended to those in Chapter 11, in which the institutional linkage of benefit levels to minimum wages of households with a non-participating partner, is seen to be crucial for the outcomes of the policy.

Chapter 11 also shows that there is a serious risk involved in designing an individualistic social assistance system. The benefits are intended for people who are searching for work, but remain unemployed. However, it may be very difficult to prevent a large increase of ineffective labour supply. Many partners, who currently do not participate, may declare themselves as searching for a job and collect the benefit. Individualization of social assistance benefits was seen to yield unfavourable macroeconomic outcomes when more than one in six partners collect the benefit on improper grounds. These results have been presented to staff members of unions and to politicians at a number of occasions and broadened the scope of the discussion on the issue.

At the CPB the risk of an individualized social assistance scheme was a reason to shift the focus of the Dutch social security system in the long term Balanced Growth scenario (Central Planning Bureau, 1992b) to the introduction of a negative income tax. Chapter 12 shows the negative income tax to be capable of reducing unemlpoyment without decreasing employment in the long run within the concept of mini welfare state and with a certain degree of collective reinsurance. The inclusion of a negative income tax in the CPB scenarios has started a new discussion in the Netherlands on the pros and cons, which continues to the present day.

This section shows the many ways MIMIC is applied to various policy issues, which all are directly related to actual policy discussions in The Netherlands and may also be of interest for other countries facing comparable economic questions. Therefore, the model is relevant to advise people and institutions engaged in the field of economic policy. Of course the model has specifically been designed for this purpose. Nevertheless, the occurrence of new subjects usually asks for adjustments on the model to implement new instruments or to extend the modelling of behaviour of economic agents. Also, frequently actual policy proposals are too detailed to be implemented directly, despite the large number of policy instruments that are already present. Many details of the social security system are not incorporated in MIMIC and the disaggregation of the household sector is not always suited for the type of question raised. For that reason, there is much to be gained by operating the model at a place like the CPB. If necessary CPB specialists on the tax and social security system provide adequate inputs for the model and monitor the simulation results. Other specialists, operating large micro databases on the household sector, manage to identify the size of various subgroups of the household categories of MIMIC. Thus impulses can be scaled down to analyze the consequences of policy measures which only apply to these subgroups.

13.2 Model structure: consistency and adequacy

Consistency

Although MIMIC has proven to be highly relevant judged by its prominent role in the discussion on economic policies, one can question in what degree MIMIC meets the other two criteria on model building mentioned in Chapter 1, namely consistency and adequacy. With respect to consistency, it can be argued that MIMIC takes an intermediate position in between more traditional estimated macro economic models and sophisticated applied general equilibrium models. For example, compared to FKSEC, the empirical macro economic model of the Central Planning Bureau (1992a), MIMIC shows a higher degree of consistency in various aspects. Firstly, because of the integration of the structure of statutory tax and premium rates in the model of income distribution and labour supply of households in MIMIC, a consistent picture can be given of the behaviourial responses of economic agents to various policy measures. Since FKSEC lacks such a detailed description of the system of taxes and social premiums, crucial variables like average and marginal tax rates and the replacement ratio are computed rather crudely in FKSEC. Secondly, MIMIC shows a higher degree of consistency in the modelling of firm behaviour. In contrast to FKSEC both price setting behaviour, factor demand and incidental wage components are derived from one theoretical concept of the firm. In addition, the model of the firm shows a high degree of consistency with other submodels of MIMIC. For example, search costs are consistently related to the ratio between the number of matchings and vacancies, which follow from the model describing the matching process between vacancies and unemployment. Likewise, the productivity characteristics of workers are determined by the productivity standard used by the unemployed in accepting jobs and by the minimum productivity standard set by employers to meet the minimum wage. In a similar way, the model of contractual wage formation is made consistent with the matching model and the model of search behaviour of the unemployed, by relating the threat point of employees to the ratio between the number of matchings and unemployment. Consistency between the model of the firm and the model of contractual wage formation is realised by assuming that the bargaining parties use a simplified model of firm behaviour, which has basically the same characteristics as the model of the firm.

Although the submodels in MIMIC exhibit a high degree of internal consistency, the model can be criticized for inconsistencies in the theoretical specification of the different submodels. This especially applies to the use of different utility functions for various aspects of economic behaviour of the same economic subjects. For example, the utility function of unemployed used in the search model is intertemporal and defined for a representative unemployed worker, whereas the utility function of households in the labour supply model is static and heterogenous in the weight of consumption and leisure. Although the situation of the unemployed (from which 90% receives an unemployment benefit) typically differs from that of partners considering labour market participation (who are not entitled to unemployment assistance), one would ideally prefer a uniform model of labour supply behaviour for all labour market participants. A further inconsistency between different submodels concerns the specification of the utility function for workers in the contractual wage model which differs from that in the labour supply model. For the purpose of analytical clearness a Stone-Geary utility function is assumed with employment and the difference between net wage income and threat point income as arguments. It is clear that more consistency would be obtained if, for example, a utilitarian function would have been used in which a utility function of individual workers with consumption and leisure as arguments is aggregated for the group of workers represented by the union.

Although this kind of inconsistencies reduces the quality of MIMIC from a theoretical point of view, one can wonder in what degree they diminish the reliability of the simulation results. As yet there is no indication that important links are lacking in the simulations, which would have been included if a fully consistently integrated model of labour supply, search behaviour and wage claims by workers would have been applied. As far as the system of unemployment benefits is considered to be of special relevance for labour supply decisions of partners, explicit attention has been paid to this, like for example in the simulation results of individualisation of social assistance benefits.

Apart from the inconsistencies between different submodels, MIMIC also exhibits some inconsistencies between different parts within submodels. For example, in the submodel of firm behaviour the minimum productivity standard set by employers in screening the pool of applicants is derived by an ad hoc decision rule and assumed to be exogenous in the intertemporal model for firm behaviour. The reservation wage is dealt with likewise in the search model of the unemployed. In both cases, a consistent way of modelling would require too complex a model and is left for future research. Again, the empirical consequences of these inconsistencies seem to be limited. For example, in the calibration procedure of the search model the effects of the replacement ratio on search intensity and reservation wage are simultaneously analyzed in order to be sure that the influence of reservation wage on unemployment duration is in line with micro-econometric research.

A different type of inconsistency relates to the exogeneity of the number of disabled persons. Empirical research shows that the ratio between net disability benefit and net wage influences the inflow into disability schemes. This indicates that the decision to participate in disability schemes is partly economically determined. In the current model version this kind of economic behaviour is simulated by exogenous impulses. A more consistent way would be to endogenize the inflow into and the outflow from the disability schemes along the same lines as search behaviour of the unemployed. This is the more relevant since part of the disability problem is actually a hidden unemployment problem.

Adequacy

With the concept of adequacy, the question of empirical reliability of the analysis performed by MIMIC can be posed in light of its scope of research, the economic consequences of institutional changes on labour market. Again, no univocal judgement can be given. On the one hand, several strong points can be mentioned if MIMIC is compared with other models of the Dutch economy. Firstly, MIMIC shows a high degree of adequacy by using a detailed micro economic data basis of the income distribution. This enables an accurate analysis of the budgetary effects of changes in statutory tax rates, social premiums, basic allowances and tax bracket borders. Moreover, since the structure of the tax and social premium system is also included in the labour supply model, a more specific analysis of labour participation reactions caused by different tax measures can be given. Furthermore, the disaggregation of households with respect to labour market position of breadwinners and type of social benefit received makes the model very suited to analyze questions about the effects of individualisation of the tax and social security system. The adequacy of the analysis is further enforced by the disaggregation of labour over different levels of education. Especially the distinction between low-skilled workers with a minimum productivity from other types of workers has proved to be very useful, since many policy proposals, like a reduction in the minimum wage or an increase in the work-related basic allowance, are targeted to improve the labour market position of this group. Finally, from the point of adequacy the disaggregation of the firm sector in exposed and sheltered sectors can be considered to be highly relevant, because of the open character of the Dutch economy.

Besides pros MIMIC clearly has some cons if evaluated in light of the adequacy criterium. Firstly, as applies to all applied general equilibrium models, the overall empirical validity of the model for the Dutch economy is uncertain, since no year to year simulation has been performed in order to check whether the model is able to reproduce the actual economic development in the past. This is due to the fact that, at the one hand, MIMIC contains many variables for which no longitudinal data are available, and, at the other hand, MIMIC includes no lag structures which would be required to describe the slow adjustments in actual economic processes. Although individual blocks of the model have been constructed in line with results from empirical macro or micro research as much as possible, we have no check on the empirical reliability of the interaction between these blocks. Therefore, for this purpose some simulation results of MIMIC have been compared with those of the FKSEC model of the Central Planning Bureau, which has been econometrically estimated and has shown to be able to describe the economic development in the Netherlands over the last two decades reasonably well.

Inadequacy of the model also arises if it lacks some economic mechanisms which may be relevant for specific policy measures. For example, MIMIC does not take account of the possibility that raising marginal tax rates on labour income might hamper the upgrading of the working population by discouraging education or inducing emigration by high-skilled workers. Although there is no direct empirical evidence of the relevance of these mechanisms, it might be expected that increasing the marginal tax rate for high incomes may have adverse effects on average labour productivity for this reason. This might somewhat bias the analysis about the effectiveness of different tax measures in favour of a reduction in the tax burden for low incomes. Another possible relevant mechanism, which is lacking in MIMIC, relates to the exogeneity of labour supply by breadwinners and single persons. It can be argued that in case of radical institutional reforms, like the replacement of the current social insurance benefits by a negative income tax, labour supply of breadwinners and single persons will also be affected. However, as with the former point, the empirical basis for modelling this kind of behaviourial reactions is weak. Thirdly, MIMIC can be criticized for the fact that labour supply of partners with children is modelled without considering the costs of child care, which it will provoke. If a shortage of qualified child care places is a major obstacle for active labour market participation, changes in partner labour supply envisaged by MIMIC may be overestimated[76]. Fourthly, MIMIC does not take account of the existence of the underground economy and the informal economy. This implies that a reduction in taxes and social premiums might be more effective than suggested by the simulation results, since it would improve the competitiveness of the official economy against the underground and informal economy. It is noted, however, that simulation results from a small general equilibrium model of the

[76] A preliminary study to the consequences of inclusion of child care costs in the labour supply model of MIMIC is Gielen (1993).

Dutch economy including an underground and informal sector (Graafland, 1990a) show that the quantitative effects on the official economy because of this mechanism are very small.

As for any model, we can conclude that the simulation results of MIMIC must be carefully interpreted. In a final judgement on all kinds of policy proposals qualitative considerations about relevant mechanisms not included in the model will also play a role. However, compared to other instruments the number of such missing mechanisms has been further diminished by the construction of MIMIC, since it captures many relevant institutional aspects of the Dutch economy in a coherent way. The outcomes of the model therefore provide a good basis for discussing the value of different economic policies. This may also be manifest from the large number of real-life policy issues to which MIMIC has already been applied.

References

Aarts, L.J.M. and P.R. de Jong (1992), *Economic Aspects of Disability Behaviour*, Elsevier Science Publishers, Amsterdam.

Alessie, R., and A. Kapteyn (1991), 'Habit Formation, Interdependent Preferences and Demographic Effects in the Almost Ideal Demand System', *The Economic Journal* 101, pp. 404-419.

Ando, A. (1981), 'On a Theoretical and Empirical Basis of Macroeconomic Models', in J. Kmenta and J.B. Ramsey (eds.), *Large-Scale Macro-Econometric Models*, North-Holland, Amsterdam.

Antonides, G., and W.F. van Raaij (1990), Inkomen en de Voor- en Nadelen van Werk, Ministry of Social Affairs and Employment, The Hague.

Arrow, K.J., and G. Debreu (1954), 'Existence of an Equilibrium for a Competitive Economy', *Econometrica* 22, pp. 265-290.

Atkinson, A.B., and J. Micklewright (1991), Unemployment Compensation and Labour Market Transitions: A Critical Review, *Journal of Economic Literature* 29, 1679-1727.

Ballard, C.L., D. Fullerton, J.B. Shoven and J. Whalley (1985), *A General Equilibrium Model for Tax Policy Evaluation*, The University of Chicago Press, Chicago.

Ballard, C.L., and L.H. Goulder (1985), 'Consumption Taxes, Foresight and Welfare: A Computable General Equilibrium Analysis', in Piggott and Whalley (1985b), pp. 253-282.

Bandara, J.S. (1991), 'Computable General Equilibrium Models for Development Policy Analysis in LDCs', *Journal of Economic Surveys* 5, pp. 3-67.

Beer, P. de (1987), 'De Bezwaren tegen het Basisinkomen Gewogen', *Socialisme en Democratie*, pp. 50-58.

Berg, G.J. van den (1990), 'Non Stationarity in Job Search Theory', *Review of Economic Studies* 57, pp. 255-277.

Berg, P.J.C.M. van den, G.M.M. Gelauff and V.R. Okker (1988), 'The FREIA-KOMPAS Model for the Netherlands: a Quarterly Macroeconomic Model for the Short and Medium Term', *Economic Modelling* 5, pp. 170-236.

Bergman, L. (1986), 'ELIAS, a Model of Multisectoral Economic Growth in a Small Open Economy', in: B.C. Ysander (ed), *Two Models of an Open Economy*, Almqvist and Wiksell International, Stockholm.

Bergman, L. (1988), 'Energy Policy Modeling: A Survey of General Equilibrium Approaches', *Journal of Policy Modeling* 10, pp. 377-400.

Binmore, K.G., A. Rubenstein, and A. Wolinsky (1986),' The Nash Bargaining Solution in Economic Modelling', *Rand Journal of Economics* 17, pp. 176-188.

Björklund, A. and B. Holmlund (1991), 'The Economics of Unemployment Insurance: The Case of Sweden', in: A. Björklund, R. Haveman, R. Hollister and B. Holmlund (eds), *Labour Market Policy and Unemployment Insurance*, Clarendon Press, Oxford, pp. 101-178.

Blades D. (1983), 'Service Lives of Fixed Assets', OECD Working Papers, no. 4.

Blanchard, O.J., and P. Diamond (1989), 'The Aggregate Matching Function', NBER Working Paper, no. 3175.

Blanchard, O.J., and S. Fischer (1989), *Lectures on Macroeconomics*, The MIT Press, Cambridge.

Blanchflower, D.G., A.J. Oswald and M.D. Garrett (1989), 'Insider Power in Wage Determination', NBER Working Paper, no. 3179.

Boland, L.A. (1989), *The Methodology of Economic Model Building*, Routledge, London.

Bolhuis, E.A., and W.J. Vossers (1986), 'Pensioenfondsen in Nederland', Central Planning Bureau Occasional Papers, no. 38.

Borges, A.M. (1986),'Applied General Equilibrium Models: an Assessment of their Usefulness for Policy Analysis', *OECD Economic Studies* 7, pp. 8-43.

Bovenberg, A.L. (1985), 'The General Equilibrium Approach: Relevant for Public Policy?', *The Relevance of Public Finance for Policy Making*, Proceedings of the 41st Congress of the International Institute of Public Finance, Madrid, 1985, pp. 33-43.

Bovenberg, A.L. (1986), 'Capital Taxation in Growing Open Economies', *Journal of Public Economics* 31, pp. 347-376.

Bovenberg, A.L., and L.H. Goulder (1991), 'Introducing Intertemporal and Open Economy Features in Applied General Equilibrium Models', *De Economist* 139, pp. 186-203, also published in Don *et al.* (1991), pp. 47-64.

Britton, A. (1989), *Policymaking with Macroeconomic Models*, Aldershot, Brookfield USA.

Bruyn-Hundt, M., and S. Gustafsson (1991a), 'De Individualisering van Belasting- en Premieheffing', *Economisch Statistische Berichten*, pp. 800-801.

Bruyn-Hundt, M., and S. Gustafsson (1991b), 'Incentives for Women to Work: A Comparison between The Netherlands, Sweden and West Germany', Report of the Netherlands Scientific Council for Government Policy, W59.

Budd, A.P., P. Levine and P.N. Smith (1987), 'Real Wage Adjustment and Long Term Unemployment', in: R.B. Cross (ed.), *Unemployment, Hysteresis and the Natural Rate Hypothesis*, Oxford, Blackwell, pp. 41-64.

Cain, G., and H. Watts (1973), *Income Maintenance and Labour Supply*, Academic Press, New York.

Calmfors, L., and J. Driffill (1988), 'Centralisation of Wage Bargaining', *Economic Policy*, pp. 13-61.

Carruth, A.A., and A.J. Oswald (1987), 'On Union Preferences and Labour Markets Models, Insiders and Outsiders', *The Economic Journal* 97, pp. 431-445.

Central Bureau of Statistics (1986), *Sociale Maandstatistiek*, The Hague.

Central Bureau of Statistics (1987a), *Arbeidskrachtentelling 1985*, The Hague.

Central Bureau of Statistics (1987b), *Bijdragen tot de Statistieken betreffende de Kapitaalgoederenvoorraad 1986*, The Hague.

Central Bureau of Statistics (1987c), *Woningbehoefte Onderzoek 1985/1986 Huisvestingssituatie, Woonlasten en Verhuizingen; Landelijke Kerncijfers*, The Hague.

Central Bureau of Statistics (1988), *Huishoudens 1985*, The Hague.

Central Bureau of Statistics (1989a), *Personele Inkomensverdeling 1985*, The Hague.

Central Bureau of Statistics (1989b), *Samenvattend Overzicht Financiën van Ondernemingen 1987*, The Hague.

Central Bureau of Statistics (1989), *Loonstructuur Onderzoek 1989*, The Hague.

Central Planning Bureau (1983), 'FREIA, een Macro-economisch Model voor de Middellange Termijn', Central Planning Bureau Monograph, no. 25.

Central Planning Bureau (1990a), *Economisch Beeld 1991*, Sdu Publishers, The Hague.

Central Planning Bureau (1990b), 'ATHENA, een Bedrijfstakkenmodel voor de Nederlandse Economie', Central Planning Bureau Monograph, no. 30.

Central Planning Bureau (1991), 'Een Analyse van het Overig Inkomen en de VPB Grondslag ter Verklaring van de VPB-tegenvaller', Central Planning Bureau Working Paper, no. 40.

Central Planning Bureau (1992a), *FKSEC, a Macroeconometric Model for The Netherlands*, Stenfert Kroese, Leiden.

Central Planning Bureau (1992b), *Nederland in Drievoud*, Sdu Publishers, The Hague.

Central Planning Bureau (1993a), 'Microtax-International', Central Planning Bureau, Working Paper, no. 51.

Central Planning Bureau (1993b), 'Macro-economische Gevolgen Voorstellen Enquêtecommissie Uitvoeringsorganen Sociale Verzekeringen', Central Planning Bureau, Working Paper, no. 61.

Central Planning Bureau (1994), 'Elections in the Netherlands. The economic consequences of five party platforms', Central Planning Bureau, Working Paper, no. 65.

Cooper, R.J., K.R. McLaren and A.A. Powell (1985), 'Short-run Macroeconomic Closure in Applied General Equilibrium Modelling' in Piggott and Whalley (1985b), pp. 411-440.

Deaton, A., and J. Muellbauer (1980), *Economics and Consumer Behaviour*, Cambridge University Press, Cambridge.

Debreu, G. (1959), *Theory of Value*, John Wiley and Sons, New York.

Decaluwe, B., and A. Martens (1988), 'Developing Countries and General Equilibrium Models: A Concise Empirical Survey of 73 Applications to 26 Countries', *Journal of Policy Modeling* 10, pp. 529-568.

Don, F.J.H., Th.C.M.J. van de Klundert and J. van Sinderen (1991), *Applied General Equilibrium Modelling*, Kluwer Academic Publishers, Dordrecht.

Draper, D.A.G., A. Nieuwenhuis and H.S. Tjan (1987), 'VINSEC, een Model met zes Produktiesectoren van de Nederlandse Economie voor de Middellange Termijn', Central Planning Bureau Occasional Papers, no. 40.

Driehuis, W., M.M.G. Fase and H. den Hartog (1988), *Challenges for Macroeconomic Modelling*, North Holland, Amsterdam.

Eijgenraam, C.J.J., and E.M. Verkade (1988), 'BETA, een Bedrijfstakkenmodel van de Nederlandse Economie', Central Planning Bureau Occasional Papers, no. 44.

Emmerij, L.J. (1985), 'Basisinkomen hier en Basisbehoeften daar', Werkgroep PvdA Voor Basisinkomen.

Erlich, S., V. Ginsburgh and L. van der Heyden (1987), 'Where Do Real Wage Decreases Lead Belgium', *European Economic Review* 31, pp. 1369-1383.

Farber, H.S. (1986), 'The Analysis of Union Behaviour', in: O. Ashenfelter and R. Layard (eds.), *Handbook of Labour Economics*, vol. II, Elsevier Science Publishers, pp. 1039-1089.

Farmer R.E.A. (1991), 'The Lucas Critique, Policy Invariance and Multiple Equilibria', *Review of Economic Studies* 58, pp. 321-332.

Feldstein, M. (1983), *Behavioral Simulation Methods in tax policy Analysis*, University of Chicago Press, Chicago.

Fischer, S. (1988), 'Recent Developments in Macroeconomics', *The Economic Journal* 98, pp. 294-339.

FNV (1990), 'Economische Zelfstandigheid en Solidariteit', Nota en resolutie vastgesteld tijdens het FNV congres op 12 en 13 november 1990 te Amsterdam.

Freeman R.B. (1986), 'Demand for Education', in O. Ashenfelter and R. Layard (eds.), *Handbook of Labour Economics* 1, North Holland, Amsterdam, pp. 357-386.

Fullerton, D. (1982), 'On the Possibility of an Inverse Relationship between Tax Rates and Government Revenues', *Journal of Public Economics* 20, pp. 3-23.

Fullerton, D., Y.K Henderson, J.B. Shoven (1984), 'A Comparison of Methodologies in Empirical General Equilibrium Models of Taxation', in Scarf and Shoven (1984), pp. 367-414.

Fullerton, D., A.T. King, J.B. Shoven and J. Whalley (1981), 'Tax Integration in the U.S.: a General Equilibrium Approach', *American Economic Review* 71, pp. 677-691.

Gelauff, G.M.M. (1986), 'Het Capaciteitsblok van FK'85', Central Planning Bureau Research Memorandum, no. 16.

Gelauff, G.M.M. (1992), *Taxation, Social Security and the Labour Market*, dissertation, WIBRO, Helmond.

Gelauff, G.M.M., F.A.M. van Erp, J.J. Graafland, A.E. van Hien and A.G.H. Nibbelink (1991), 'Towards an Analysis of Tax Effects on Labour Market and Allocation, a Micro/Macro Approach', *De Economist* 139, pp. 243-271, also published in Don *et al.* (1991), pp. 105-133.

Gelauff, G.M.M., and J.J. Graafland (1991), 'Analyzing Taxation and Labour Market with an AGE Model for The Netherlands', Central Planning Bureau Research Memorandum, no. 86.

Gelauff, G.M.M., and V.R. Okker (1988), 'ZOEM: a Condensed Version of the FREIA-KOMPAS Model for the Dutch Economy', Central Planning Bureau Research Memorandum, no. 49.

Gelauff, G.M.M., A.R.M. Wennekers and A.H.M. de Jong (1985), 'A Putty-clay Model with three Factors of Production and Partly Endogenous Technical Progress', *De Economist* 133, pp. 327-351.

Gielen, A. (1993), 'Work, Children and the Labour Market', thesis, Katholieke Universiteit Brabant, Tilburg.

Ginsburgh, V., and J. Mercenier (1988), 'Macroeconomic Models and Microeconomic Theory', in Driehuis *et al.* (1988), pp. 291-335.

Gordon, R.J. (1990), 'What is New-Keynesian Economics?', *Journal of Economic Literature* 28, pp. 1115-1171.

Gorter, C., P. Nijkamp and P. Rietveld (1993), 'Unemployed Job Seekers in The Netherlands', *De Economist* 141, pp. 70-95.

Goulder, L.H., J.B. Shoven and J. Whalley (1983), 'Domestic Tax Policy and the Foreign Sector: The Importance of Alternative Foreign Sector Formulations to Results from a General Equilibrium Tax Analysis Model', in Feldstein (1983), pp. 333-367.

Graafland, J.J. (1990a), 'Tax Policies and Interaction between Hidden and Official Economy', *Public Finance* 45, pp. 70-89.

Graafland, J.J. (1990b), *Persistent Unemployment, Wages and Hysteresis*, Dissertation, WIBRO, Helmond.

Graafland, J.J. (1991a), 'Effecten van Marginale Belasting- en Premiedruk op Loonvorming', Central Planning Bureau Research Memorandum, no 78.

Graafland, J.J. (1991b), 'Minimum Wages, Unemployment Benefits and Equilibrium Unemployment: A Simulation Model for the Netherlands', Central Planning Bureau Research Memorandum, no 87.

Graafland, J.J. (1992a), 'Insiders and Outsiders in Wage Formation: the Dutch Case', *Empirical Economics* 17, pp. 583-602.

Graafland, J.J., (1992b), 'From Phillips Curve to Wage Curve, *De Economist* 140, pp. 91-104.

Graafland, J.J. and J.P. Verbruggen (1993), 'Macro Against Sectoral Wage Equations for The Netherlands' *Applied Economics* 25, pp. 1373-1383.

Grift, Y.K., F.G. van Herwaarden, E.J. Pommer, J.J. Siegers and L.A.H.M. Smit (1991), 'Individualisering van Uitkeringsrechten', *Economisch Statistische Berichten*, pp. 1032-1040.

Groot, W., and G. Jehoel-Gijsbers (1990), 'De Invloed van Uitkeringshoogte op Werkloosheidsduur', *Economisch Statistische Berichten*, pp. 177-181.

Hagemann, R.P., B.R. Jones and R.B. Montador (1987), 'Tax Reform in OECD Countries: Economic Rationale and Consequences', OECD Working Paper, no 40.

Hahn, F. (1981), 'General equilibrium theory' in D. Bell and I. Kristol (eds), *The Crises in Economic Theory*, Basic Books, New York.

Hamermesh, D.P. (1985), 'Substitution between Different Categories of Labour, Relative Wages and Youth Unemployment', *OECD Economic Studies* 5, pp. 57-85.

Harris, R. (1984), 'Applied General Equilibrium Analysis of Small Open Economies with Scale Economies and Imperfect Competition', *American Economic Review* 74, pp. 1016-1032.

Hasselman, B.H. (1991), 'Investment, Q and financing', Central Planning Bureau Research Memorandum, no. 77.

Henderson, Y.K. (1991), 'Applications of General Equilibrium Models to the 1986 Tax Reform Act in the United States', *De Economist* 139, pp. 147-168, also published in Don *et al.* (1991), pp. 7-28.

Hersoug, T. (1984), 'Union wage responses to tax changes', *Oxford Economic Papers* 36, pp. 37-51.

Hersoug, T., K.N. Kjaer and A. Rødseth (1986), 'Wages, Taxes and the Utility-maximizing Trade Union: a Confrontation with Norwegian Data', *Oxford Economic Papers* 38, pp. 403-423.

Herwaarden F.G., van, E.J. Pommer and E.M. Hooijmans (1990), 'Gecumuleerd Beleid', Social and Cultural Planning Bureau Cahier, no. 76.

Hoel, M. (1990), 'Efficiency Wages and Income Taxes', *Journal of Economics* 51, pp. 89-99.

Hoel, M. and R. Nymoen (1988), 'Wage Formation in Norwegian Manufacturing: an Empirical Application of a Theoretical Bargaining Model', *European Economic Review* 32, pp. 977-997.

Jackman, R., R. Layard, and C. Pissarides (1989), 'On Vacancies', *Oxford Bulletin of Economics and Statistics* 51, pp. 377-394.

Jackman, R., and S. Roper (1987), 'Structural Unemployment', *Oxford Bulletin of Economics and Statistics* 49, pp. 9-36.

Jager, N.E.M. de (1993), 'The Implications of a Basic Income from an Economic Point of View', thesis, Katholieke Universiteit Brabant, Tilburg.

Jensen, S.E.H., S.B. Nielsen, L.H. Pedersen and P.B. Sørensen (1993), 'Tax Reform, Welfare and Intergenerational Redistribution', Research Paper 1993-1, EPRU, Copenhagen

Johnson, N.L., and S. Kotz (1970), *Distributions in Statistics; Continuous Univariate Distributions*, Wiley and Sons.

Jorgenson, D.W., and K.Y. Yun (1986a), 'The Efficiency of Capital Allocation', *Scandinavian Journal of Economics* 88, pp. 85-107.

Jorgenson, D.W., and K.Y. Yun (1986b), 'Tax Policy and Capital Allocation', *Scandinavian Journal of Economics* 88, pp. 355-377.

Jorgenson, D.W., and P.J. Wilcoxen (1990), 'Intertemporal General Equilibrium Modeling of U.S. Environmental Regulation', *Journal of Policy Modeling* 12, pp. 715-744.

Keeley, M.C. (1981), *Labour Supply and Public Policy: A Critical Review*, Academic Press, New York.

Keller, W.J. (1976), 'A Nested CES-type Utility Function and its Demand and Price-index Functions', *European Economic Review* 7, pp. 175-186.

Keller, W.J. (1980), *Tax Incidence: A General Equilibrium Approach*, North Holland, Amsterdam.

Keller, W.J., C. Zeelenberg, R.D. Huigen and P. Kooiman (1988), 'Effecten van Belastingheffing: een Toegepaste Algemeen Evenwichts Analyse', in *Belastingheffing en Belastinghervorming*, Stenfert Kroese, Leiden.

Kidd, D.P., and A.J. Oswald (1987), 'A Dynamic Model of Trade Union Behaviour', *Economica* 54, pp. 355-365.

Killingsworth, M.R. (1983), *Labour Supply*, Cambridge University Press, Cambridge.

Klein, L.R. (1947), *The Keynesian Revolution*, MacMillan, New York.

Klein, L.R. (1983a), *The Economics of Supply and Demand*, Basil Blackwell, Oxford.

Klein, L.R. (1983b), *Lectures in Econometrics*, North-Holland, Amsterdam.

Layard, P.R.G., and S.J. Nickell (1987), 'The Labour Market', in: R. Dornbusch and P.R.G. Layard (eds.), *The Performance of the British Economy*, Oxford University Press, pp. 131-179.

Lever, M. (1991), 'Union Wage Setting and Unemployment in The Netherlands', *Applied Economics* 23, pp. 1579-1585.

Lindbeck, A., and D.J. Snower (1987a), 'Efficiency Wages versus Insiders and Outsiders', *European Economic Review* 31, pp. 407-416.

Lindbeck, A., and D.J. Snower (1988), 'Cooperation, Harassment and Involuntary Unemployment: An Insider-Outsider Approach', *American Economic Review*, pp. 167-188.

Lucas, R.E. (1976), 'Econometric Policy Evaluation: A Critique', in K. Brunner and A. Meltzer (eds), *The Phillips Curve and Labour Markets*, Carnegie-Rochester Conference Series 1, North-Holland, Amsterdam, pp. 19-46.

MacCurdy, T. (1981), 'An Empirical Model of Labour Supply in a Life Cycle Setting', *Journal of Political Economy* 89, pp. 188-209.

Malcomson, J.M. (1987), 'Trade Union Labour Contracts, an Introduction', *European Economic Review* 31, pp. 139-148.

Malcomson, J.M., and N. Sartor (1987), 'Tax Push Inflation in a Unionized Labour Market', *European Economic Review* 31, pp. 1581-1596.

Malinvaud, E. (1977), *The Theory of Unemployment Reconsidered*, Basil Blackwell, Oxford.

Mankiw, N.G. (1988), 'Recent Developments in Macroeconomics: A Very Quick Refresher Course ', *Journal of Money Credit and Banking* 20, Part 2, pp. 436-449.

Mankiw, N.G. (1990), 'A Quick Refresher Course in Macroeconomics', *Journal of Economic Literature* 28, pp. 1645-1660.

Manning, A (1987), 'Collective Bargaining Institutions and Efficiency. An Application of a Sequential Bargaining Model', *European Economic Review* 31, pp. 168-176.

McDonald, I.M., and R.M. Solow (1981), 'Wage Bargaining and Employment', *American Economic Review* 71, pp. 896-908.

McKee, M.J., J.J.C. Vissers and P. Saunders (1986), 'Marginal Tax Rates on the Use of Labour and Capital in OECD Countries', *OECD Economic Studies* 7, pp. 45-101.

Melo, J. de (1988), 'Computable General Equilibrium Models for Trade Policy Analysis in Developing Countries', *Journal of Policy Modeling* 10, pp. 469-503.

Meyer, R.H., and D.A. Wise (1983), 'The Effects of the Minimum Wage on the Employment and Earnings of Youth', *Journal of Labour Economics* 1, pp. 66-100.

Ministry of Social Affairs and Employment (1989), *Rapportage Arbeidsmarkt*, The Hague.

Ministry of Social Affairs and Employment (1990), 'De Ontwikkeling van de Laagste CAO-Lonen in de Periode 1983-1988', The Hague.

Moffitt, R.A., and K.C. Kehrer (1981), 'The Effect of Tax and Transfer Programs on Labour Supply: the Evidence from the Income Maintenance Experiments', in: R.G. Ehrenberg (1981), *Research in Labour Economics*, JAI Press Inc., Greenwich, pp. 103-150.

Morrison, G.J., and E.R. Berndt (1981), 'Short-run Labour Productivity in a Dynamic Model', *Journal of Econometrics* 16, pp. 339-365.

Mourik, A. van, and J.J. Siegers (1991), 'Labour Market Conditions and Labour Force Participation: the Case of The Netherlands', *Applied Economics* 23, pp. 87-94.

Nash, J.F. (1950), 'The Bargaining Problem', *Econometrica* 18, pp. 115-162.

Nash, J.F. (1953), 'Two Person Cooperative Games', *Econometrica* 21, pp. 128-140.

Nelissen, J.H.M. (1991), 'Household and Education Projections by Means of a Micro-simulation Model', *Economic Modelling* 8, pp. 480-511.

Nickell, S.J. (1978), *The Investment Decisions of Firms*, Cambridge University Press, Cambridge.

Nickell, S.J., and M. Andrews (1983), 'Unions, Real Wages and Employment in Britain 1951–79' *Oxford Economic Papers* 35, pp. 183-206.

Nickell, S., and S. Wadhwani (1990), 'Insider Forces and Wage Determination', *Economic Journal* 100, pp. 496-509.

Nieuwenhuis, A. (1986), 'Twee Bekende Stelsels Vraagvergelijkingen en hun Mengvorm', Central Planning Bureau Research Memorandum, no. 15.

Nooteboom, B. (1987), 'De Economische Voordelen van het Basisinkomen; een Basis voor het Midden- en Kleinbedrijf', *Economische Statistische Berichten*, pp. 149-152.

OECD (1988), *Employment Outlook*, Paris.

OECD (1989), *Economies in Transition: Structural Adjustment in OECD Countries*, Paris.

OECD (1990), *Employment Outlook*, Paris.

OECD (1991a), *The Tax/Benefit Position of Production Workers*, 1987-1990, Paris.

OECD (1991b), *The Role of Tax Reform in Central and Eastern European Economies*, Paris.

OECD (1991c), *Employment Outlook* 1991, Paris.

OECD (1992a), *Historical Statistics*, 1960-1990, Paris.

OECD (1992b), *Employment Outlook* 1992, Paris.

Opstal, R. van (1990), 'Minimumloon en Werkgelegenheid; een Empirische Analyse op Micro-data uit 1979 en 1985', Central Planning Bureau Research Memorandum, no. 69.

Oort, C.J. (1986), *Zicht op Eenvoud*, Rapport van de commissie tot vereenvoudiging van de loonbelasting en de inkomstenbelasting, The Hague.

Oswald, A.J. (1985), 'The Economic Theory of Trade Unions: an Introductory Survey', *Scandinavian Journal of Economics* 87, pp. 160-193.

Ours, J.C. van (1991), 'The Efficiency of the Dutch Labour Market in Matching Unemployment and Vacancies', *De Economist* 139, pp. 358-378.

Paulus, A.T.G. (1991), 'A Negative Income Tax in The Netherlands? A General and Emancipatory Point of View', *Journal of Economic Studies* 18, pp. 105-120.

Pereira, A.M., and J.B. Shoven (1988), 'Survey of Dynamic Computational General Equilibrium Models for Tax Policy Evaluation', *Journal of Policy Modeling* 10, pp. 401-436.

Pesaran, M.H., and R.P. Smith (1985), 'Evaluation of Macroeconometric Models', *Economic Modelling* 2, pp. 125-134.

Phelps, E. (1988), 'Comment on "Recent Developments in Macroeconomics: A Very Quick Refresher Course"', *Journal of Money Credit and Banking* 20, Part 2, pp. 456-458.

Piggott, J.R. (1985), 'Introduction', in Piggott and Whalley (1985b), pp. 1-24.

Piggott, J.R., and J. Whalley (1985a), *UK Tax Policy and Applied General Equilibrium Analysis*, Cambridge University Press, Cambridge.

Piggott, J.R., and J. Whalley (1985b), *New Developments in Applied General Equilibrium Analysis*, Cambridge University Press, Cambridge.

Pissarides, C.A. (1986), 'Unemployment and Vacancies in Britain', *Economic Policy*, pp. 499-559.

Pissarides, C.A. (1990), *Equilibrium Unemployment Theory*, Basil Blackwell, Oxford.

Prins, R. (1991), 'Arbeidsongeschiktheid in Internationaal Perspectief', *Economisch Statistische Berichten*, pp. 64-72.

Prins, R., T.J. Veerman and S. Andriessen (1992), *Work Incapacity in a Cross National Perspective*, VUGA, The Hague.

Ravestein, A. van, and H. Vijlbrief (1988), 'Welfare Cost of Higher Tax Rates; An Empirical Laffer Curve for The Netherlands' *De Economist* 136, pp. 205-219.

Ridder, P.B. de (1987), 'Enkele Elementen van Aanbodeconomie in Model', in A. Knoester (ed.), *Lessen uit het Verleden*, Stenfert Kroese, Leiden.

Robins, P.K. (1985), 'A Comparison of the Labour Supply Findings from the Four Negative Income Tax Experiments', *The Journal of Human Resources* 20, pp. 567-582.

Robinson, S., and L. D'Andrea Tyson (1984), 'Modeling Structural Adjustment: Micro and Macro Elements in a General Equilibrium Framework', in Scarf and Shoven (1984), pp. 243-274.

Saunders, P., and F. Klau (1985), 'Taxation, Disincentives and Distortions', *OECD Economic Studies* 1, pp. 160-188.

Scarf, H., and J.B. Shoven, (1984), *Applied General Equilibrium Analysis*, Cambridge University Press, Cambridge.

Schaaijk, M. van, and A. Verkade (1988), 'Eenvoud Verzekerd: Microtax 88', Central Planning Bureau Research Memorandum, no. 43.

Schaaijk, M. van, A. Verkade and R. Waaijers (1990), 'Micro Simulation as an Instrument for Policy Evaluation in The Netherlands', Paper for Forschungskolloquium des Sonderforschungsbereiches, Frankfurt, June 1990.

Shoven, J.B., and J. Whalley (1972), 'A General Equilibrium Calculation of the Effects of Differential Taxation of Income from Capital in the U.S.', *Journal of Public Economics* 1, pp. 281-321.

Shoven, J.B., and J. Whalley (1973), 'General Equilibrium with Taxes: A Computation Procedure and an Existence Proof', *Review of Economic Studies* 40, pp. 475-490.

Shoven, J.B., and J. Whalley (1984), 'Applied General-Equilibrium Models of Taxation and International Trade: An Introduction and Survey', *Journal of Economic Literature* 22, pp. 1007-1051.

Shoven, J.B., and J. Whalley (1992), *Applying General Equilibrium*, Cambridge University Press, Cambridge.

Siebrand, J.C. (1988), 'Macroeconomic Modelling for Economic Policy' in Driehuis *et al.* (1988), pp. 99-149

Sims, C.A., (1982), 'Policy Analysis with Econometric Models', *Brookings Papers on Economic Activity* 1:1982, pp. 107-164

Sinderen, J. van (1990), *Belastingheffing, Economische Groei en Belastingopbrengst: een Evaluatie van Aanbodeconomie*, Wolters Noordhoff, Groningen.

Slemrod, J. (1983), 'A General Equilibrium Model of Taxation with Endogenous Financial Behaviour', in Feldstein (1983), pp. 427-458.

Smit, L., J. Siegers, Y. Grift, E. Pommer, F. van Herwaarden and M. Bottema (1991), 'De Financiële Gevolgen van Individualisering van Uitkeringsrechten', Economisch Instituut, Centrum voor Interdisciplinair Onderzoek van Arbeidsmarkt- en Verdelingsvraagstukken, Rijksuniversiteit Utrecht.

Social Economic Council (1992), 'Herziening Belasting- en Premieheffing', Publicaties van de SER, no. 9.

Soest, A. van (1989), 'Minimum Wage Rates and Unemployment in The Netherlands', *The Economist* 137, pp. 279-308.

Soest, A. van (1990), *Essays on Micro-econometric models of Consumer Demand and the Labour Market*, dissertation, Tilburg University, Tilburg.

Soest, A. van, and A. Kapteyn (1990), *Minimum Lonen, Loonkosten en Werkgelegenheid*, Ministry of Social Affairs and Employment, The Hague.

Solow, R.M. (1985), 'Insiders and Outsiders in Wage Determination', *Scandinavian Journal of Economics* 87, pp. 411-428.

Stadt, H. van de, A. Kapteyn and S. van de Geer (1985), 'The Relativity of Utility: Evidence from Panal Data', *The Review of Economics and Statistics* 67, pp. 179-187.

Stevens, W.F.C. (1991), *Graag of Niet*, Rapport van de Commissie voor de Belastingherziening, SDU Juridische en Fiscale Uitgeverij, Den Haag.

Stiglitz, J.E. (1991), 'Alternative Approaches to Macroeconomics: Methodological Issues and the New Keynesian Economics', National Bureau of Economic Research Working Paper, no 3580.

Stuart, C.E. (1981), 'Swedish Tax Rates, Labour Supply and Tax Revenues', *Journal of Political Economy* 89, pp. 1020-1038.

Theeuwes, J.J.M. (1988), 'Arbeid en Belastingen', in *Belastingheffing en Belastinghervorming*, Stenfert Kroese, Leiden.

Theeuwes, J.J.M., and I. Woittiez (1992), 'Advising the Minister on the Elasticity of Labour Supply', Rijksuniversiteit Leiden Research Memorandum 92.06.

Verbruggen, J.P. (1992), *Van Macro naar Meso, een Trendmatige Ontwikkeling in de Nederlandse Modelbouw*, Wolters Noordhoff, Groningen.

Vijlbrief, J.A. (1992), 'Unemployment Insurance in The Netherlands, Sweden, The United Kingdom and Germany', Research Memorandum 1992-18, ALERT, Free University, Amsterdam.

Werkplaats Basisinkomen (1989), 'De Economische Effecten van een Basisinkomen', Discussiepaper t.b.v. de Studiedag van de Werkplaats Basisinkomen en de Vakgroep Sociale Zekerheids Wetenschap KUB, 16 juni 1989, Tilburg.

WRR (1985), *Waarborgen voor Zekerheid: Een Nieuw Stelsel van Sociale Zekerheid in Hoofdlijnen*, Sdu Publishers, Den Haag.

Zalm G. (1988), 'Modellen en Economische Politiek', *Beleidsanalyse* 3.

Zeelenberg, C., R.D. Huigen, P. Kooiman, H. van de Stadt and W.J. Keller (1991), 'Tax Incidence in The Netherlands: Accounting and Simulations', Central Bureau of Statistics Statistical Essays, no. 42.

Name index